CHINA DIARY

CHINA

PAUL PADDOCK

DIARY

CRISIS DIPLOMACY IN DAIREN

IOWA STATE UNIVERSITY PRESS / AMES

OTHER BOOKS BY PAUL PADDOCK:
WITH WILLIAM C. PADDOCK

Hungry Nations
Famine—1975

923.273
P123

© 1977 Iowa State University Press

Ames, Iowa 50010. All rights reserved

Printed by
The Iowa State University Press

First edition, 1977

Library of Congress Cataloging in Publication Data

Paddock, Paul.
    China diary.
    1. United States—Foreign relations—Russia. 2. Russia—Foreign relations—
United States. 3. Dairen—History. 4. China—History—Civil War, 1945–1949.
5. Diplomats—United States—Biography. 6. Paddock, Paul. I. Title.
E183.8.R9P3   327′.0951′8   77–3229
ISBN 0–8138–0240–7

CONTENTS

51553

FOREWORD

China Diary provides some revealing side-lights about our China policy in the late 1940s. The former American Consulate had little impact on that policy. However, Dairen's status as a free port was one of the provisions of the Yalta agreement. To those of us in Dairen it seemed that decision makers in Washington made too little of this fact and its implications. Washington officials regarded Dairen as a useful listening post to hold onto as long as possible. For the most part it was not appreciated that the conditions under which the Dairen Consulate operated were more like those of the Soviet Union or Eastern Europe than those of other posts in war-torn China. Furthermore, it probably was not sufficiently understood that the very existence of an American Consulate in Soviet-occupied Dairen could be a major problem for both the Soviets and Chinese after October 1, 1949. This is why decisions about the post were slow and often unrealistic. We were painfully driven out of Dairen.

This book is an account of how "Zeke" Paddock, as he was known to a former generation of Russian and Chinese experts, tried to keep the Consulate in Dairen open under conditions which were extraordinary and even bizarre. More importantly it is an account of Paddock's persistent struggle to protect our Chinese employees and his achievement of arranging the repatriation of stranded Europeans. Paddock was something of a model in his efforts to protect human rights which have come up front so far again in our foreign policy.

Scholars will find *China Dairy* useful for the light it sheds on the U.S.-Chinese Soviet geopolitical relationship. The perspective of Dairen was truly a narrow one, but the base was unique. No other American foreign service post was similarly exposed to what later proved to be a focal point in Soviet-Chinese friction.

This book does not of course represent in any way my own current opinions about China and Russia. My professional life has centered in particular on U.S. relations with the latter country. And I am still in the Foreign Service. But I made some comments on the book during the drafting stage and the final version is factual as I recollect events and piece them together with my own fragmentary records.

CULVER GLEYSTEEN
Coordinator of Cuban Affairs
Department of State

PROLOGUE

In 1948 the State Department appointed me the new American Consul in Dairen. The Dairen consulate was called "the only American post in Communist China," but this was a misnomer; the Russians had occupied this city in Manchuria ever since the war with Japan ended in 1945. Although they quickly admitted Chinese Communists into Dairen's civil administration, the Soviet army itself remained firmly in charge of Dairen and the whole Kwantung Peninsula, with Port Arthur at its tip. Thus an American official in Dairen would have to deal with both Chinese and Russian bureaucrats, whether military or civil, separately or together. It was a tough and touchy situation at a time when the cold war between the democracies of the West and the aggressive Communism of the Soviet Union was swiftly growing hotter.

My tour of duty in Dairen, from late spring of 1948 to autumn of 1949, encompassed the period when the Chinese Communist Party (CCP) under Mao Tse-tung's leadership consolidated its military control throughout Manchuria and moved on to conquer mainland China. At this time, too, the cold war was at its apex, embracing Russia's coup in Czechoslovakia, the Berlin blockade, the initiation of the Marshall Plan in western Europe and the Soviet-inspired and Soviet-supplied guerilla operations in a dozen countries.

Some background details are important in telling the story of the Dairen consulate in the postwar years — a story that has never before been fully told in print.

Almost as soon as it was signed, the Yalta Agreement proved to be a false illusion of concord: Russia made permanent its military occupation of all eastern Europe and extended its domain in Asia. Kwantung had been an easy conquest, and by agreeing to share it with China — as the Yalta pact already in February arranged — the Russians could legitimately retain control over this highly desirable territory. One can speculate too that, psychologically, the Russians had a particular chauvinistic impetus to seize Kwantung, since this region had been the scene of their bitter and humiliating defeat by the Japanese in the Russo-Japanese War in 1905.

In almost every century, some cities and areas of land are separated from their "natural" country and, due to quirks of geography, history, and shifting boundaries, they must cope with an artificial, semi-independent status or with foreign domination. Sometimes this period lasts for only a few years, as in the case of Trieste and Tangier; sometimes it takes several decades of turmoil before the territory is restored, as with Danzig and Singapore.

Kwantung was a prolonged example of the latter. For half a century separated from China, this narrow finger of land dangles down from the great land mass of Manchuria and forms the Gulf of Chihli, the route of the sea trade to Tientsin and Peking. Good natural harbors make it a launching place into the Yellow Sea and the Pacific and a convenient landing location for ships carrying cargo or troops.

Kwantung, the southern tip of the Liaotung Peninsula and the southernmost portion of Manchuria, was an integral part of China until 1898. In 1896 Russia extended its railroad to Dairen (Dalny in Russian, Dairen in Japanese) from Siberia and northern Manchuria, on the lookout, as always, for a year-round ice-free port on the Pacific. In 1898, China was forced to lease Kwantung to the Russians: Dairen's harbor, unlike Vladivostok — Russia's chief Pacific port—was free of ice the year through. From a fishing village, Dairen grew swiftly into one of the busiest ports in east Asia, but in 1905, with the Treaty of

Portsmouth ending the Russo-Japanese War (which was fought, in part, over the rivalry between the two countries on Manchuria), Russia lost the Kwantung lease to Japan. The Japanese completed the ambitious Russian designs, constructing an impressive city with an improved harbor at Dairen. The city thrived as a center of commerce and industry. Investing heavily in construction of building, extension of railroads, expansion of Manchurian agriculture, and development of new industries, Japan began to consider the whole northeastern Chinese province as its own possession. From about 1911, Chinese war lords ruled the area, until in 1931, it was occupied by Japan. The "puppet" nation of Manchukuo was set up, with Henry Pu-yi, of the deposed Chinese Manchu dynasty as ruler.

The wheel of power turned again at the close of World War II when the Russians regained the area. The Soviet Union declared war on Japan on August 8, 1945, two days after the first atomic bomb fell on Hiroshima. At once Soviet troops rushed in to occupy all of Manchuria. (A unit landed in Dairen on August 22.)

On August 14 the Soviet Union and the Chinese Nationalist government (with Chiang Kai-shek at its head) signed the 1945 Sino-Soviet Treaty and Agreements. (By chance, this was the day that the shooting war in the Pacific stopped; formal surrender took place on September 2.) The treaty put into detailed form the vague phrases of the Yalta Agreement (February 1945) concerning northeast Asia. For one thing, Soviet Russia confirmed its recognition of the Chinese Nationalist government as the sovereign power over all Manchuria, including Liaotung Peninsula.

As for Kwantung, the treaty divided the region into two units: one comprising the city of Dairen only, the other including the rest of the peninsula. Dairen was proclaimed a "free port," open to the trade and shipping of all nations. The harbormaster there would be a Russian, but the city administration itself would be Chinese.

The much larger territory surrounding Dairen, called the Port Arthur Naval Base Area, was to be used jointly by China and the Soviet Union. Russian representatives were named as paramount in the governing commission, and Russia, charged with the base's defense, was given the right to maintain its own military forces there. The Chinese, however, were to conduct the civil administration here too.

All very well, perhaps, so long as the Russians and Chinese could get along with each other. But the treaty also provided that Dairen was to come under the Russian military regime of the Naval Base Area in the event of war with Japan. When signing, the Nationalist Chinese were considering the possibility of some future war. The Soviet Union, however, later claimed that the war with Japan was not over until a peace treaty was signed. Until then, it announced, Soviet troops would stay in Dairen—which might be for several years. In fact, it was not until September 8, 1951, that the United States and forty-eight other non-Communist nations signed a peace treaty with Japan in San Francisco. For the record, the USSR still has not signed such a treaty, and so remains technically in the state of war with Japan to this day.

In addition to keeping its troops in Dairen, Russia installed Chinese "administrations" in both Dairen and the Port Arthur Naval Base Area consisting of local puppets and Chinese Communist Party members. Representatives of the Chinese Nationalist government were never allowed to exercise the official duties granted by the treaty. Only on one occasion (June 1947) were they even allowed to set foot in Kwantung—and then they were so harassed that they feared for their safety and promptly left.

Before the Russian occupation, the Communists had been an insignificant political and military element in Manchuria. When the Chinese Communists began to rush their cadres northward into Manchuria from their wartime stronghold in Yenan, the Russians armed them, primarily with the equipment they received when the Japanese forces surrendered. Although the Soviet Union continued to maintain what it publicly called "correct" diplomatic relations with the Chinese Nationalists, it was at the same time providing the Chinese Communist Party with advice, weapons, and economic support: at first covertly, then more and openly as the CCP achieved significant military victories.

Meanwhile, Soviet troops hampered the Nationalist forces from moving easily throughout the area, refusing for instance, to let them land at Dairen. Under this Russian umbrella of protection the Communists were able to establish firm control over most of the Manchurian countryside. The Nationalists, however, managed to occupy the major cities—except for Dairen.

Kwantung became a silent outpost on the cold-war front. Although top Soviet officials and their Chinese Communist allies met together periodically in Moscow and Siberia to plan their strategy, it was easier for the second echelon and the lower action men to carry on consultations in Port Arthur and Dairen. Kwantung lay beyond the prying eyes of the Chinese Nationalists and the Western powers. There, the Russian police units had quickly organized a thorough surveillance system over the local population, the sort of subjugation they were similarly imposing throughout eastern Europe. Thus, whatever might be happening in Kwantung and whatever Communist policy decisions were made, it was safely beyond the ken of the outside world — or might have been, except for a single "keyhole": the American consulate at Dairen.

The State Department of the United States had reopened its prewar consulate in Dairen a half-year after the Japanese surrender. Since Dairen was supposed to be a "free port," a return to its once-vigorous commerce would naturally reinvolve American and other foreign business interests and their representatives: a primary *raison d'etre* of a consulate in a foreign land. The Russian hold on Dairen, however, prevented this reawakening of trade.

The American consulate was the sole foreign mission in Kwantung. The State Department kept it open, recognizing a significant value in being able to note the day-to-day events and trends in Russia's relations with the Chinese. The Manchurian branch of the Chinese Communist Party was making full use of

Dairen. Through it, agents transited to Korea, Nationalist China, Hong Kong, and the rest of the Western world. Gold bullion and other financing were easily and secretly carried back and forth. And since Chinese Communist publications, as well as a wide range of Soviet periodicals and books, were available in the stores, new propaganda themes could often be spotted before they surfaced in the West.

By the time my vice-consul and I arrived in Dairen, the "communization" of the city was nearly complete. The Russian military and secret police and the Chinese Communist officials and the Chinese police were in firm control of every phase of local life. We estimated that about 10 percent of the male population was in the police force, either uniformed or in plainclothes. In the one-mile walk between the consulate and my house, I passed six police stations. Every family possessed a registration book. If any member wanted to spend the night away from his house, he had to sign in with the police. When anyone escaped from the city, as on a coastal junk, his entire family was made to suffer the consequences.

Our main dealings, inevitably, were with the Kommandatura, the Russian army headquarters from which all real power in Dairen emanated. Our relations with the Kommandant, or Major General—baffling, annoying time-consuming, beset by evasions and neglect and downright rude refusals—eventually came to symbolize our whole exposure to Communist bureaucracy, from the lowliest officials to that faraway, nebulous but most potent hierarchy in Moscow's Kremlin, the ultimate source of all big decisions.

We two Americans were the only non-Russian foreign officials in Dairen. Nor were there any foreign journalists. Thus, our reportage of events in Dairen became all the more necessary and vital in supplying information that could be given to the free world and its communications media. Information gathering for one's own nation is an important basic function of a foreign-service officer, so that policy makers at home would be well acquainted with the prevailing mood of a populace, the current political and economic situations, and any significant changes or activities in a foreign land. Doing our proper work in a Communist country, we unavoidably ran the risk of being arrested and imprisoned as "spies."

This very isolation from our own people and government and way of life both intensified and personalized the crux of the conflict between East and West. In our constricted corner in China we experienced the cold war's progression in a very human dimension—sometimes scary, sometimes amusing, always frustrating, and forever fascinating.

The files of the State Department are full of stories of diplomatic mishaps and adventures by its personnel around the world. The records of the Dairen story however, were long absent from those files. A month after my return to Washington from Dairen, wanting to review some of my reports, I found that most of the material I had sent to the department was missing. I looked for it too, without success, in the political offices. By this time, the Communists were mopping up the last sectors of resistance in mainland China. In the midst of such excitement, the fact that this set of official governmental documents had, apparently, drifted into oblivion did not arouse much interest. Nor was the Dairen material in the files during the next few years, as I checked each time I was in Washington.

Now a quarter of a century later, when I applied to the National Archives in Washington to review whatever they might have on Dairen, not expecting to locate much, I was startled to find that most of my telegrams and reports were properly ensconced there. Where had they been? I have no idea.

Copies of the daily issues of all the Dairen newspapers, plus a collection of Chinese Communist books which we carefully sent to the Library of Congress for permanent filing, did reach that complex organization. However, they too were missing in the years after my return. Today, the newspapers are still definitely missing, but many of the books have surfaced and are now properly in place.

Fortunately, Culver Gleysteen, the vice-consul with me, sent a copy of each of these newspapers and books to his alma mater, Yale University, and they are now on file at the Sterling

Memorial Library there. They form a unique collection for scholars because it is unlikely that duplicates, other than what is at the Library of Congress, are available anywhere else. Even in the Communist world many would have disappeared by now if the contents contained some new policy endorsement superseded by later changes in the Communist Party line.

Although most of this account is in the form of a loose "diary" relating most of what happened in a chronological sequence—this account has been written largely from memory, except for the material I consulted that is now stored in the National Archives and some letters to my family. The State Department for years decreed that its officers could not keep diaries or other personal documents without special permission. Lacking such exact records, I may be mistaken regarding some details. Most important is that the story be told, and I am the only one left to write it.

A note on geographic names: The Chinese, Russians, and Japanese each have their own names for the places mentioned in the text, which are often found in the histories and maps dating from their separate eras of hegemony. I have adhered to the names generally used by the English-speaking world. Some day, however, everyone may be using the Chinese names of Lushun (Port Arthur), Talien (Dairen), and Luta (Port Arthur and Dairen combined).

My Dairen story must be read with an awareness of the special climate and extreme anxieties that the cold war was causing throughout the world in the immediate postwar years. Today, in this era of detente, most of the older generation has forgotten the extent of their former fears of the Russians; or at least their memories have blurred that period into a neutral shade. As for younger readers, the tensions of those days are usually beyond their comprehension. Perhaps one had to live through that epoch in order to make much sense of it now. And by now, a large part of both age groups have become accustomed to or bored with the never-ending confrontations between the two major powers and the polemics of opposing ideologies. Dairen, in 1948 and 1949, was a paranoid time in history.

The cold war's first stirrings came when the Bolsheviks gained control of most of Russia by 1920 announcing that their goal was to make all the rest of the world communistic too. The invasion of Russian soil by the Allies provoked fears of the West that have not yet been set to rest. In the two decades afterwards, many of the nations of the West—mostly democracies combined with a system of free-enterprise—reacted nervously and aggressively to the Soviet Union's challenge. A brief lull came during the Second World War, when the Allies combined to defeat Nazi Germany. But by the end of 1945 the enmity and distrust between the two camps broke out anew. The American public was initially shocked by the Soviet Union's attitudes; having accepted the Soviet Union as a sincere ally, not only for the war's duration but in solving future postwar problems, America and the rest of the world suddenly had to face a new period of hostilities. It was as if a bomb had been thrown into a quiet room; though unexploded as yet, it was ticking away.

I was stationed at the American embassy in Moscow at the time of the Yalta Conference in early 1945. It was a memorable moment when several of the men who had taken part in it arrived at the embassy afterwards in an exultant mood of success. They truly believed a sizable block of the world's problems had been resolved. Yet before the end of the year the elusive rapport was gone; we were looking into the threatening abyss of the cold war.

The policies, the goals, of each of the two sides—the West and Russia—were highly complex, and it is both simplistic and wrong to consider them in terms of black and white. The tendency of the left to look upon the Soviet Union as the unfortunate victim of capitalist machinations is as mistaken as the practice of the right to regard Russia always as the willful instigator of unprovoked villainies and the source of all the world's evils.

Looking back now, one can see that the cold war was inevitable in the immediate postwar years. Most of the top officials of the United States, both civilian and military, had become convinced of Russia's perfidy and of the impossibility of reaching permanent agreements and a stable peace through negotiations. But even if the West had been overflowing wholly with goodwill and trust, it is highly doubtful that a real accord could have been reached with Stalin—by this time a pathologically suspicious and devious tyrant. Many influential people hoped for a reconciliation between the two sides if only each would understand the pressures of the other's domestic problems as well as the urgent need of the whole world for a long and settled peace. But that sensible accommodation proved to be impossible. Both Stalin and the leaders of the West were convinced that the other side was lying in wait for the first sign of weakness in order to begin all-out warfare and conquest. Outright, acute paranoia on a national and international scale became the standard response.

During the cold war, which began its open course in 1945, we won some confrontations and lost some. The leaders of the West managed to confine the Soviet empire's expansion, whether through luck, counterforce, the attractive image of freedom, or economic influence. Significantly, only by military action has Russian Communism won and kept its areas, not by the persuasion of its ideology.

The end of the cold war is by no means in sight despite periodic detentes, during which each side decides, for whatever reasons, to coexist with the other for the time being. As many an expert has pointed out, the conflict will probably continue, despite transitory respites, until capitalism collapses, due to its inability to adapt to new social and economic pressures, or the Soviet system collapses due to the internal strivings of its subject peoples. (The techniques of fear and repression, however, have been refined by the Communist police into such an effective science that successful rebellion by any minority has virtually become impossible.)

The events of Dairen of 1948-49, which I describe hereinafter, took place when our disputes with Russia were at their most intense pitch. But, gradually, I sensed another conflict growing—one which did not directly involve the United States or other nations of the West. Throughout all the years since the original 1898 "lease" to Russia, China actually remained the "sovereign" nation in Kwantung, even though Russia and Japan in their successive periods of dominion gave it scant heed. During my service in Dairen, I became increasingly aware of the potential rivalry between the Chinese and Russian forms of Communism. The point of sovereignty in Kwantung would become crucial as the Chinese Communists took over all of mainland China in 1949. When would the new masters of China exercise their right of sovereignty and push the Russians out of the Port Arthur Naval Base Area and Dairen? Or would the Russians manage to stall them, and continue to keep their troops for a long while in this strategic piece of land now under their hegemony? And for how long would orders from Moscow take precedence over the plans of Peking?

Here, then, is the account of my experiences deep within the Communist world during a period of constant danger that one of the confrontations in Europe or Asia might burst into a shooting war. Dairen, where Russians, Chinese, and Americans collided, was just such a "hot spot." In retrospect, I see the situation in Dairen as a microcosm of the cold war itself—a war that went on for years without an effective truce.

CHINA DIARY

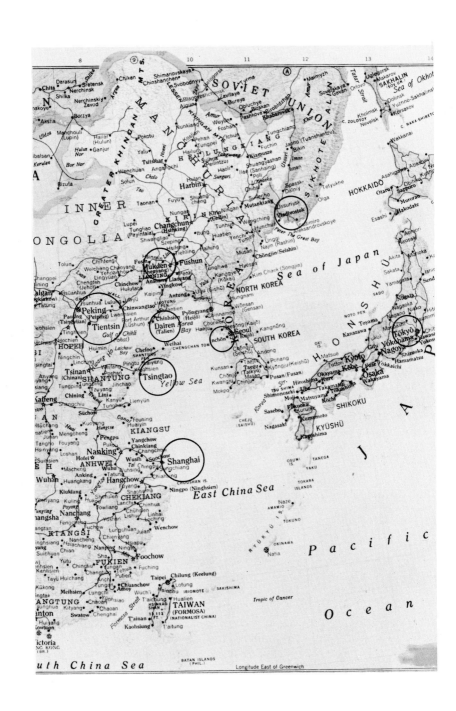

CHAPTER I
ASSIGNMENT: DAIREN (WINTER-SPRING 1948)

My assignment as American consul in Dairen came in the winter of 1948. I was a forty-year-old bachelor stationed as Deputy Chief of Mission at the American embassy in Kabul, Afghanistan. An Iowan, who wanted to see and experience more of the world than the American Middlewest offered, I had entered the State Department's Foreign Service five years after my graduation from Princeton University. I had already served in Mexico City, Batavia (now Djakarta), Melbourne, Auckland, Casablanca, and Moscow.

The announcement of this transfer to Dairen reached me, not in Kabul, but in the corridors of our embassy in Delhi, India, where I was on a special visit of a few days. One of the staff, passing by, told me that I had just been posted to Dhahran. I knew I was scheduled for a new assignment—but surely not at that dismal place perched at the desert's edge in Saudi Arabia! Among us that post had long been infamous: the job was dull, the facilities primitive, the social life nil. The principal work occurred whenever the local American oil officials assumed "their man" could accomplish great deeds by waving his diplomatic status in front of the Saudi Arabians after their own billions of dollars had failed to influence.

After two years in Kabul—then very remote and rugged—I was ready for something like London or Rome. (Afghanistan, however, has forever remained my favorite country in the Foreign Service.) As I stood in a corner mentally composing a tough telegram to Washington protesting Dhahran, another staff member came by and congratulated me on *Dairen,* mentioning Manchuria. Immediately, the challenge of handling that strange post at the border of the Communist world swept aside all thoughts of the pleasantries of Europe.

(And I never did lose this stimulating sense of the excitement of operating beyond the outskirts of normal diplomacy. Only once while in Dairen did the frustrations pile too high. While I was walking home after an especially harsh confrontation with the Communist officialdom, a dog came sniffing at my heels. I gave it a healthy kick and sent it squalling. Never had I kicked a dog before. The shock swept away my gloom, and I ended up laughing. With perspective thus reestablished, no matter how, for me Dairen became the most absorbing post in the Service.)

I learned that the previous American Consul in Dairen had departed when his wife became seriously ill. The Russians gladly flew them out. A vice-consul was left in charge. For more than half a year now the State Department had been trying to get a new consul into Dairen. The catch was that the only transportation route then available—through Vladivostok, the seaport in Siberia—required a Russian transit visa. The Department would appoint a new man. He would apply for a visa and then get no answer: a standard Russian-diplomacy ploy when it did not intend to act. After two months or so the Department would reassign that officer and appoint another. Again no answer to the visa application. Meanwhile, the lonesome vice-consul in Dairen was long overdue for transfer, and his wife was pregnant. The Department had to decide whether to close down the consulate—the goal, obviously, of the Russian procrastination—or to try something else.

My orders were to make the usual application for the Vladivostok transit visa, but to assume it would not be granted. I was to proceed to Shanghai, charter a vessel, and sail directly into Dairen—an expensive but perhaps necessary plan. On the basis of the 1945 Sino-Soviet Treaty an American-flag vessel had the legal right to enter the port. But this direct action would risk creating a dangerous political or even military confrontation with Russia which controlled the area since the end of the Second World War.

Stopping in Washington "for consultation" brought out nothing new in these orders. Go to Shanghai, charter a vessel and sail to Dairen. (This assumed, of course, I would not receive the Russian transit visa via Vladivostock, already applied for at the time of my assignment.) Since none of the State Department officers with whom I spoke knew any more than I about how to charter a ship, or about Dairen itself, their advice was not helpful. However, as a newly appointed officer is expected to do, I read through the accumulated files on Dairen and our consulate there, acquainting myself as best I could with its history and economy and population, and learning many details about the living conditions there which were described in the annual post reports.

In San Francisco, I ordered a large amount of supplemental food items from a wholesale grocery firm accustomed to dealing with diplomats abroad. Basic foodstuffs were to be acquired in Shanghai. These were primarily typical American semi-luxuries like canned meats, even the opprobrious Spam which we all had learned to hate during the war, and canned pumpkin, corn, sweet potatoes, cranberry sauce; also things like tapioca, powdered sugar, and a variety of soups plus many spices. A post report had mentioned that food flavorings were unobtainable in Dairen. By a lucky accident, my order of a few cans of lemon juice somehow resulted in getting two full cases. When our spices had gone, we sprinkled that wonderful juice on almost everything.

I had never been to China itself, but I was familiar with the comparatively sedate Chinese sections of cities in Indonesia and Southeast Asia. Now, tossed into springtime Shanghai by air transport from the States, I found that the turmoil of that busy port bludgeoned my senses.

The core of Shanghai had not changed physically from the prewar days, when it was the great entrepôt for East Asia. The traditions and thought patterns of the palmy days of the colonialist French and International Concessions too were unchanged. As soon as the Japanese departed the "old China hands"—foreign business agents, journalists, cosmopolitan drifters—hurried back or surfaced anew, together with the taipans, the hustlers, and the weird eccentrics for which Shanghai had always been notorious. Not so many now as in the old days, perhaps, but enough to make it appear the same, at least according to those who had been there before. For me, once I got used to it, Shanghai was a delight. Just the way I had pictured it: noisy, gaudy, gay, delightful.

I did not know how much of the current hubbub was natural Chinese big-city turbulence and disarray, how much an expression of the anxieties of the times. China became a republic January 1, 1912, following the Wuchang Uprising led by Dr. Sun Yat-sen, and, after years of fighting the Japanese and finally defeating them—a feat accomplished by Chinese Communists in cooperation with the Nationalists—the Chinese civil war revived. It was a fight to the death between the Nationalist/Kuomintang Party and the Communists. The Communist forces, led by Mao Tse-tung, were hundreds of miles away, beyond the northern horizon, concentrating on Manchuria. The Chiang Kai-shek government, with its capital in Nanking, and still bolstered by the United States, appeared to be strong enough to resist toppling. (General George C. Marshall, sent to China by President Truman in 1946, spent a whole year fruitlessly trying to arrange some sensible settlement between the two factions, to avoid a conflagration that might consume all of China.)

It could well be many years before a resolution was achieved—or so it seemed to a newcomer, a passerby, like me. The city of Shanghai seemed solid and impregnable within its rhythm of business activity. The immediate crisis now was inflation: big inflation. It had reached the point where one U.S. dollar was equivalent to one million Chinese dollars. The government's non-stop printing presses turned out new bills by the ton. Affluent people carried their loads of paper money around in string sacks. At the end of each day banks were swamped with the chore of counting reams of paper. I had a luxurious room at the famous Metropole Hotel and lived lavishly off my United States money, dining on the most elaborate meals for a dollar or so. Most of the time, I felt too good to feel guilty.

While knowledgeable people in various governments, embassies, and big corporations were guessing as to what the future would hold for China, most of the Chinese people themselves were drifting along, as most people do, trying to get from one day to the next, coping with each new problem as it arose. For nearly half a century they endured continual uproar, with armies marching, cities burning, bandits looting, and foreigners living among them enjoying a living standard far above theirs. Instability, uncertainty and exploitation marked their physical, political, social, and economic lives. After the collapse of the Manchu Empire in 1912 came signs of progress, especially with the Republic of China under Sun Yat-sen. His successor, Chiang Kai-shek, the head of the Kuomintang or Nationalist Party, quelled the regional war lords, tried to stem the growing power of the Communist Party through sheer extermination, and ineffectually fought off the successive invasions of the Japanese which resulted in their occupying most of the heavily populated centers of commerce, industry, and agriculture. But now the Japanese conquerors were gone. The Nationalists were in control of the cities, the Communists—with their peasant following—of the northern countryside around Yenan and Hunan, their headquarters since the Long March of 1934—1936, the Communist armies' astounding 8000-mile trek through central China to escape Kuomintang pursuit. By now Mao Tse-tung had clearly emerged as their prime strategist and leader, and he fully intended to wrest the remainder of China from Chiang's unsteady grasp. Expecting assistance from the USSR in Manchuria, Chinese Communist troops in the guise of civilians began to infiltrate Manchuria—the northeastern province containing the most productive mines and the best farmland.

The situation was interesting to China-watchers; but for the populace itself the period was a miserable and never-ending struggle for survival.

While enjoying the panorama of Shanghai spectacles all around me, I was getting acquainted with Dairen's new vice-consul. Culver Gleysteen had already been waiting a month in Shanghai for his Vladivostok transit visa. Raised in Peking, where his father had been a well-known missionary-educator, Culver was fluent in Chinese. Having been away at school in the United States, he escaped Japanese internment with his parents and two of his brothers. After graduating from Yale he did his military service, completing special Chinese language courses in the Navy Language School in Boulder, Colorado. Returned to civilian status, he had now passed his written examinations for the Foreign Service. But as is the way with such matters, it would be a year before Culver would receive his first official assignment. To fill in the time, he had accepted an appointment as "Vice-Consul of Non-Career" in Dairen.

Aged twenty-two, Culver somehow seemed older and wiser than his years. Very quickly, from our talks and various undertakings, I discerned in him certain agreeable character traits: intelligence, good humor, resourcefulness, self-confidence, patience, reliability, flexibility, common sense. The pressures of official problems never seemed to ruffle him. I felt most fortunate to be assigned such a good man to work alongside me in the future. Dairen would obviously be a hard test for both of us. We prepared ourselves by going through the available materials on Dairen and Manchuria at the Shanghai consulate general.

Our first step in getting to Dairen itself was to arrange for the chartering of a ship. (Actually, the very first step had been to go to the Russian consulate general and ask whether they had received authorization for our transit visas. The answer was "No." Nothing else to explain or mitigate the abruptness of the bare response. Just "No.") The plan to charter a vessel was kept secret within the top levels of the State Department, of the consulate general in Shanghai, and of the embassies in Nanking and Moscow. Public announcement would be made only after the ship was on its way to Dairen.

Our embassy in Moscow did, however, inform the Russian Foreign Office of the plan to use a freighter, emphasizing that if visas were granted, the charter would be cancelled and Culver and I would use the monthly Russian ship to Vladivostok.

It was originally planned for me to arrange the charter myself. Instead, the State Department now contacted the president of the Everett Steamship Line, and he agreed to let us use one of his ships. Based in Manila, this was an American-owned firm, but the ships flew the Philippine flag. Norbert Everett agreed to this chartering, he said, only to accommodate the government. Changing the route to include Dairen would take four extra days, costing $7,200, with demurrage at $1500 per extra day. Any undue delay would throw their tight Orient-interport trade off schedule, a delay that would take months to regain.

A flood of telegrams between Washington, Manila, Shanghai, Nanking, and Moscow worried about this and that. If the ship is to go directly from Shanghai to Dairen, will it not be called coastal trade? If so, will that not violate decrees of the Chinese Nationalist government based on the 1945 Sino-Soviet Treaty? But if the ship goes to Korea first, should it be to the port of Pusan or Inchon? Would not a Korean-flag vessel be better after all? What should be done about the assorted foreigners stranded in Dairen who will use every pressure for passage out with the ship? Can we, asks the British ambassador in Manila—who had, in the best tradition of the diplomatic world, learned of this so-secret ship—arrange for it to bring out of Dairen 122 boxes of personal effects of British consular personnel, all dating from the time of Pearl Harbor? Can fifty drums of gasoline be shipped as "office supplies"? (Yes, they can be called "office supplies"; but the U.S. Maritime Commission has bareboat charters on Everett ships, and its regulations forbid carrying gasoline and passengers on the same ship. No, thundered Everett, the commission has no bareboat charter; we own our own ships, or at least this one, and we allow gasoline and passengers to mix.)

The State Department, that sincere but amorphous body, had assured Culver and me that our tour of duty at Dairen would last for eight months only, and that a diplomatic courier would bring us mail and supplies each month. The eight months were, of course, an arbitrary number for the length of our assignment; some personnel officer had decreed it as the maximum time one ought to be kept at such an isolated post.

Culver and I struggled to determine what office and personal supplies we would be needing in Dairen for the eight months. We could expect to get nothing there except a few foodstuffs like fruit and fish. The city had long been cut off from the world, first by the war and then by the Russians, and no one ever expected to able to buy much in any Communist city.

Shanghai, on the other hand, had recovered from the war insofar as commercial activities were concerned. Whatever we needed was there—if only we could find where in that vast metropolis. Culver's Chinese came into use as he tracked down items from one place to another to the next. Also, the American military commissaries supplied us with basic items. The grocery "supplement" from San Francisco, in transit, would arrive in plenty of time.

The Dairen consulate had a prewar Chevrolet and a jeep. The advisability of taking in a new car had been discussed in Washington and again in Shanghai. Each time it was decided not to do this because there was always the possibility the Russian transit visas might be granted; then the transporting of the car via Vladivostok would involve too many problems.

While making what he called his "scavenging rounds," Culver heard by chance that the State Department had actually shipped an American car to the Dairen consulate a year and a half earlier. It had gotten only as far as Tsingtao, the port halfway between Shanghai and Dairen, where the U.S. Navy had a base from which a supply ship to the consulate had been periodically sent. By the time the car reached Tsingtao, this service had stopped, so the car remained forgotten in a marine warehouse. Eventually, we learned that it was a fine new Oldsmobile untouched by driver's hand. Without further ado, I had it sent to Shanghai and included it with our other supplies.

Having a new car, plus the old Chevrolet and jeep already in Dairen, raised the question of gasoline. In Communist countries, and certainly in Dairen, gasoline was closely rationed and controlled. To prevent the authorities from hamstringing the consulate, it was decided to take an extra-large supply of gasoline with us. But how much gasoline?

A pet idea of policy officials in both the Department and the embassy in Nanking was now revived. This was for me to drive as often as feasible from Dairen to confer with the American consul general at Mukden, three hundred miles to the north. Going by train was impracticable because of Communist restrictions preventing most travelers from using what was considered to be primarily a military means of transport. The Chevrolet was too decrepit for such a trip; but as soon as we acquired the new Oldsmobile, that handicap was overcome. Why the Mukden consul general himself could not drive to Dairen was hazy. Was it because the Russian authorities would not have admitted him? Apparently, it would be different with the Dairen consul going in the opposite direction; but why it would be different was equally vague. Anyway, we added to our growing stock of supplies more drums of gasoline, oil, and spare automobile parts.

Meanwhile, the Department by-passed one available Everett freighter in order to give the Russians one more month of grace about the visas.

By now, the Russian Foreign Office presumably had passed on to its consulate general in Shanghai the information about the chartering of an Everett Line ship. When I called there, explaining that I would be sailing on a freighter the middle of May, the official still had no word about granting our visas.

The contract with Everett stipulated it would be cancelled at any time, right up to the last minute, if the visas were received.

I continued to give no public indication that I would be leaving Shanghai soon. For whoever might be interested, Culver and I said we were waiting for Russian visas—a well-known situation locally. Despite all the carefully maintained secrecy, two American reporters in Shainghai did learn about the charter, but they agreed not to release the story until after we sailed. It was surprising that others had not caught on to our arrangement with Everett. The antennas of shipping companies were always activated to pick up reverberations of any unusual charter. It had been necessary, also, to go through the formality of getting official permission of the Chinese Nationalist government for the ship to land in Dairen; and that bureaucracy was no vault of secrecy. Furthermore, in those days Shanghai certainly had as large a quota of spies of assorted backgrounds and allegiances as those other centers of espionage: Vienna, Istanbul, and New York.

By now there was little for me to do except to continue to read the Shanghai consulate general's background files on China, receive briefings about the current political complexities, and, after hours, to enjoy the social life—always pleasant in diplomatic circles when you are merely visiting and have no official obligations. Every day, someone would be giving a luncheon or dinner with elaborate Chinese dishes. Then there were events like attending midnight Easter mass at the Russian Orthodox Cathedral, one of the largest Eastern churches outside Russia. Between times, I wandered all over the city.

I remember especially well when Tillman Durdin, the *New York Times* correspondent, and his wife Peggy took me to dinner at their favorite Chungking-food restaurant. He had been on my refugee ship out of Java, and I had known Peggy in Auckland, where she operated what was probably the most popular Red Cross "rest and recuperation" hostel for American servicemen in the South Pacific Command. At that time, Tillman was in Chungking, reporting from that far-inland, wartime capital of Chiang Kai-shek. That night in Shanghai we walked almost two miles through the slums of the city, the streets barely lit and the stones slippery with refuse, and ended up at a ratty hole-in-the-wall. Even after all my years in Asia, I would have hesitated to eat there on my own. The food proved to be great; but only the most diligent and intrepid culinary enthusiasts could ever have found such a place—and returned to it. Alas, I have never seen the Durdins since then. Such is life with professionals who work abroad, parting after a pleasant and unexpected meeting, and knowing you may never see each other again.

Another time, two pleasant representatives of Northwest Airlines sought me out and treated me to dinner. I learned that Dairen was scheduled to be a stop on their route as soon as it "opened up." (It will still be quite a while before Northwest flies into Dairen!)

Everett now gave us a definite date. The *Coastal Champion*, 3805 tons, would arrive at Shanghai on May 14 and sail at noon the next day. The Russian consulate general again had no visas.

Two days before the ship was due, the Shanghai representative of the Everett Line reported second thoughts about this charter. A message from Manila had stated that the company could not go through with the agreement unless the State Department guaranteed that it would be responsible for any damages to the ship or crew that might be caused if the Dairen authorities fired upon it or otherwise tried to prevent its landing.

There was some reason for their apprehension. The Soviet Union claimed that the 1945 Sino-Soviet Treaty and Agreements gave it the right to keep its troops in Dairen until it signed a peace treaty with Japan. China challenged the Russians interpretation of the document. As soon as Soviet troops arrived, in August of 1945, the Russians closed the port to non-Russian ships, or at least to those not under Russian charter. When China realized that it did not have the force to make Russia withdraw its troops from the city, it issued an official edict that closed the port. Thus the port was now doubly closed by decrees by each of the two powers.

The National Chinese government had already granted our *Coastal Champion* special permission to sail into Dairen. The ship's status with the Russians there, however, remained unsettled and uncertain.

In chartering this vessel and sending it to Dairen, the State Department was acting on the basis of rights established in the Yalta Agreement (that Dairen was "internationalized") and in the 1945 Sino-Soviet Treaty (that Dairen would be a free port). But no one, no country, had yet put the Soviet ban to the test. Would the Russians passively allow the *Coastal Champion* to enter the port? Or would they use some means to prevent it? It was a moot point.

The Everett Line was convinced that real danger existed and feared that the Russians might stop the ship from landing. Its demand for assurances that the Department would pay for damage set off a new blizzard of telegrams. The Department asserted that there would be no trouble since the United States had the legal right to send in the vessel. I went to the local Everett representative, and in my firmest official manner said there was nothing to fear. Everything would be all right; just relax and adhere to the signed contract. When he repeated that to Manila, the answer came back: No guarantee of damages, no ship. Despite continuing telegrams, neither side changed its posture an iota.

In desperation the Department did come forth with an alternative: The *Coastal Champion* was scheduled in any event to call at the Korean ports of Inchon and Pusan before going on to Dairen. Culver and I were to board the ship with all our supplies and go with it to Korea. It would probably be possible from there to charter a Korean flag vessel to take us to Dairen.

Right on the dot, the *Coastal Champion* arrived and anchored directly opposite the Bund. It was still scheduled to sail the following morning. But never, no never, the company emphasized, would it go to Dairen unless the Department guaranteed payment for damages that might be inflicted by combative authorities at Dairen.

Although Shanghai is the port for the Yangtze River basin, it is actually located on a small tributary or inlet (today really a canal) called the Whangpoo. From the juncture of the Whangpoo and the Yangtze it is another thirty miles to the ocean. The broad street along the Whangpoo waterfront is called the Bund; at this point, the Whangpoo is over a quarter-mile wide. Besides being the port area, the Bund is the commercial center of the city. Lined with tall skyscrapers, its appearance is something like Michigan Avenue in Chicago if, say, the chaos of an Asiatic port were also going on along the lake shore. Thus, when our freighter did come, it was anchored in full view of Shanghai, and the Russians were, of course, aware of its arrival.

The ship began to unload its Shanghai cargo. Our pile of freight—about three tons—was put on a lighter and sent out to the ship, ready for loading the next morning.

As I went to bed that May night of 1948 in the Metropole Hotel, the State Department and the Everett Line were still at loggerheads, and for all I knew, the ship might not be allowed to leave.

* * *

At 4 a.m. my telephone rang. The duty officer at the American consulate general told me he had just received a telegram from the State Department. The Russian Foreign Office had just granted transit visas for Culver and me to go through Vladivostok to Dairen. The Russian message specifically stated, "In connection with the foregoing the necessity for the voyage of the vessel *Coastal Champion* ceases to exist."

The Americans had not been trying to bluff the Russians, because we were legally and openly going to sail a ship to Dairen if the visas were not received. (The later disagreement with Everett was outside that subject.) But because of the extreme tension between the two countries, we all felt a wonderful bounce of euphoria when the Russians declined to fight us.

From the Russian point of view, a successful dispatch of the *Coastal Champion* into Dairen would not only have resulted in their humiliation in front of the Chinese Communists but would have caused elation among the Chinese Nationalists. After this demonstration that the United States refused to conform to the Russian fiat, other nations might send shipping to Dairen too. (That would have been only a hypothetical advantage, however, because no trade was possible there except through the Russians.) The Soviet Union had obviously decided, at this particular time and on this particular point, that a direct showdown with the United States was not worth the risk.

The Russian transit visas authorized us to go through Vladivostok from Shanghai to Dairen. The only way to get to Vladivostok was on the Russian passenger ship *Smolny*, which left Shanghai about once a month, usually on its return voyage from other ports in south China or elsewhere. Except for freighters, it was the single sea link between Siberia and east Asia, nor was there any regular air service. The *Smolny* was notorious in the area because rumors were rife in all the ports that its crew kidnapped Russian refugees and carried them off to Siberia. However, it was not unusual for the ship to carry Americans and other non-Communists: anyone, in fact, who had received a Russian visa, such as one to travel between Vladivostok and Moscow on the Trans-Siberian Railroad.

The *Smolny's* next arrival in Shanghai was scheduled for May 29, two weeks away. Since all matters, such as purchase of supplies, had already been finished, this period of waiting allowed me to take my only trip to Peking.

As the sailing date approached, Culver and I decided to repay our social obligations by asking "everyone" to see us off. We alerted the Russian shipping officer that we were inviting friends aboard; to our surprise, no objections were made.

Giving a farewell party on the mystery ship *Smolny* automatically guaranteed full attendance. Over a hundred guests came, slyly looking around to see if any kidnappers were aboard. In the tradition of old-time diplomats, we served only champagne. Cheap due to our duty-free status, it was made even cheaper by the inflated exchange rate for our U.S. dollars. We took over the rear deck: the afternoon sun shone while the champagne corks popped. It was a fine affair.

As the ship's lines were cast off and we started to move, I noticed my string sack with its packets of Chinese paper money in five thousand dollar denominations, each bill worth one U.S. nickel. When I began to throw them at the friends on dock, some of the packets broke open. Bills floated every which way while the dockhands scrambled for the money. Happy to be off and away at long last and effervescent with champagne, I found myself actually acting out the familiar fantasy of being rich enough to throw money to the throng. It was a sensational way to leave port.

We were well out into the Whangpoo River, with the skyline of the Bund beginning to grow small, when the boat that was to take off the pilot approached. A dozen friends who had wangled their way aboard had taken an armful of our champagne with them. One found the boat's steam whistie and kept blowing it until a police ship came to investigate. The pilot boat captain amicably steered within a few feet alongside the *Smolny* as we continued on down the river. Our friends started opening the champagne bottles. They popped the corks across the space between, and the foam blew all over them.

It was a memorable departure.

CHAPTER II

EN ROUTE
TO KWANTUNG
(JUNE 1948)

The *Smolny* took five days to sail from Shanghai to Vladivostok. It was comfortable enough—although we were glad to have along an insecticide bomb for our cabins. The dining room and small lounge were drably furnished; unchanged, probably, since before the war. The food also was drab; the best victuals were the thick soups, usually sauerkraut or soup-pickle soup. The bread was the wartime-Russian type: dark gray, soggy and sour. Breakfast consisted of tea and two hardboiled eggs, occasionally rotten.

Built in 1929, in Leningrad, for passenger service to Hamburg and London, the 5000-ton *Smolny* made its way to the Pacific during the 1945 San Francisco conference for the organization of the United Nations. The Russians equipped it with elaborate American radio gear and made it their communications center for direct contact with Moscow.

In addition to Culver Gleysteen and me, our party included a diplomatic courier, George Miller, and a Chinese radio operator, Chao Shou-yu. Chao would replace the radio operator who had gone to Dairen when the consulate was opened after the war and was to leave with Vice-Consul Patch upon our arrival. He was about thirty years old and seemed both competent and wonderfully even-tempered. His credentials as an American employee were impeccable: our Shanghai people had checked him out thoroughly.

It was hard to picture the roly-poly Chao walking nearly two thousand miles from Shanghai to Chungking, China's wartime capital; but he had done it to escape the Japanese occupation and then to take part in the fighting against the invaders. Unmarried, Chao had accepted this job at Dairen, not only because of the high salary, but also because he wished to get away from the unrest in Shanghai. Yet I could not help but wonder, and worry, whether his new situation might not prove to be equally hectic and tense for him, if not downright dangerous.

Among the passengers was a group of Chinese Nationalist consular officials and wives en route to posts in Vladivostok and Zaisan in Kazakh Soviet Socialist Republic (Kazakhstan), Central Asia. An able, and amiable group, they expected to stay for three years at their posts without any opportunity to import supplies. Later, when Russia shifted its diplomatic recognition from the Nationalists to the Communists, I wondered what happened to these diplomats, especially the ones lost to view in Central Asia. Were they allowed to leave Russia freely, or were they turned over to the Chinese Communists?

The few Soviet passengers were of unknown backgrounds and unknown official capacities. They did not mix with anyone else. The rest were White Russian repatriates, mostly mothers and children and single men. The men spent their time playing Mah-Jongg, the Chinese game played with tile pieces. In the Chinese fashion, they whacked the pieces on the table, producing as much noise as in any Shanghai cafe. I speculated on how long this exuberance would last after they reached Vladivostok; in Russia one seldom hears noisy goings-on except from drunks.

Although there is a province of Russia called White Russia (Byelorussia), the term "White Russian" ordinarily is applied to the refugees who fled the country (and the "Red Russians") at the time of the Revolution or later in the 1920s while it was still possible, though with great difficulty, to escape from the Bolsheviks. Groups of these White Russians found refuge in every country in Europe and also in the United States, but one of the largest concentrations of these exiles was in China, especially Shanghai. There most of them lived a rough hand-to-mouth existence, at the mercy of the Chinese officials and later of the Japanese.

Watching these White Russian passengers, I thought about how the twentieth century had indeed been a time of political chaos, with helpless and homeless peoples flooding in this direction and that. Since 1914 few countries in the world had not been wrenched by wars and dictatorships that forced thousands, even millions, to seek safety in flight. Stable nations in the midst of flux were the United States, Canada, Great Britain, Switzerland, Sweden and a handful of others, including sections of Latin America. It was difficult for many Americans to believe the bizarre adventures that so many of these uprooted persons experienced or to understand the emotional stresses that came from trying to adjust to a new culture while aching to return to their homeland.

In 1946 Russia had decreed that anyone who had been a Russian national in 1917 could apply for Soviet citizenship. Usually this included their families too, especially the children. In Shanghai many of the White Russians did apply; they received citizenship and acquired a Soviet passport. A passport was a precious document to them, because most of them were without any papers that established their national identity and enabled them to travel outside China. Mere possession of a Soviet passport did not mean, however, that the new citizen could return to Russia. Each case was settled individually by Russian consular officials. Normally, children and healthy persons under forty were allowed entry without undue trouble.

And here on the *Smolny* was this small group of White Russians going of their own free will to Russia, even though they had heard all the anti-Communist stories and must have feared that many were true. Yet the longing to return to their own country was so great they were now ready to risk their freedom. (Their life in Shanghai had probably been a battle of survival, so most of them were not giving up much in the way of physical comforts.) They had been fired with nationalistic pride by the great victories Russian armies had won over the Germans and by the extraordinary endurance of the Russian people during the war years. Now they were returning from their exile to whatever uncertainties awaited them. I understood their motives but could not help but feel sorry for them and be concerned over their fates.

The one moment of excitement on our voyage came when we were passing through the Tsushima Strait between Japan and Korea. An American light bomber buzzed the *Smolny*, swooping down low and making a terrific screech that was frightening. I suppose this was part of the cold war "game" that required buzzing Russian ships because they buzzed ours. I did not like it at all. Childish, senseless and annoying, it somehow seemed symptomatic of the larger issues dividing the world. Tensions were already fierce enough between the West and Russia: how could one be sure that mere "child's play" like this buzzing of ships might not suddenly become serious and precipitate deadly consequences?

Culver and I were already concerned about traveling into the Soviet sphere. When we sailed from Shanghai, the news events of the week included a number of cold-war crises around the globe. France had demanded guarantees of armed support from the United States if it were to continue to join projects opposed by Russia; the State Department formally charged that Russia had violated ten postwar agreements on Germany, seven on Austria, six on Bulgaria, three on Romania, three on Hungary, four on Korea, one on Poland and also, for good measure, three of the Chinese-Russian agreements. In the Philippines fighting against the rebel Huks was resumed as their leader publicly admitted he had been a longtime Communist Party member. The United States announced it would send "nonaggressive weapons" to Iran (tanks, guns, fighter planes). Plus ongoing stories concerning the Russification of Czechoslovakia (of which Russia had gained control a few months earlier), the efforts of the Western allies to set up a viable West German government with a reformed currency (over the vehement objections of Russia) and crises with Russia in the "internationalized" cities of Vienna and Trieste.

And by the time we reached Dairen three weeks later, there

were more happenings. Congress passed a bill admitting 205,000 displaced persons into the United States, 40 percent of whom must be from the Baltic nations and eastern Poland (regions seized and incorporated into Russia); Greece began its biggest offensive against Communist guerrillas; Hungary refused to return the Greek children the Communists had kidnapped and sent there. In Vietnam, France signed a treaty with pro-French groups giving independence to the country, but the Communists continued the civil war. In Korea, the new National Assembly elected Syngman Rhee as chairman and asked the United States to continue its military occupation until the country could defend itself; the Communist North Koreans boycotted the session. Russia arbitrarily continued to hold up surface traffic into Berlin for varying periods. A rather typical news story told of a band of Russian soldiers in still-occupied Vienna who invaded a British-operated police station, freed two Russian secret-police agents, and abducted a United States plainclothes officer; the American had broken up an attempt by the two Russians to kidnap an Austrian girl who had quit working for the Russians to work for the U.S. Army.

We reached the entrance to the harbor of Vladivostok in the early evening of June 2. Although there were still two hours of daylight, the ship anchored outside for the night. The crew gathered informally on a corner of the deck and danced sedately to music from a loudspeaker—the only time on the voyage there had been any sign of liveliness at all. The next morning at seven o'clock the ship made the passage up "The Golden Horn," a narrow inlet four miles long, really the inner harbor. In shape it did resemble that other stretch of water called "The Golden Horn," at Istanbul; here, however, it was flanked by rolling, grass-covered hills. The most notable sight was two dozen or so extremely old and rusted, played-out freighters scattered along the shore.

We docked at a pier between two coastal steamers. An hour later assorted port officials came aboard. A Russian-bureaucracy style vaudeville act was now performed as the local diplomatic agent gathered together some of the Russian passengers but made no effort to speak to the Chinese and American diplomats—although he constantly had to step over our feet in the small lounge. Then he left with his charges. After an hour more of waiting for something to happen, I went to the captain's cabin to protest. He took me to the Intourist woman whose duty was to look after travelers, whether diplomats or otherwise. After considerable prodding and threatening to complain to the Russian officials still on board, I got her to agree, if sullenly, to telephone the American consul.

Within a quarter of an hour Oscar Holder was dockside. Although Shanghai had informed him of our coming, no one had told him that the ship had arrived. Now he was not allowed aboard, although by this time the local Chinese consul was meeting his colleagues on shipboard.

The frustrating and grotesque "vaudeville" act was resumed as I stood around for another hour waiting for some kind of action, any kind of action. Finally, I went up and talked to the border-patrol man, who was recognizable by his green cap; I assumed his job must somehow involve my getting ashore. He and two plainclothes men thereupon led me to a dark corner and muttered that they must examine my baggage. Even though I had a diplomatic visa, it was only a transit visa. To be entitled to customs exemption, they said, I must also have a "laissez-passer." It was the first time I had ever needed that quaintly antiquated document of old-time diplomacy. I refused to open my bags unless Holder could be present. After more blather, he was allowed to come aboard.

In the end, Holder and I agreed to the baggage examination, and would leave it up to our embassy in Moscow to protest to the Soviet Foreign Office about this infringement of the traditional rights of a diplomatic visa. Nevertheless, it took another three hours before the customs men deigned to make their inspection. All passengers except the American group had long since left.

During the period of waiting I had a panoramic view, as if from box seat in a theater, of the passengers in the small, low-lying steamer docked next to us. Obviously settlers on their way to some point up the coast, they totaled around two hundred, but had split themselves up into tight little groups of a dozen or so. One or two people in each group always remained to guard the stack of tin trunks, bedrolls, string bags and whatnot. Meanwhile, the others were going constantly to and from shore on errands that were mystifying to me, since their effects already were aboard. In one crate, incongruously, was a racing bicycle—I thought it might be war loot from Eastern Europe.

It was all a still and somber business. No one laughed; even the babies did not cry. There were no guards anywhere, so these people could not have been political prisoners or forced immigrants; they looked like solid, rather well-dressed farmers and technicians, on the way with their families to a new life somewhere in the vastness of the Siberian coast. Yet, their quietness—what seemed to me to be their desperate quietness—caught at my throat; looking down from my "box seat," I felt a great compassion for them.

The examination of our luggage, when it came at last, was perfunctory. The officials seemed to be looking at the strange American articles mainly from curiosity. In Culver's luggage they sealed two books, *Speaking Frankly* by former Secretary of State James F. Byrnes and *I Chose Freedom* by Victor A. Kravchenko. It was four o'clock when we left the ship. The unloading of our cabin baggage was handled by dock hands whom Holder himself had engaged.

The American embassy in Moscow did send a protest to the Foreign Office concerning this irregular episode. But at the same time it sent out a circular telegram saying that the importance of securing complete Soviet documentation could not be overemphasized. Actually, weeks before, Holder had duly applied for laissez-passers for us with the local diplomatic agent but had been told they would not be necessary. It is always an up--and-down battle, This securing of "complete Soviet documentation."

We were to remain in Vladivostok for ten days and then board the *Ilyich*, already in port, for the voyage to Dairen.

Since we had no duties or errands, we could just relax or take walks around town. We stayed in the consulate building. (Holder's telegram to us in Shanghai had included the perceptive statement, "Placing anybody in the local hotel would not be a humanitarian gesture, so hope your party won't mind a bit of crowding under this roof.") Our ten days at the Vladivostok consulate was like a long house party for everyone. The staff was hungry for visitors.

Except for Dairen itself, Vladivostok was perhaps the most isolated post in the American Foreign Service. The staff consisted only of Holder and his wife, a vice-consul and another officer. The latter was supposed to have "cultural relations" with the local Russians, but this surely was as frustrating and pointless a job as ever was invented, considering the enforced seclusion of the Americans from any contacts with the citizenry or officials. During the war, the consulate had also included a United States Navy mission, to facilitate the immense Lend-Lease shipments (on Russian-flag vessels), but this was closed in 1946.

When I was stationed at the Moscow embassy towards the end of the war, an officer from the embassy or the navy would sometimes be sent to Vladivostok as a replacement. The tour of duty was then limited to six months at this "hardship post." A group of us would go with him to the railroad station for the Trans-Siberian Express, which left around noon. It was always a lively send-off, with drinks, funny gifts, and jokes about whether at least one of his three sleeping-compartment roommates would be, in the mixed Russian custom, a beautiful blonde. The train trip at that time took fourteen days, for Moscow is actually closer to New York than it is to Vladi- vostok. In winter it grew dark at four in the afternoon and light at nine the next morning; there was only a single, low-watt bulb in the ceiling, too dim for reading. Confined for a near-eternity inside the small world of a railroad car, it was a truly tedious trip. The train would chug off, we would go back to the office, life in Moscow would continue. Two weeks later a wan telegram would come to us announcing our friend's arrival.

In truth, we had already forgotten about him. Vladivostok was limbo. None of us ever wanted to go there.

I now found the city of Vladivostok, with a population of about 250,000, an oddly intriguing place. Almost everything looked as it must have in the day of the Czars. The few gray stucco Soviet buildings, ugly boxes, were ramshackle structures compared to the Czarist-regime's stone buildings, once painted yellow with white trim. Most of the houses, except for the old-time "mansions" (any two-story house), were built of wood embellished with considerable hacksaw fretwork. The side streets were paved with cobblestones but rather quickly petered out into dirt paths. The city had a primitive, pioneer-settlement appearance due to the lack of trees and landscaping and also because the buildings were widely scattered over the barren hillsides. Yet it was a picturesque place, partly because some portion of the beautiful harbor was always in view.

Vladivostok's history, too, tantalized me. It once enjoyed a few years of a glamorous if ephemeral social life—rather an artificial, "hothouse" existence. When the Bolshevik Revolution swept over Russia in 1917-18, a civil war developed between Red Russians and White Russians. An unruly legion of Czech war prisoners seized control of much of the Trans-Siberian Railway. Meanwhile, the Allies, as part of an overall plan to keep part of the German forces pinned down in Eastern Europe, landed troops in Vladivostok. Now this provincial outpost suddenly found itself the capital city of an autonomous area covering a quarter of Siberia (although the boundaries fluctuated wildly from month to month).

Amid all the turbulence, thousands of refugees escaped in one way or another, out of European Russia and got to Vladivostok. The small British and American units departed within two years, but the sizable Japanese forces remained, at one time occupying several hundred miles of the interior behind Vladivostok. They agreed to leave only when forced to do so as part of the Washington Conference in 1922. Even after the entry of Communist troops later, Vladivostok still continued its own semi-capitalist way of life.

During all these years cultural traditions completely lost in the rest of Russia managed to survive. Titled folk—the familiar Russian princes and countesses—were in goodly number and gave their cachet to social events. The great trading and banking houses of the Far East, British, Swiss, German and the rest, maintained branches here. All who visited or lived in Vladivostok during that period lasting a half-dozen years looked back upon it fondly as a carefree time: the sort that takes place when a war-front is just over the horizon. Responsibilities are neglected, for no one knows what the future holds. Eventually, of course, as the wheel of politics turned, the Reds communized the city. Those who could, fled to China, to swell the White Russian colonies already there.

* * *

Fortunately for us, Oscar Holder was an experienced Russian hand. He said it would be wise to check up on the transfer of our goods from the *Smolny* to the *Ilyich*. These goods consisted of 119 cases of commissary supplies, 22 cases of office supplies, 1 auto, 50 drums of gasoline, 2 cases of grease, 2 cartons of lube oil, 1 case of tire tubes, 2 cases of tires, plus miscellaneous pieces of personal effects.

The problem of loading these supplies on the *Ilyich*, did not come from officialdom's hindrances. The persons involved in the transfer were professionally anxious to get the job done smoothly and with dispatch. We maintained pleasant relations with the dock superintendents and their men. The trouble lay rather in the primitive equipment available. The dock area had several cranes given to Russia under Lend-Lease, but they were either in need of repair or were just not used. Everyone seemed more comfortable moving cargo by hand or by ships' hoists.

The crisis was the brand-new, shiny Oldsmobile. When we first went to the docks, the car already had been rolled off the low-lying *Smolny* and was parked a few feet away. We had it towed over to the *Ilyich*. It took a week to get it on board.

The *Ilyich*, 13,000 tons and built in 1932, had been a

German cruise ship operating before the war between Europe and the Caribbean. After somehow escaping four years of bombing, it was allotted to the Russians as war booty by an Allied commission.

Now, the ship towered above us at the dock. Gazing up at it was like looking straight up at the side of a three-story building. How to get the Oldsmobile up there?

First, the ship lowered its own set of ropes with a cargo net and the car was pushed into the middle. While I stood gawking, the ropes tightened and began to pull it upward, like a sack of potatoes. Luckily, everything was going slowly; as the ropes began to crush the four fenders, I gave a yell to stop the hoist.

We began a search all over Vladivostok for a platform on which to fasten the car. In a bewildered voice, the dock superintendent kept saying he knew one was around somewhere: three years before two Cadillacs were brought in from the United States by Molotov, the Russian foreign minister, and there had been no trouble then. Each night, a woman guard stood at the car. A platform of sorts finally did appear. The car was placed on it, a two-by-four was put under each wheel and held in place by one nail. I told the men to use more nails, and I also had the wheels lashed to the platform by wires. My precautions were justified, for the platform and car took off at a rakish angle; halfway up, the cables became caught on a projection, and the load dangled precariously for a while above us before the cables were freed and the precious cargo finally delivered safely on board.

Our departure from Vladivostok illustrated the hazard of traveling in Russia without firm schedules. The Intourist woman was to let us know every four hours whether or not it was time to board. She never did. The consulate itself would telephone various port officials, and eventually, we would get a rather positive answer that the ship would not sail for another four hours. We could then leave the consulate to go into town, but had to be back for the next session of telephone calls. After three days of this dawdling, the Intourist woman telephoned at 5:30 *a.m.* to say that we must be on the ship in fifteen minutes!

Once aboard, we were confronted by the same border-patrol official and his two plainclothes men as at our arrival. Although the diplomatic agent had assured Holder our baggage would not again be examined, they still insisted on it. This time around the border-patrol man spoke freely on a variety of subjects. He wanted to know why there was not more friendship between Russia and the United States and why the Americans wanted war. He said how bad for the world it was when Roosevelt died; that President Truman was "no good" but former Vice-President Wallace was "good." The men insisted on keeping the cabin door shut. When I eventually commented that we seemed to be conspirators plotting a revolution, and that persons outside might think I was bribing them, they hastily opened the door and kept it open.

After two hours they finished and we sailed immediately. The Dairen group waved, and the Vladivostok group on the dock waved back. Miller, the courier, would be returning from Dairen to Vladivostok in about two weeks. Once a month a courier was scheduled to travel through this city to service the Dairen consulate. We were like neighbors on the old frontier separated by rivers and mountains; here were our nearest friends. I felt both the pangs of parting and the excitement of venturing into an unknown terrain.

Again we sailed through the Golden Horn with its rusting, abandoned ships, and then out into the open sea.

Only then did we realize that the *Ilyich*, at least on this voyage, was a Russian troopship. It carried several hundred soldiers and officers of all ranks, with their families: mostly army, some navy, a few civilians. The military were miscellaneous replacements for the several Russian divisions and other units stationed in Dairen and Port Arthur.

The voyage to Dairen took five days. Traveling on a Russian troopship was interesting. I thought of the group of American "Russian experts" whom I had known at our embassy in Moscow during the war, several of whom later became prominent ambassadors, professors, and writers. Always frustrated because of the constant restrictions preventing natural contacts with the local people, they would have exulted in this opportunity to watch Russian activity.

For me, the most intriguing aspect was that things were done so differently from the way they are done in democracies. As one example, the *Ilyich,* built as a luxury cruise ship, had its spacious public rooms firmly locked. There was no place on the ship where a person could sit down, except for a few nailed-down benches on the top deck. Yet, one could look through the glass doors at the empty, elegant lounges, bars, and writing rooms, left unchanged from the last prewar cruise, although the chairs had been stacked against the wall. The narrow corridors were packed with military personnel and their families squatting on the floor playing cards, smoking, talking, sleeping (although each person had his own bunk in one of the staterooms). I could not imagine any non-Communist, non-dictatorship people on a five-day voyage not fulminating in protest at this senseless exclusion from the public rooms, and either forcing the captain's permission or just breaking the locks. Latins would have been inside within the hour, Africans in two, Americans in three—and the British before the end of the day.

Without any lounges and without deck chairs, our party spent the first days, which were cold, reading in bed, each cabin lit with a single dim bulb. Later, when it warmed up, we sprawled out on the floor of the top deck.

Since no meals were served to the passengers at large, each family had brought its own food supplies aboard to last for the trip. There were no cooking or heating facilities so everything was eaten cold.

Only for the American party and a dozen Russians of probable high-echelon importance was a dining room provided, where we were given regular meals. The food was better than the *Smolny's* although it sometimes offered an odd menu. For breakfast, one day, each of us received a can of crabmeat, served in the can with the lid cut off. It was excellent crabmeat which, the label proclaimed came from Kamchatka, but nothing else was given us to eat.

We guessed that the Russians at their own table included several generals, while the rest had the air of high-ranking political commissars or maybe police types. This may have been the reason why they all ate mostly in stony silence. How could they trust one another, even with small talk?

Actually, the only lively place on the entire ship was the swimming pool. But there was no water in it. Instead, the resourceful mothers had turned it into a nursery pen, dropping their children down its steep sides. It was the safest playground I had ever seen, for the children could play there indefinitely and were unable to get out. Often there would be several dozen of the little folks down there; from above they resembled a mass of wriggling caterpillars. They obviously relished their own quarters and certainly had a far better time on shipboard then anybody else.

For the adults there was no social life at all on board, except for one evening when the loudspeaker played music and there was dancing on the promenade deck. Although a few women danced, most of the couples were men. But the program did not provide dance music continuously, so they tried unsuccessfully to dance to Moussorgsky and Glinka as well.

Occasionally we would hear the sounds of an accordion or a balalaika. Yet the musicians never came together to play as an impromptu group, unlike any other informal gathering of the military I had ever been with. All in all, the *Ilyich* mirrored a most somber world. It was a hushed, dour ship. By 1948 one could not blame the war for such earnest stolidity. Moreover, these passengers were all off on a voyage which, to them, must have seemed as exotic as going to the South Seas.

Again in Tsushima Strait two American light bombers buzzed us. Then they flew over to another Russian ship and buzzed it too. This cold-war policy of buzzing seemed an inane and irritating exercise—especially when you went through it yourself on an "enemy" ship.

We reached Dairen in midmorning on June 17. In the distance, beyond the harbor, the city itself stretched out upon rounded hills that came down close to the sea.

The dock facilities, relics from the Japanese days in Dairen, looked considerably better than Vladivostok's, but little of the equipment was in use. Only a few freighters were in sight. The once-thriving Dairen was now nearly an empty port. But then, of course, we knew that Manchuria, for which Dairen was the principal outlet, was at an economic standstill while the Nationalists and Communists struggled for dominion.

Hardly anyone stood on the dock awaiting the ship. But Vice-Consul Isaac Patch was there to greet us warmly. He had served at the Moscow embassy while I was there; we were old friends. Here, quite visibly, was a happy man. Our coming meant that at last, a year and a half overdue, Patch was going home with his wife, their two small children and the new one who was scheduled to arrive in two months' time. The beaming relief that he exuded made me wonder sharply what problems this post would hold for us.

Here no customs, immigration, or quarantine people met the *Ilyich*. No formalties of any kind. As soon as Patch came aboard to greet us, we left. Obviously, the Russians considered transportation and trade with Dairen to be a domestic, within-the-empire affair.

After Patch hired pushcarts for our cabin luggage, we all squeezed into the consulate's ancient Chevrolet and drove into the city.

Our first view of Dairen, seen through the car windows, was hardly prepossessing. There was almost no traffic in the streets at all in late afternoon and most of the pedestrians seemed to walk in a dispirited way, as if life held few joys for them. Dairen, we knew, once had been a bustling metropolis with many factories, a huge railroad yard and the third busiest port in East Asia (next to Shanghai and Hong Kong). International monies had built large, sturdy, Victorian-style buildings six or seven stories high; there had been luxurious hotels, imposing business offices, splendid homes. Many of them were still there, but they were badly in need of care: general repair, scrubbing, paint, window-polishing. Did nobody notice?

We had expected a better-looking place than this, to be sure..

The over-all impression was not so much of faded elegance and depressed vitality as it was of a moribund condition. We almost felt as if we had entered a paupers' morgue.

We had arrived at the Russian cold-war fortress of the Kwantung region.

We had come to Dairen.

CHAPTER III

INTRODUCTION
TO DAIREN
(LATE SPRING 1948)

During our first few days in Dairen, and before he was to leave in the return voyage of the *Ilyich*, my old friend Isaac Patch did what he could to ease our adjustment period to this unique consular post within the Communist hold. He acquainted us, of course, with the routine procedures at the consulate—some of which needed plenty of explaining—and let us know that few of the normal functions of consular officers would be appropriate here: Culver and I would be the only Americans in town. And he told us particulars of the consulate's recent history in relation to the changes in Dairen itself.

All the while Patch was taking us around town to see things and meet a few officials—a total of fewer than a half dozen, both Russian and Communist Chinese—and about fifty non-Chinese civilians. The populace, for a half-century, had lived under other nations' thumbs. No wonder the place had a lackluster look; no wonder the people themselves seemed apathetic or even hostile. The main population appeared, basically, Chinese, but it was a mix of subracial elements that included the taller, darker Manchus from the north, Chinese from the south (most of them originally emigrants, to work in factories and fields), and even North Koreans from the east.

Dairen's population was nearly 750,000 at the beginning of World War II. After the arrival of the Russians, the figure fell to perhaps 175,000, as a number of the Japanese were repatriated, and a large number of Chinese left—mostly those with money.

By the time of my arrival in June 1948, the population had stabilized at over 200,000 which included the Russian military, although reliable figures were impossible to obtain.

The first thing the Russians did following their occupation of Dairen in 1945, aside from quickly establishing police control over the population, was to loot the industrial equipment. "Looting" is indeed the correct word. Both in Kwantung and all Manchuria, the Russians systematically stripped machinery and technical goods, sometimes whole plants, and sent them to Siberia. In Dairen this period lasted for a year, the Japanese prisoners doing most of the physical labor.

Russia justified this action by claiming all Japanese property as spoils of war, theirs by right of conquest. They disregarded the rights of Nationalist China who, as the sovereign power, and also an ally, was legally the correct receiver of Japanese property. And, of course, Russia did not even enter the war with Japan until two weeks before the fighting stopped.

Ironically, the Russians, who in the early days of their occupation had rushed to ship away to Siberia much of the industrial and port equipment of Dairen, later had to replace much of the equipment in order to prop up the city's economy. At first they had been unsure of their position in Dairen, fearful that the Chinese Nationalists or perhaps a truly internationalized government would gain control. Thus, a direct result of their success in sealing off the city to outside trade was to force back onto themselves the responsibility for the area's economic life, even in its present stumbling, sickly state.

Currently manufactured in Dairen—although on an insignificant level—were electric light bulbs, cement, peanut oil, salt, and glass. Small-arms ammunition for the Chinese Communists was also produced. To support even this minimum output, Russia was forced to bring in coal and other raw materials as well as food. Kwantung had never been self-sufficient in food production; apples were the region's only agricultural export of consequence. However, soybeans, grown by the millions of tons in the rich farmlands of Manchuria, were the primary produce sent out from the port before the Russian takeover, accounting for more than half of the exports. The beans themselves were sent away fresh or dried, but mostly they were processed in Dairen factories to make an amazing variety of products, ranging from bean oil, bean cakes, bean curds, soy sauce, breakfast foods, and milk substitutes to fertilizers, stock feed, paints, linoleum, celluloid, and soap.

In Japanese times, a chief sector of Dairen's industrial economy had been the chemical industry (ammonium sulfate and soda ash). Then, other important manufactures included machine tools, cement, and glass, controlled by the Japanese supercompanies (the Zaibatsu). And the largest railroad building and repair yards on the East Asia mainland were here.

Now, however, Dairen had lost its reasons for existence. Due to looting, most of the factories were empty shells, and there was little traffic through the port. All trade had stopped with battle-mauled Manchuria as Chinese Nationalists and Communists carried on their death struggle. Unavailable now were the soybeans from the northern countryside, where the feuding armies fought, and the vital coal and iron ore from Manchurian mines to supply the crippled factories with fuel and metal. The few Russian freighters coming here merely carried supplies for the military and whatever materials were needed to keep the local economy from collapsing completely. The products coming out of Dairen's factories only partially filled the ships for the return voyage to Vladivostok. Nevertheless, Kwantung and Dairen remained important to Russia because of their strategic military location. And some day, the economy would surely revive.

But right now Dairen was dead as a town could get. The streets were nearly devoid of traffic. Automobiles were a rarity, and there were only occasional streetcars, a few pedicabs, and horse-drawn droshkies. It was like looking up the main street of a middle-sized American city at high noon and seeing one car and fifty pedestrians. The larger stores, now state-owned, had nearly empty shelves. Some small shops were still privately owned and contained a heterogeneous assortment of prewar merchandise. Even for the necessities, prices were exorbitant. I could only guess at the degree of unemployment in the city and the resulting misery. From observation I estimated that three-quarters of the Chinese population were undernourished.

Patch gave us an informal review of the Dairen consulate's recent history. An unarmed United States Navy vessel had brought in the first postwar American consul, H. Merrill Benninghoff, in April 1946, six months after the surrender of Japan. In Washington the administration people at that time apparently regarded Dairen, despite the Russian presence, as merely one more prewar post to reopen in East Asia, to staff and to utilize for the usual functions performed by any other consulate. Although it was realized that the political complexities in Dairen were unique, they knew that American officials under Russian jurisdiction anywhere would have awkward troubles: and that is about as far as their worries then went.

Benninghoff at first had a staff of three Americans and a Chinese radio operator who received the consulate's incoming messages, broadcast twice a day from the United States Information Service office in Shanghai. The group led a more or less normal life, moving freely around the city and going swimming at nearby beaches. A small U.S. Navy ship brought mail and supplies to them from our military base at Tsingtao. This was organized to come monthly; actually, it made only four irregular trips. The Russian restrictions on the crew were tightened progressively and, eventually, they were not even allowed off the ship to play catch alongside. Nor was the ship's doctor allowed to visit Vice-Consul Patch's sick daughter.

When Benninghoff was assigned to Dairen, the British also sent a man to reopen their consulate, but he died before arriving. By the time a new man was designated and ready to go, the cold-war political situation had frozen to such a degree that the British government could not get him to Dairen.

Although the handwriting on the wall forecasting trouble with the Russians over the American consulate in Dairen may have been apparent for some time, the actual crisis occurred on December 18, 1946, when the Navy ship brought in as passengers two American reporters from *Life* magazine and Scripps-Howard, and a representative of the Standard Oil

Company who wanted to check on its prewar refinery. They were the first nongovernment Americans to arrive on the ship.

Benninghoff had informed the Kommandant two days earlier about the oil man, but had been given no warning at all about the newspapermen. The Russians, disturbed over these unannounced visitors (or pretending to be disturbed), forbade the three men to leave the ship. They used the incident as an excuse to stop further trips of the vessel.

The Soviet Consulate General sent a formal memorandum to Benninghoff, entitled "Regulations Relating to the Calling of American Ships at, and Entry of American Citizens into, Dairen." It stated that permission had to be obtained through the Russian Foreign Office in Moscow in advance of the arrival of any American ship and it recommended two weeks be allowed for this. It ended with: "As the Port is closed for trade and navigation, entry of American businessmen is not held to be a necessity." Since the memorandum also specified that only commercial ships would be allowed to enter, the Navy ship from Tsingtao was thus automatically eliminated.

The proper time for the United States forcefully to have questioned Russia's interdiction of shipping into Dairen was when the Navy vessel was forbidden to return. In the opinion of the State Department, the Russians were acting illegally in imposing this ban. Nevertheless, someone within the hierarchy of the American government ordered acquiescence. The United States sent two notes to Russia (January 3 and August 21, 1947) protesting the barring of foreign shipping to and from the international free port of Dairen, but these had only the effect of all such notes sent merely "for the record."

And so the haphazard and costly courier service via Vladivostok was begun. But only three couriers reached Dairen during all of 1947; so far, by mid-1948, there had been two.

No non-Communist journalists ever entered Dairen. Nor was any representative of the two American oil companies owning refineries there allowed to inspect their property. Although the Russians openly operated the plants, they never compensated the owners.

The State Department's strenuous efforts to send in replacements for both Benninghoff and Patch were always stymied by the refusal of the Russians to grant transit visas through Vladivostok. During September 1947, when Mrs. Benninghoff became seriously ill, the Russians obligingly flew her and the consul to Korea. By this time, two of the staff members had left; until our arrival, Vice-Consul Isaac Patch and his family were the only Americans in Dairen. No wonder he met us with open arms! We provided his ticket to freedom.

To my surprise, we found the consular office and our housing rather splendid.

The consulate quarters were spacious. On his arrival, Benninghoff had leased the entire office compound of the prominent trading firm of Bryner. The Bryners, a Swiss family who had been in the Far East for two or three generations, had built up a major merchandising organization with offices in several coastal cities and, at one time, mining operations north of Vladivostok. (Yul Brynner, the actor, who added an extra "n" to his name, is a member of this family.) The head office was in Shanghai and, before the war, Dairen had been one of its principal branches. The Bryners, as Swiss neutrals, were able to continue in business during the war, but with the advent of the Russians it closed out all operations. Now it was at least getting some cash return from the building in the form of American rent.

The office, built in the 1930s by a prosperous Manchu merchant family, was located near the port. In the traditional fashion of Far East trading houses, the building enclosed a large open compound about 100 by 150 feet, with a well in the center and a number of storage rooms called "godowns" around it. A high wall and a solid gate made it a small world of its own—able to withstand street rioting and other unpleasant events. Dairen would not seem to offer that sort of excitement, but the privacy and security thus obtained gave the feeling of seclusion from the vicissitudes outside. And who knew when and if the civil strife that currently engulfed the rest of Manchuria might afflict Dairen, with our consulate the inevitable target of a mob furious at the Americans for supporting their enemies, the Chinese Nationalists? At such a time of crisis the layout of the courtyard would offer us excellent protection.

I took over the house which Benninghoff also had rented from the Bryner firm. It was on a street nicknamed "Millionaires' Row," but the places were not all that grand: merely eight big brick or stone residences facing what must have once been an attractive park. The other houses on the Row had been confiscated for high-ranking military and civilian officials. (For instance, the head of the KGB, the Russian secret police, lived in one.) Beyond the park was a steep hill five hundred feet high. It had been thickly forested, but after the Russian occupation, when fuel became scarce, people cut down the trees. Now it was barren and eroded. Yet we often climbed up its slopes, discovering that from the top we could get a marvelous view of the city and the harbor. Looking down at Dairen, one could better appreciate its design. In their early tenure of the town the Russians had adapted the plan of Washington, D.C., dividing the place into several large circular areas joined together by wide straight boulevards. The Japanese had completed the city's construction, and in Dairen's heyday—the 1920s and '30s—it had been a most imposing-looking city, said to resemble some of Europe's best. But the war had ruined both heart and skin. The once-lush, well-tended gardens were gone, the buildings but ghosts of their former elegance. Seen from above, Dairen with its concentric circles linked together by streetcar lines rather resembled a spider web: but one that was old, dusty, and dilapidated—abandoned by the creature that had made, maintained and used it.

The Bryner house was a double one. The other half of the house was occupied by the widow of the Swiss consul who had recently died: the last of the foreign consuls except for us. In my half, the Bryner furniture was still in place, including such refinements as a grand piano, but the upholstery in the overstuffed pieces was ragged and stripping away. Actually, most of the furniture in use was from the prewar American consulate. The rear attic window gave a partial view of the harbor which turned out to be most convenient for us. Denied already entry to the harbor area, from the window we could at least get some notion of the daily general traffic in the port—the comings and goings of freighters and junks—as well as spot unusual ships at certain of the docks. In front was a little garden with several high gardenia bushes. A Japanese rock corner made a pleasant landscaping feature. A five-foot wall separated my garden from that of the other half of the house and also from the street. Outside, at least one Chinese policeman was on duty day and night: we were under perpetual surveillence.

Culver settled into Patch's house, a half-mile away. (He also adopted Patch's dog.) Small but comfortable enough, the house had a little swimming pool, fifteen feet by eight, fed by its own spring.

When the Swiss widow left Dairen a few months later, Culver moved into the other side of my house. However, I retained Patch's house under official United States rental, as the future home for the American clerk we were expecting to be assigned to Dairen. It was handy for both of us to live under the same roof, eliminating the problem of Culver's going between the Patch house and mine. During our first weeks, when he was on foot at night, he would regularly be halted by a policeman confronting him with a rifle pointed straight at him, cocked and ready for firing, and demanding to see his papers. Since it was months before we received night passes, this usually was an unpleasant and sometimes prolonged experience. Accordingly, we always used a car after dark.

We regarded our Chinese staffs in the office and at home as an efficient, hard-working group. I had a cook and, in the universal term of the Far East, also a "Number One Boy." The cook was superb; he had worked for the British consulate before the war and then stayed on as caretaker of their building. In his sixties, or perhaps seventies, he was quiet and self-effacing, having learned the value of a low profile during these troubled years. Culver too had an excellent cook, inherited from the widow of the Swiss consul, and a Number One Boy. We shared an "ahmah," the local name for laundress.

At the office, in addition to Radio Operator Chao, who came with us from Shanghai, we had a chauffeur, a messenger and two clerks: Ch'en Liang-hung, who did the accounts, and Chao Yi-sien, the Head Clerk (distinguishing between the two Chaos in our telegrams later on would be a chore.)

Head Clerk Chao was a highly intelligent and dignified North Chinese who had worked for the American consulate in Dairen since 1927. At the time of Pearl Harbor, the Japanese interned the American staff in the consulate building and he had been held with them. When the Americans were repatriated, the Japanese immediately seized Chao, tortured him, and kept him in prison for over a year—all because he had been a loyal American employee. Upon the arrival of the Russians he must have become fully aware of the dangers of working again for the Americans. Yet when Benninghoff sailed into Dairen, Chao was there on the dock to greet him. In the finest sense he typified the absolute loyalty and trustworthiness of the old-time employee once a major feature in the Far East.

An unexpected defect in the office was the antiquity of our three safes. Here we were, deep within the Communist world where we had to worry about every word, every piece of paper. Yet one safe dated from the opening of the consulate in 1904, and the other two from the 1920s! The 1904 safe was a big black iron cube: the kind one sees bandits breaking open in films of the Old West. Certainly, any half-experienced safecracker could fiddle with the dial and open it. Still, it seemed to us to be the most secure and we put our code material there. There was really no sure way to protect it. But the reliable Chao had his living quarters off the office area, and someone was at hand most of the time. Nevertheless, the vulnerability of our safes was a constant worry. For extra security, I changed the combinations on all the safes every few weeks.

Almost as soon as we arrived, we learned that communication to and from the consulate was not a simple two-way affair. All messages addressed to the consulate, such as from the State Department or the Moscow embassy, were radioed at an established time twice a day from the United States Information Service (USIS) center in Shanghai. This was standard procedure for all our consulates in China, each having its own scheduled time to receive messages. Radio messages can of course be picked up by any receiver. There is no way for the host government to verify whether a post has receiving equipment —at least this is the theory—except by its police actually entering the premises, which would violate the traditional diplomatic immunity.

Outgoing messages are a different matter. Radio-transmission equipment can be spotted immediately by the local authorities. In those days, few countries except close allies allowed a diplomatic post to send out its own messages. Although many American embassies and consulates, including Dairen, had transmitting equipment, the host government determined whether or not it would allow outgoing radio communications. Nationalist China had given permission to some American posts to have their own broadcasting stations, such as at Shanghai and elsewhere, such as our Mukden consulate.

In Dairen Benninghoff had broached this subject with the Russians several times and had been refused—the usual situation throughout the Communist world. Once I asked the Department whether this matter could be taken up again with the Russians, but it said nothing would be served "by stirring up the question." Also, I was warned that should the consulate use the transmitter without the prior authority of the Russians, it might be confiscated and even cause the closure of the consulate. Only in an extreme emergency could it be used—with the knowledge that it would surely be a one-time operation.

The whole concatenation of sending messages from Dairen to Washington seemed preposterous at first to us, but soon we became accustomed to the routine.

Our messenger delivered our messages to the Russian Consulate General (why there I never knew), which gave them to a Russian army unit to transmit to its opposite number in Vladivostok. There they were delivered to the American consulate, which copied them onto Russian telegraph forms and then delivered them to the local telegraph office, which sent them on to Moscow, where they were delivered to the American embassy, which copied them again and delivered them to the Russian overseas telegraph office. From there they were sent to the State Department in Washington, probably through the Western Union office.

Our messages—both those in code and "in clear"—were further complicated because the English alphabet is not the same as the Cyrillic Russian. Since the Russians had no facilities to transmit in English letters, we had to transpose each letter into two numbers before giving the messages to the Russian consulate general. A telegram went in that form all the way to the State Department, where it was finally decoded.

Almost every message we sent out was the kind that really had to be coded. We did not have any of the then-newfangled coding machines. Since all our coding had to be done by hand, a lot of our time was taken up by the telegram-sending.

Through sad experience we learned not to include on the telegrams any uncoded instructions like "Priority," "Urgent," "Night Action." Such terms are supposed to alert the code room of the receiver—as at the Department—to decode these telegrams first. But when we used those terms, the telegrams invariably were delayed in reaching Washington by an extra three or four days.

This complex system of getting messages out of Dairen actually worked accurately and effectively enough, although the Russians in Dairen often held them up before sending them on to Valdivostok. The average time from the date the Department would telegraph us until it received our answer back in Washington was eight days. This slow and indirect communiction added to our sense of isolation and to being left much to our own resources.

* * *

Before Patch left on the *Ilyich*, he accompanied me on my

"requisite official calls," introducing me to Dairen's official-dom. I was limited, in many cases, to the Russian Kommandant and the Chinese mayor.

We first visited the Kommandant. Major General I. Levushkin was in charge of the Dairen Kommandatura, the Russian military headquarters for the city. Everybody jumped whenever the Kommandant gave an order. He was subordinate, however, to the lieutenant general in Port Arthur. Although his official title was, confusingly, Chief of Civil Administration of Dairen, the Russians had set up a separate civil government for all of Kwantung, called the "Kwantung Administration." This was staffed by local Chinese in the titular top positions; the real work was carried on by their aides, usually assigned from the Chinese Communist Party in Manchuria.

Like so many Russian officers I had encountered, Levushkin was a stolid, expressionless person. He acted bored with my call; yet I also sensed he was irked, or maybe amused, by my being there at all. No doubt he had been briefed as to the reasons for the delays in getting the new American consul to Dairen and had already received orders about his upcoming relations with me.

The mayor of Dairen, Hsu Hsien-chai, was a short, wizened man lost behind a big desk in a huge room. He and the two aides with him seemed inordinately embarrassed by our presence. Completely unable to carry on even small talk, they gave audible sighs of relief when we left.

In contrast, the Russian consul general, Ivan Baronov, and his staff of three officers were friendly and sophisticated. Easily carrying their part of the conversation, they were on a par with the Russian embassy people whom I had known in Afghanistan. Under normal circumstances, if they had been allowed to take part in the life of the diplomatic corps, we could have become friends. I daresay this small group felt rather lonely in Dairen; their kind of educated Russian was rare there. They came to the street door with us, saying their gracious goodbyes as we climbed into our Chevrolet. Our chauffeur stepped on the starter; no response. The battery was dead. Getting out, Patch,

Culver and I pushed the decrepit car down the slight hill to start it. Meanwhile the Russians stood there, grinning sympathetically. Only other diplomats will understand the grotesque irony of having to push your car after making an official call.

* * *

We received the license plates for the Oldsmobile within a few days of our arrival. The car created a sensation as the chauffeur drove us around the city. An elegant light gray in color, it was the first postwar automobile to be seen in Dairen. We were delighted to note that within two weeks the Russian Consul General was driving a fine new Russian Zis—the equal to ours in size. Culver and I always wondered how the Russians had been able to bring in such a car so fast. Anyway, in the diplomatic game of keeping up with the Americans, the Russians had held their own.

Culver and I never did get drivers' licenses. Culver drove the Chevrolet and jeep regularly without a license, but I almost never drove a car in Dairen. I always traveled with the chauffeur or, occasionally, with Culver at the wheel. The danger of a trumped-up accident is omnipresent in hostile foreign posts; such events are always more serious if the principal officer is the driver.

Whenever I was a passenger in the car, the American flag was required to fly properly above its front fender, for all to see.

CHAPTER IV

CONSULAR WORK
(EARLY SUMMER 1948)

Protocol required me to honor the Fourth of July by inviting top local officials to some sort of social affair. Throughout the diplomatic world, entertaining on one's National Day is a chore that cannot be avoided by an ambassador or consul. Yet the form the function can take is infinite in variety.

Accordingly, for the Glorious Fourth in Dairen, I gave a buffet luncheon. I sent invitations only to the persons on whom I made official calls and to those foreigners who had maintained social relations with Patch; it was obvious no others would come. All the invited guests did appear—a total of forty-five. The menu indicated what my fine cook was capable of when we had important guests and when our supplies were still plentiful. It included veal aspic, chicken cutlets with a chicken thigh bone stuck into each one (a Russian dish), fish salad shaped like a fish with the head and tail attached in the French style, and apricot ice cream made from ice-cream mix and fresh apricots.

The most successful item, however, was American beer, which the guests had never had before. They kept drinking it long after we had used up the cold beer and were serving it warm, straight from the cartons. The Russian consul general and his staff and their wives thoroughly enjoyed themselves and stayed on and on. Our most jovial and psychologically most uncomplicated guests were the officers of a Norwegian freighter in port. A few days earlier, Culver had happened to meet one of the crew, John Finney on the street. A member of Culver's class at Yale, Finney was seeing the world as a seaman before settling down. (He is now a *New York Times* correspondent in Washington.) Through him, Culver had met the officers and invited them to our affair. The freighter captain brought with him a gift of a huge Norwegian goat cheese eight inches square and a foot high. Extremely rich, only a thin sliver is eaten at a time. A thorough extrovert, the captain, kept slicing the cheese and forcing it on everyone— which was fine, except for the Chinese mayor and his aides. Many Asiatic peoples, including the Chinese, seldom eat dairy products and cheese often nauseates them. (This type of Norwegian cheese keeps indefinitely; Culver and I were slicing away at it a half-year later and still finding it delicious.

When all the officials had gone and only a dozen guests remained, I brought out some firecrackers. Although my cook had informed me that shooting off firecrackers was illegal, I told him to buy some anyway, "from under the counter." After all, this was the Fourth of July—and we *were* in China. Traditionally, firecrackers were a major part of Chinese celebrations, and great sums were spent on them. The Communists, however, had forbidden them now as bourgeois and wasteful. We shot them off in the small garden and could see the police guards—always stationed outside the house and office—running around like headless chickens, wondering what they should do. It was all rather satisfying emotionally, if also childish on my part.

Rumors about the Norwegian freighter, the *Nortuna*, had titillated Dairen for weeks. The convolutions of local officialdum left the poor captain dazed and wondering how he ever became buried in such a pile of feathers. Daily he would wander disconsolately into the consulate and weep on our shoulders. From him we learned a fine vocabulary of vile Norweigian oaths.

The *Nortuna* was an 11,000-ton vessel flying the Panamanian flag, and was owned by a joint Norwegian-French-American company chartered in New York. It had entered Dairen on June

18 from Manila: the first non-Russian, non-Chinese commercial vessel to have arrived since the Russians forbade all trade with the rest of the world. It was, at least, the only one we or the general public ever knew about. Immediately, it was rumored that trade would soon open up again between Dairen and the "outside."

The ship brought no cargo. In the early morning on the 20th, it began loading cement, but work suddenly ceased at 10 a.m. Coolies—and freight cars full of cement—stood by idly the rest of the day. The captain tried in vain to learn what had happened. It was rumored in port that sudden orders had come from Moscow to halt shipment. Yet work recommenced the next day, and by the 24th the loading of 10,000 tons of cement was completed. The Russian harbormaster, however, said the vessel could not leave until the 29th; typically, no reason was given.

The *Nortuna* actually did not sail for another two weeks. The only excuse given to the captain was that the cement buyers had not yet paid up; but who the mysterious buyers were, or where located, the Russian shipping official refused to say. The sorely frustrated captain did not even know what his next port would be. He sent many telegrams to his home office, but never received a reply. In the end, total demurrage cost the Russians $12,000.

The captain had additional complaints as well: on his arrival, he had been told that in purchasing supplies he would be charged the official rate of 53 Kwantung yuan per one U.S. dollar, whereas he soon learned that the local exchange market was 2200 yuan. Fortunately, he did not need to buy anything. The crew members supplied themselves with money by selling cigarettes illegally at 300-500 yuan per package.

Although the *Nortuna*'s officers were all Norwegian, the crew was a mixture of many nationalities. After a few days, aware of how well they looked in contrast to the Russian sailors and most of the civilian Russians, the crew took special care of their appearance when going ashore; In port, too, the entire exterior of the ship was painted, the crew working with an unusual willingness just to show the Russians and Chinese what a shipshape vessel should look like compared with the unpainted, dingy ones in the harbor.

Early on July 12, the Russian harbormaster announced that no one except the captain would be allowed ashore because the crew were having too many fights with the local people. This was patently false because the men had been exceptionally well behaved. The captain believed the real reason was that the authorities did not want the men to mix with the population. Then, out of the blue, the official returned three hours later to say that the ship must sail immediately.

After the *Nortuna's* departure the story circulated that the family of the Ataman Grigorii Semenov had escaped as stowaways on the ship. He was the infamous, brutal White Russian Cossack leader in Siberia who had sold out to the Japanese during the turbulent days of the Russian Civil War (about 1920), when Japanese troops moved inland from Vladivostok for several hundred miles. Afterwards, Semenov fled and reached Dairen. He brought with him a large amount of gold and loot, which the Japanese confiscated. However, they gave him a comfortable pension. When the Russian military arrived in Dairen, one of their first acts was to send Semenov off to Moscow, where he was executed. His family, all women, remained in Dairen. The story of their escape on the *Nortuna* made big news locally—until it became tacitly accepted that the Russians had themselves spread this story to hide the fact they had arrested the women and sent them to Russia. Years later I learned from John Finney that the *Nortuna* sailed from Dairen to Petropavlovsk in the Kamchatka Peninsula of Siberia, where its cargo of cement was discharged. From there it went empty to Valdivostok. It had carried no stowaways.

When reporting the prolonged duress of the *Nortuna* to the Department, I speculated that some Russian official must have blundered in allowing this ship to come here. The surprised authorities were uncertain how to handle it. Once here, the long delay after loading may possibly have been an intentional ploy to see if the Chinese Nationalist government would protest. Nanking showed no interest.

Yet it was to be nearly a year before any other foreign commercial ship came to Dairen.

A curious incident during the *Nortuna* stay involved Culver and Finney. They drove to a rather isolated section of Dairen called Rokotan, looking for the swimming beach there. However, in error they took a road that led to the entrance of a Russian military equipment camp. Instead of merely shooing them away, the guard became excited and decided to report to the ranking police officer. While looking for him, the guard took the young men throughout the entire camp. Culver and Finney saw the storage depot area, the extensive military-vehicle section and the quarters of the three to five thousand soldiers who manned the station. When they did find the officer, he gave them a lecture about not driving on military roads; and that was that. Perhaps he did not realize what a fine Cook's tour the two Americans had had—all rather amusing because no nationality is so secretive about its military installations as the Russians.

* * *

Our first "monthly" courier arrived promptly in the middle of July on the *Ilyich*. It was to be five months before another reached us. To meet him at the port involved getting a special permit from the ship's captain. I had a long talk with the Captain while waiting for the paper to be prepared. It was the only really relaxed, "normal" conversation I had with a Russian all the time I was in Dairen.

Before the war he had been a pioneer ship captain in exploring for a commercial sea lane across the north of Siberia between Archangel and Vladivostok. By now this route had become a routine operation, the average voyage taking two months; the ships making it, however, were all small, three to five thousand tons. It still remained, nevertheless, a dangerous undertaking because when there is a north wind, the ice jams and the wind can crush a ship's hull. It is a frigid place, too: the average temperature in summer is just above freezing.

This talk, carried on in my halting Russian, reawakened my interest in learning the Russian language. I wanted something constructive to do in my spare time. The worse handicap, I knew, would be the lack of anyone with whom I could converse informally. We never had social contacts with Russians, and when infrequently we called on an official, he almost always had an interpreter at hand.

When I was in Moscow during the war—a time of unusually relaxed relations between Russia and its allies—a maximum of two or three hundred carefully screened persons were allowed to associate with the diplomatic corps. Although it was taken for granted that these were informers, picking up whatever bits of information they could get from us and then reporting them to the authorities, we found that talking Russian with informers provided as good practice as with anyone else. However, in Dairen we did not even have informers to use as conversationalists. Casual contact with the local Russians was impossible, for they were careful not to be seen with us out of a well-founded caution or downright fear of troubles with the police.

Then I thought of the charming Russian woman in her late thirties who had attended our Fourth of July celebration at the consulate. A friend of the Patch family, she had been a frequent visitor at the Americans' residences. Mrs. Schumann was quite willing to give Russian lessons to both Culver and me.

Although I had spent a year in Moscow and had worked hard at the language, my ability remained superficial and was made even weaker by my two years in Afghanistan since those studies. For Culver it was a new language. In the summertime, we settled down to lessons every day, and they continued throughout our stay in Dairen.

Russian really is a dreadful language. Every verb has two separate forms: "I spanked the baby yesterday" is quite different from "I spanked the baby every day last week." For every verb one must learn two separate words, often with no apparent connection. And every noun and adjective has six cases. For a noun, this means twelve endings in the singular and plural. An adjective, in addition, has three genders for us to worry about, which means a total of thirty-six endings to remember in the singular and plural. And the use of a number in a sentence follows a different set of rules. Trying to say, "Three nice ladies broke five pretty teacups on May eleventh" was torture.

Our instructor was the wife of Edmund Schumann, the chancellor of the former German consulate in Dairen. With the other German men, Schumann had been taken off to internment in Siberia in 1945. His wife—handsome, intelligent, resourceful—was a born "survivor." One got the feeling that somehow she could cope with almost any adversity life might present. She had found work in a Russian office and even had a small apartment for herself and her three children. Edmund Jr., was seventeen years old, Marlene fourteen, and Karen seven. Compared to the other German wives, Mrs. Schumann lived rather comfortably, which inevitably caused jealousy and resentment toward her.

Mrs. Schumann's unique background undeniably helped her maintain a sense of adaptability and inner strength as well as set her apart from the particular problems of the people in the small German community in Dairen. She was actually a native Russian; her family, originally from Leningrad, had been among the refugees who managed to reach Vladivostok during the Revolution. They were there during the exciting time when the city lived its brief semi-capitalist career. However, her father died, and the family did not get away before the Soviets solidified their control. In 1929, she married Edmund Schumann, who was then secretary in the German consulate in Vladivostok. This was during a brief period when Russia and Germany had friendly relations, so when Schumann was transferred to another post, his wife was able to obtain a Russian exit visa.

Mrs. Schumann's case is the only one I know where there were no complications in leaving Russia. The extreme difficulty in getting exit visas for the Russian wives of foreign diplomats, journalists, and other men stationed in the Soviet Union has caused many personal tragedies. When I was in the Moscow embassy during World War II, although there was friendship between the United States and Russia, the half-dozen Russian wives of American diplomats and journalists continued to be refused exit visas. A technique developed to deal with this. When some high American official, such as the Secretary of State, was having talks in Moscow he would, at the proper time, make a personal appeal to Stalin for two or three of the wives; sometimes the visas then would be granted. Otherwise, when a husband eventually would be transferred to another country, he would be faced with the tragic decision of whether to leave his wife behind or to give up his career and try to stay in Moscow. In a few cases the husband would find a niche and be able to remain. A decade might pass and still no visa. Often the continued tension and uncertainty would break up the marriage, and the husband finally would return home alone. From the Russian point of view, any citizen who marries a foreigner and wants to accompany him abroad is a traitor. This phobia is part of the Communist ethic which make those countries seem like absolute prisons to outsiders. The situation today remains essentially unchanged.

That Mrs. Schumann possessed an authentic Russian exit visa, was now a German citizen, had diplomatic status, and was not a White Russian (a term implying she had left the Soviet Union illegally) would be important factors later on in her efforts with the local Dairen authorities to get permission to leave.

Our association with Mrs. Schumann made us more alert and sensitive to the big problem of the handful of foreigners still living in Dairen—most of them desperately anxious to leave. We soon discovered that their problems were becoming our problems too.

An oddly assorted group of nationalities made up Dairen's foreign colony or colonies. ("Colony" is the term used to describe those foreigners living in a city abroad if there are enough of them to make a little community by themselves—such as the "American colony," the "Italian colony," and so forth.) Before Pearl Harbor, a full hive of such colonies represented most of the world's trading countries here.

Dairen long had been recognized as one of the most cosmopolitan posts that a consular officer or the agent of a trading house or of an international bank could have in the Far East. For one thing, it was a free port, with a wide range of luxury articles in the stores at cheap prices. Social life was centered in the International Club (which did not admit Japanese or Chinese to membership). Dairen was also a major summer resort for people from Shanghai and Manchuria; the coastal weather was temperate even in winter, and the beaches were good. The Japanese had built beautiful hotels that offered excellent services; they had also constructed golf courses and other recreational facilities. This sort of pleasure-taking changed in the late 1930s, when the Japanese imperialists became nasty and arrogant: then it became distasteful to have relations with them in business or diplomacy or social affairs. The number of foreigners in Dairen, however, was not reduced.

With Pearl Harbor came the internment of the British and Americans. Although the Germans, Italians, and French—considered allies—were left free, they still were trapped here since there was no way for them to return home. And so this part of the original foreign colony stayed on throughout the war, including a miscellany of neutral and other nationalities, such as Eastern Europeans. Apparently, they had a rather relaxed life, untrammeled by the worries of the rest of the world. Dairen was not a bad place for sitting out the war. Towards the end, it was bombed slightly but nothing like the cities of Japan.

When the Russians arrived in Dairen shortly after Japan's collapse, the troops were officially given three weeks of looting—the same policy as sometimes was allowed when the Russians moved into the cities of Turkestan some seventy-five years earlier. After three weeks, any soldier caught stealing in

Dairen was shot (at least, that was the general's published edict). Actually, it was two months before the Russian troops became a disciplined force. Except for the Japanese civilians, the ones who suffered most were the Germans. Their homes were ransacked, daughters raped, and men interned (all of which and more the Germans themselves had done wantonly in Russia).

Twenty-two of the German men and five of the women were transported to Siberia. Before they left, the wives had the chance to bring them clothes and personal possessions. In great confusion they debated whether it was better to take their husbands good, warm clothes and extra little things they could use to trade for necessities, or whether one should assume that everything would be stolen by the Russians. As a result, some prisoners went off to camps in Siberia with practically nothing, while others even had fur coats. The reports later received were that the Russians had let them keep their belongings. The men were in various camps for about five years before finally being allowed to go to Germany—some as early as 1949. And they all did get back.

Seventy-six German nationals were left in Dairen. Although the Germans elsewhere in China already had been repatriated by this time, those in Dairen had been stranded because of their isolation within the Russian area. Except for a few, mostly elderly men and teen-age boys, all of this German group were women and children. Jammed together in an old hotel building shortly after the Russian occupation, they were not molested by the authorities, except for periodic police questioning. Left to their own devices as to survival, eventually some obtained jobs in the state-owned trusts; others sold their jewelry and any other possessions they had been able to carry with them from their homes, and lived meagerly and frugally.

During the first year of the Russian occupation most of the non-German, non-Japanese, "miscellaneous foreigners" caught in Dairen by the war managed to leave. Then the situation froze. It became much more difficult—and by now, no one had been able to get out for ten months. Our arrival may have sparked the hitherto-dormant decision levels of Moscow to think about Dairen, because suddenly it was announced that an evacuation ship would be coming shortly to take foreigners to Japan. Also, some of the Japanese civilians still held by Russia were to be repatriated later in the summer on a special ship. It looked as if the Russians had decided to "clear the decks."

The miscellaneous foreigners still in Dairen numbered about fifty. Some had not been able previously to get their exit visas; some had stayed on voluntarily, hoping the Communists would let them resume their businesses; and some who had lived in Dairen all their lives, had been unable to bring themselves to leave this place they considered their home. The eastern Europeans had no country of their own to which to return since Communist governments were now in control. By now, however, almost all were desperate to go. They believed that this evacuation ship might be their last chance to escape out of the Russian realm because of the steadily tightening exit controls.

In order to leave, each foreigner had to have an exit visa. To get this he first had to produce a permit allowing him to enter Japan, which entailed getting clearance from the occupation authorities there, the Supreme Commander for the Allied Power or SCAP. In remote, cut-off Dairen, telegraph services were unreliable and prohibitively expensive, and one needed special police permits even to use them. As for mail, it was practically non-existent. Most letters received were smuggled in from Shanghai and Peking.

It would have been a simple matter for the Kommandant to set up a desk in the headquarters building to transmit applications for the SCAP clearances to the Russian representative in Tokyo. Any other government would have done this. Instead, the Russians sat back, crossed their arms and said that the foreigners' exit problems were not their concern at all. Yet these were not enemy nationals; they were from a dozen countries, several of which had been Russia's allies.

So the foreigners came to the American consulate for help in communicating with SCAP—although these assorted aliens were clearly not our responsibility. Out of compassion I agreed to act as the transmission channel. At times I considered myself foolish, for this resulted in a clerical madhouse for a while, with telegrams being rushed back and forth to Tokyo; ("rushed" is the wrong term; even under ideal conditions when SCAP could act quickly the time lag was between one and two weeks). And naturally, all the responsibility—and ill will—was placed on the consulate for delays and misunderstandings. Each evacuee was supposed to have an immigration visa to a third country, or adequate funds to pay for a prolonged residence in Japan while arranging such a visa. SCAP bent over backwards to supply needed assistance. In the end nearly all the applicants did get away, except for a few whose exist visas the Russians rescinded at the last minute or were not given them at all. About a dozen remained in Dairen, plus the Germans and an unknown number of Poles, Czechs, and other Eastern Europeans, who apparently still wanted to stay.

In these first months I did not know of the high cost of our telegrams; the bill was paid by our embassy in Moscow. Later, when I counted up the cost to the United States in behalf of these persons, many thousands of dollars, plus the labor of SCAP personnel in Japan, I sometimes half-regretted letting myself become involved. Typical Russian intransigence had trapped these unfortunate persons in Dairen. Yet those same responsible officials stayed passively and indifferently on the sidelines, took in the American telegraph money, and saw to it that the Americans were blamed for any mishaps that occurred. Ultimately I found satisfaction and pride in the consulate's invaluable help in enabling the foreigners to leave Dairen. A humane action, it was initiated entirely by Americans.

A month and a half before the Japanese repatriation ship was due, two exceedingly nervous Japanese men came into the consulate. Claiming to represent all the Japanese in Dairen, they gave me a letter which they wished me to send to General Douglas MacArthur, Commander-in-Chief of SCAP. The letter described their poor living conditions and begged for the removal of the entire group. The two men acted terrified throughout the interview, obviously concerned as to what would happen to them when the policeman outside the door reported their visit to the consulate. But they had come in desperation.

At the time of the mass repatriation of Japanese civilians in the preceding year, the Russians announced that only 3000 remained in Dairen; this letter claimed that there were actually 9000. (Since the Japanese residents in Dairen during the 1930s numbered some 150,000—almost one-quarter of the city's total population—it was expected that many of them had been unable to get away.)

Among the Japanese residents in Dairen it was mostly specialists (such as doctors, nurses and engineering technicians) and their families who had been forced to remain, but they had been assured they would be allowed to go to Japan a year later. They had been promised a double raise of rations after two months and a triple raise in half a year. However, the food they received was primarily corn flour, often spoiled, and a little kaoliang, a local grain. Reading between the lines of the letter, I realized that the worse hardship for them was being forced to attend daily a two-hour lecture on Communist doctrine.

Now, learning that a repatriation ship would be coming shortly, they feared that many or most of them might be kept in Dairen for another year. The same promises as before were being made; it would be easy for the Russians to continue to hold several thousand of them due to the discrepancy in the figures of Japanese said to be here. And, clearly, a single ship could not take them all away.

Those Japanese specialists who were especially useful and who would not sign "contracts" to stay, were now being threatened that the Russians would send them away to remote places in Manchuria. The contracts were worded to seem voluntarily signed. The letter told of a group of eighteen Japanese doctors and nurses from the Dairen Red Cross who, two years previously, had been "invited" to visit Antung in Manchuria as representatives of the International Red Cross. There they had been divided up into small medical units; nothing had been heard of them since.

I duly telegraphed the contents of the two Japanese letters to SCAP. When the Japanese repatriation was arranged a month later, two ships arrived instead of the expected one. Doubtless, the letter in alerting SCAP to the presence of 9000 instead of 3000 Japanese in Dairen and SCAP's consequent notification to the Russians had played a key role in the repatriation of the bulk of the Japanese remaining in Dairen. Many, however, still remained—how large a number we never learned. No other repatriation ship came for a year. And by then, I had learned more intimately the reasons for the foreigners' anxiety to get away from Dairen.

Just now, the news we were receiving from the State Department broadcasts seemed none too encouraging to Americans in an isolated post in a Communist enclave, where it took at least a week to get some response from our chiefs in Washington. The more we heard, the more soberly we regarded our position in Dairen.

During our first month in Dairen the Berlin Blockade began, whereby the Russians carefully cut off all motor, rail, and barge traffic into the section of Berlin governed by the Western powers. The blockade was intended to starve into submission the more than two million inhabitants of West Berlin. Russia's announced reason however, was to prevent the Allies from inaugurating a new currency for West Germany, thereby splitting Germany permanently into two parts. It insisted that economic reforms had to be applied to the country as a whole, although it already had demonstrated it would, and could, prevent such reforms through its power of veto.

To support the citizens of Berlin, President Truman instigated the American-British airlift over the objections of his own air force Chief of Staff who insisted it was impractical. It was nicknamed "Operation Vittles." Truman's decision fortunately was the right one. The alternatives had been either to launch a maximum attack on the Russians "before they got the A-bomb" or to "fight our way through" the Russian barriers into Berlin. Both of these had been urged strenuously by high-ranking military and civilian advisers. Throughout the entire time of the airlift, Russian military planes continually harassed the Allies' planes and staged "maneuvers" that included bombing and parachute practice in the flight lanes. Public opinion in the West was so tense that if there had been even one collision with a Russian plane open war might have resulted.

During our first month in Dairen we also read these headlines: In France, the Marshall Aid Pact (to revitalize the economy of West Europe) was ratified, although Communists and Gaullists voted against it. Russia's relations with Yugoslavia were reaching the breaking point after Tito thwarted an apparent attempt by Russian agents to overthrow him. The United States revealed that Russia had not yet returned, as it had agreed to do, 110 ships loaned under Lend-Lease. In Costa Rica, constitutional guarantees were suspended after discovery of a Communist plot for a coup d'etat. In Malaya, Communist-inspired guerrillas openly revolted, killing and pillaging the rubber plantations in an attempt to seize the government.

And in China, the Communists' sieges of Mukden and Chang-chun (the principal cities closest to Dairen in Manchuria) were tightening; the food supplies for almost a million civilians was nearly at the starvation level.

That was quite a lot of action around our tight little globe. The cold war was at flood force and a lot of people were being swept helplessly downstream.

CHAPTER V

COLD WAR
IN THE SUMMERTIME
(MIDSUMMER 1948)

In times of international tension like the cold war one cannot know how far the fall-out from any incident may spread. An episode taking place in New York had major repercussions for us.

On July 31, 1948, Mrs. Oksana Kosenkina, a chemistry teacher in the school for children of the Russian delegation to the United Nations, fled from the Russian consulate general to a farm operated by the daughter of the great Russian writer, Leo Tolstoy, near Nyack, New York. Kosenkina had been scheduled to return to Russia that day. The Un-American Activities Committee of the House of Representatives was in the midst of its hearings on Whittaker Chambers' charges against Alger Hiss and others regarding their alleged activities as Russian spies. Immediately upon her escape the committee sought to have Kosenkina appear for questioning.

On August 7 Russian agents "rescued" her from the farm and brought her back to the Soviet consulate building in New York City. Five days later she jumped from a third floor window onto a concrete courtyard, suffering serious injuries. The press was keeping such close watch on the building that photographs were taken showing her being carried back into the building. These pictures appeared in newspapers around the world. The sensational story, as well as that of two other Russian teachers who had escaped separately about the same time and were still in hiding in the New York area, caused even bigger headlines than the Whittaker Chambers testimony or the current Big Four meetings concerning the Berlin Blockade.

A week later, the United States ordered the recall of the Russian consul general in New York because of the tactics he had used in trying to persuade the three teachers to return to Russia. I omit the Russian side of this story and give no details of the American countercharges in this complex affair. It was the first time a high Russian diplomat had been ousted from the United States. On August 25, Russia retaliated by ending consular relations with the United States. This meant the closing of its consulates in New York and San Francisco as well as the closing of the American consulate in Vladivostok—our only consulate at that time in Russia.

The Dairen consulate, however, remained open, demonstrating the always unique status of our post. Although we obviously were under Russian control, juridically we were under Chinese sovereignty.

Culver and I followed this prolonged drama via our chief news source, the daily radio news bulletin which the State Department broadcast to all its posts around the world, and which Radio Operator Chao typed up for us.

We thought the closing of the Vladivostok consulate would affect us only by making it even more difficult to get a courier to us. We did not realize that from that time on none of our telegrams reached Washington.

The Department did wire instructions immediately for us to address our messages directly to the embassy in Moscow. When I called on the Russian consul general, he was unable to say whether the new address would be acceptable; he must first check with his superiors in Kwantung and, probably, in Moscow. Since the dispatch of our daily telegrams was not something that could hang in abeyance, I told him that henceforth I nevertheless would send all my telegrams addressed to the embassy. None were received there.

Gradually we realized we were getting no replies from the Department, obviously indicating that it was unaware that it was not getting messages from us. I made another call on the

Russian consul general; as always he knew nothing.

The Department woke up to the situation three weeks after the closing of the Vladivostok consulate. It then took another two weeks for it to arrange with the Russian Foreign Office to have our telegrams sent, still via the Russian consulate general, directly to the embassy in Moscow. Although this was exactly what I had been doing, the telegrams did arrive there from then on without trouble.

This evidence of the State Department's indifference as to whether or not it was hearing from us was perhaps the most discouraging experience I had while in Dairen. It is one thing to be isolated at a distant post. To be ignored or, more exactly, carelessly forgotten, was nerve-wracking. Ever afterwards, I knew that if the Russians, for whatever reason, created an incident that would prevent our sending out telegrams, it could be several weeks before the Department would sense something was wrong and start investigating.

I now sent copies of all our telegrams of the missing weeks, at the same time alerting our embassy in Moscow, which paid our telegraph bills, to pay for only this one set of the telegrams. The cost of these messages was extremely high, fixed according to the official rate in Dairen, which meant over a dollar for each alphabetical letter. Always conscious of the outlandish cost, I pared our words to the bone.

When the first monthly Dairen telegram bill was presented to the Moscow embassy after the resumption of service, it totaled more than that of the embassy's bill itself. The Department thereupon asked me to restrict my periodic reporting via telegrams and to limit other messages to the most urgent matters. I did this to a degree but, since I already had been using discretion, not much further reduction was possible.

This cost applied only to sending our messages to Moscow; from there they were treated as any routine messages out of the embassy, meaning it had to pay an extra charge to get them on to Washington. After two months the embassy did manage to arrange for us to address our telegrams directly to the Secretary of State, Washington, thus eliminating that extra charge.

Whatever our other problems with the Russians might be, the technical transmission of our telegrams was usually handled satisfactorily. It was rare that our coded messages arrived so garbled that the Department asked for a repeat. Transmission was slow, but at least it was accurate.

A sorry result of the Kosenkina affair for us was our missing out on the courier who had been waiting to get to us from Vladivostok. Although the consulate ceased to function officially from the moment of closing, the staff did not leave until five weeks later. We never understood what could have prevented the courier from coming on to Dairen. It ought to have been merely a matter of taking the next available ship; the Moscow embassy could have backstopped the paperwork. But removed from the frustrations imposed by the Russians, we could not know all the factors involved. Anyway, the courier, instead of returning to Shanghai, was forced to go on to Moscow via the Trans-Siberian Railroad. What happened then to Dairen's pouches we never learned. When the next courier did reach us, in December, they were not with him. But they finally did show up with the courier who arrived the following April—eight months later!

This international incident also put the end to some promising negotiations to fly our couriers from Tokyo to Vladivostok on a bimonthly Russian plane. The courier service had been considering this route only as a last resort because of the long-proven Russian undependability in providing seats and baggage space for couriers on other Russian air routes, even when space had been reserved. However, without the Vladivostok consulate staff now to oversee that terminus, the idea was shelved as too unreliable and risky for the couriers.

The subject which began to cause the greatest number of telegrams concerned getting couriers to us. It was not entirely the Russians' fault, although a major factor involved the time in making application for visas and whatever documentation they required and then waiting for a reply. A serious problem derived from the Department itself. Its worldwide courier service maintained a tight and complex schedule for its staff. Since the average round trip from Shanghai to Dairen and return took three months, it was a large chunk of personnel time to take out of the overall schedule. Worse, a pair of couriers now had to be used for security reasons, since the Vladivostok consulate's closing. There was also the great cost of the two men traveling to and from Dairen; expenses were paid in Russian rubles, and the rate of exchange was inordinately high. (I was always hoping that the Department would send the couriers to us on a small Korean-flag vessel from South Korea. This would have been quick and certainly no more expensive. But the Department steadily shied away from the prospect of more problems with the Russians—perhaps rightly so.)

Most of our time in Dairen, it seemed, we were always waiting for couriers who rarely arrived. The once-dreamed-of plan for bimonthly visits—a frequent and dependable connection with the world outside— progressively dwindled. We came to realize that we would be lucky to get any couriers again, anytime.

* * *

The protracted break in communications with Washington helped to kill off an intriguing project that had come to us mysteriously and was never adequately explained.

One day, a middle-aged Chinese man stopped Culver on the street and said he had known his parents in Peking before the war. They had a number of meetings in a park and eventually, the man admitted he belonged to the Chinese Communist intelligence agency. The consulate was "within his jurisdiction"; therefore he could meet with Culver openly. It turned out, too, that he had not known Culver's parents at all; he had used this as an initial excuse for talking with him.

In one conversation, Culver told of his wish to visit Harbin either by air or car; the agent said he would try to arrange such a trip with his superiors. The first, rather prompt reply was that the Chinese Communists welcomed the idea of the trip as a means of proving that their rule in Harbin was independent of Russia. The agent reported that he himself would be permitted to escort Culver in the consulate's jeep, flying the American flag, but that no one else, such as a chauffeur would be allowed. This could be an unusually important observation trip. No American official had been in Communist Manchuria since the war, and Harbin at that time was presumably the center of their administration for the whole northern part of China.

We first had to receive from our embassy in Nanking, or from the Department, permission for Culver to make the trip. I telegraphed the request, saying that although there was no proof of the agent's official position, I believed Culver would be safe because the Communist hierarchy would take special care regarding him, and also because he spoke Chinese fluently. The proof of the Communists' welcome would be whether indeed, they gave him a travel pass. It was all tenuous—but, of course, one plays out such leads as long as possible; if it came off, this would be a unique trip for an American official.

One week passed, and no word came from the embassy about the plan. I sent a follow-up telegram. A second week went by. By then we realized that our telegrams were not getting through. Since it was uncertain when communication channels again would be open, I told Culver to go ahead on my own responsibility and apply for a travel pass.

The difficult factor concerning such documents was the conflicting lines between governmental jurisdictions. To whom would Culver make his application? When was Dairen an integral part of the rest of the Kwantung Peninsula, and when was it a separate entity? Trying to guess the answer in advance was a useless exercise.

The military government which the Russians set up in the fall of 1945 was called the Port Arthur Naval Base Area and its "capital" was Port Arthur.

The first postwar civilian administration, organized by the Russians for all Kwantung and with its "capital" in Dairen, had consisted essentially of a mayor and a deputy mayor appointed for each town. The mayor normally was a local resident, but the deputy mayor, at least in the larger places, was usually a member of the Chinese Communist Party of Manchuria. The former was a puppet; the latter exercised the power, that is, whatever limited power the Kommandant chose to delegate. This civil administration had not been authorized at all by the Chinese Nationalist Government, the legal sovereign power. This same pattern was generally followed in later administrative reorganizations.

A year later, in November 1946, Russia brought into being, by a sort of immaculate conception, a more formal civil administration for all Kwantung. Four sub-units were formed, one of which was Dairen. This government was called the Port Arthur—Dairen United Political Administration. On April 4, 1947, its name was changed to "Kwantung Administration" (which is the term I use throughout the text). The Russians assigned to it "full" jurisdiction over the Chinese population of all the area. Non-Chinese, such as the Russians, the White Russians, the Japanese, and the miscellaneous foreigners, remained under Russian military jurisdiction.

Russia claimed the Kwantung Administration was elected by the Chinese residents, but in reality the officials had been appointed by the Russians and/or the Chinese Communist party. The Administration remained subservient to the Russian military, both in Dairen as well as in the rest of the peninsula. Although the men in its top positions may indeed have been local citizens, such minor authority as the Russians delegated was carried out by their aides, who were mostly active Chinese Communists from the outside, probably on direct assignment from the Communist forces in Manchuria.

The Russian propaganda disseminated the pretense that because Kwantung was under the control of "local" Chinese, the area was "separate" from the civil war going on between the Nationalists and the Communists. Chinese Communist soldiers who came to Dairen for medical treatment or for other reasons had to rent civilian clothes so they would not appear on the streets in uniform.

As another facet of this "separateness," no one admitted publicly that any Chinese Communist organizations operated in Kwantung, even though most local political groups were behind-the-scenes branches of parent bodies making up the Chinese Communist party in Manchuria. And constant military support was being given to the Communist forces, such as by manufacturing small-arms ammunition and by giving them specialized military training. At any one time, several hundred Chinese Communists would be in Dairen receiving officer training. Some Chinese officials held positions concurrently in the Administration and in the Manchurian element of the Communist Party. Also, many Communists were in the local police force. Above all, Kwantung provided a base area where the Chinese Communists could obtain supplies. Whether they generally received what they expected we could never judge.

Now came the problem of getting a travel pass for Culver to travel with his new-found Chinese colleague to Harbin. It turned out that he needed three approvals. First, he needed permission to leave Dairen city, the jurisdiction of the Kommandant. Second, he needed permission to travel from the Dairen boundary through the Port Arthur Naval Base Area to the Manchurian border; this could be obtained from the Kommandant acting in his subordinate role to the commanding general in Port Arthur. Third, he needed the permission of the Chinese Communist authorities in Manchuria to enter Manchuria at the Kwantung border—which, presumably, would include a permit to travel from the border to Harbin, a distance of nearly six hundred miles. This approval might be obtained from the Kwantung Administration.

"Permission" is perhaps too formal a word. It did not necessarily involve separate documents, but might be contained on a single piece of paper. We had never seen one, and thus did not know what form it took. Although travel from Dairen into Manchuria was achieved by only a handful of civilians, it was done rather regularly. What routes these persons took when in Manchuria was a mystery to the consulate; for one thing, it depended on the battle lines and guerrilla operations, and these shifted constantly.

Culver's first step was to get permission from the Chinese Communits to enter Manchuria and go on to Harbin. If granted, it would show this project did have their approval. By the time the permission was received, maybe our telegraphic communications with the Department would have reopened. Should the embassy or the Department say "no," the project could still be cancelled.

Culver called on the chairman of the Kwantung Administration to make his application and then we waited for an answer. From the beginning we assumed the pass would never be given if it depended on Russian action; behind the scenes, however, the Chinese Communists perhaps would pull strings or otherwise handle matters in such a way that the Russians would not have to come out in the open by either agreeing or disagreeing.

When no answer came from the Kwantung administration within the following week, we recognized the deal was off. (Not answering letters or applications or queries was the standard Communist tactic when the answer was really "no.") This negative response could have been due either to Russian disapproval or to a change of mind by the Chinese Communists. When he saw Culver, the agent said it was the latter—that the authorities at Harbin had remembered all the anti-American signs painted on the walls of the city and other evidences of rancorous propaganda. Having an official American guest clearly would be confusing to the populace—and possibly dangerous for him.

When we did get our replies from the Nanking embassy and the Department, the former favored the proposed trip but the latter was against it. The Department believed it possible that the entire plan had been concocted in order to leave me alone in Dairen.

Also, later meetings with the agent indicated that he was hoping to defect by escaping to a non-Communist area. The agent said the Communists in a newly occupied area near Peking had recently killed his parents and his children. But he declared that he would not enter a Chinese Nationalist area, as he might be able to do, because the Nationalists were reported to kill defectors as "renegades," instead of welcoming them.

The Department stated that if the agent were actually an authentic defector—which on the surface seemed doubtful—he might be exposed while on the trip; the resulting punishment would jeopardize Culver's position and possibly his safety.

After the travel plans fell through, the agent told Culver that he was scheduled to go within two months, to South Korea to work as a Communist agent. He asked the United States to arrange a contact there to whom he could defect; he was given an address in Seoul. Then, one day, he said his orders had been changed: he had to go to Manchuria. We never saw him again. And we never knew whether his defector role was "for real" or a part of his espionage duties.

* * *

Espionage, of course, was one of the most dramatized of international activities during the intense cold war period. The sort of work that Culver Gleysteen and I did in the Dairen consulate, that outpost in the Communist sphere—primarily information-gathering for our government—was decidedly suspect in the eyes of the Russian and local Chinese officials. To them we were spies, whom the exigencies of the moment had forced them to let inside the front door.

To all dictators and totalitarian groups, everyone who is not with them is against them; and everyone who is against them must, perforce, be a spy if he is within, so to speak, peeking distance. Thus, must foreigners living or visiting in such a country automatically are considered to be possible spies. Nor is this anything new. The Russians—that most xenophobic of peoples—have had this attitude for centuries. And the Chinese, who have long practised their own brand of xenophobia—a sort of indifferent disdain for the alien barbarian—today take for granted that each foreign diplomat is essentially a spy. To be stationed in Peking today is the same, psychologically, as being stationed in Moscow. And the diplomat who befools himself into thinking he has broken through this distrustful or hostile barrier is indeed naive. Nor will this condition be changing within the foreseeable future.

It is both interesting and sad, however, that in many Western capitals, and also in New York City, although the local populace may regard all Communist diplomats as out-and-out spies, the Communist diplomats there can have social relations with anyone wishing to accept their invitations. This is in sharp contrast to the atmosphere in Communist cities where the Western diplomats usually are efficiently isolated except from certain carefully selected individuals. All other residents socialize with the foreigners at a personal peril, which may be immediate or, depending on the political climate, latent. Right now, our relations with China and Russia are unprecedentedly friendly, so the number of local people willing to meet American diplomats is large. However, there must be many persons, experienced with their government's tactics as international politics change, who do not wish it recorded in their dossiers that they have been unduly friendly with a Western diplomat.

As a logical result of this viewpoint of Communist officials toward the foreign diplomats among them, every effort is made to infiltrate informers into the nests of their enemies, the local embassies and consulates; plus wire taps and whatever else is at hand. Years ago, this practice shocked the newcomers from democracies; now they resignedly accept it as a matter of course—which is not necessarily progress in the upward striving toward a civilized world, especially since this sort of thing now goes on in nearly all capitals, regardless of ideologies. In the Dairen setting it was natural for Culver and me to assume we had informers both in the office and in our households. But which members of the staff? Through intuition, nothing more, we rather shortly decided on our chauffeur and both our Number One Boys. We were not quite so certain about Ch'en, the accountant. Probably not either of our cooks. Head Clerk Chao definitely not. And Radio Operator Chao, who had come with us, had been checked out in Shanghai.

But if we fired the informers, whom could we get to replace them? Only other informers. Actually, it was a simple matter of protocol: to ignore their informing as long as they did not let themselves get caught openly, because then, to save face, we really had to fire them. Not long after our arrival, Culver discovered his Number One Boy going through his personal papers. Also, our "ahmah" (laundress) really seemed over-zealous. Both were dismissed, presumably to be replaced by other informers.

And, what if the servants were indeed informers? (As has been observed at many a diplomatic post, informers make the best servants. For one thing, they are more attentive.) It actually did not make much difference whether any or all of them were informers. Always conscious of risk, Culver and I never said anything of importance in their presence. We did not take classified papers to the house or even outside the one room at the office reserved for our codes and confidential files; this room we always kept locked. Our locks on the file cabinets and safes were by no means secure, but breaking into them would be more drastic and revealing than merely snooping.

Those informers inside our consulate or household staff we assumed had been told to look out for any secret spying activity on our part. This was something—for want of a better word—tangible.

The term "informer" also applies to the network of people reporting to the police any criticism a citizen may make, no matter how inadvertently, about the local regime.

Every Communist or other dictatorship country has a "secret police" organization. This is a misnomer, since much of the organization is highly visible. The men usually wear special uniforms, and everyone in town knows where the building or buildings are in which seized persons are interrogated and often tortured. The only thing secret about the secret police is which people, i.e., informers, on your block or factory shift or among your friends are reporting even the slightest derogatory comment about the power structure to the MVD. (In Russia, the KGB are today's initials; in my day, in Dairen, the secret police were called MVD, before that KNVD, and before that OGPU.) The Russians had been in Dairen three years and had firmly established a KGB apparatus that was all-pervasive and to which the Chinese police of the Kwantung Administration were subordinate.

Consequently, whenever I mention that the local people were too fearful to talk with the consulate personnel or to come to our residence and office, I mean they were afraid the MVD would take them in for questioning. The Soviet government in Moscow had declared openly that the Americans were its enemies. Thus, any local person's contact with us was fraught with the danger of immediate interrogation: a danger hammered home time and again in every propaganda medium. Any individual talking with us was well aware of the risk.

In order not to implicate the innocent, Culver and I were careful to avoid talking with anyone unless he himself made the first approach; then we assumed he knew what he was doing and had weighed the consequences. Shopkeepers, foreign-exchange dealers, and others whom we met in the normal course of our business were, perforce, in a different category, and we continued these contacts unless a shopkeeper specifically asked us not to return, as sometimes happened. On one occasion I was in the Russian department store making a purchase and talked for about five minutes with a Russian clerk. I heard later that after I left, two Russian officers from the Kommandatura reprimanded her for being friendly to "our enemy," threatening punishment if she did it again.

This subject of a local people's avoidance of Americans is more complex, of course, than putting all the blame on fear. For more than a decade, the populace in Dairen had been subjected to intense anti-American propaganda, first by the Japanese beginning in the middle 1930s and then by the Russians. Probably at no time had most individuals heard a single good thing said about Americans. No American publications or movies were available; no news items were printed about the United States unless twisted to make them anti-American.

The most effective propaganda medium was the lectures and meetings that all workers had to attend several times a week. The people were undoubtedly bored by the amount of time they had to give to these affairs and by the constant repetition. Nevertheless, the anti-American lies were pounded in hour after hour, month after month, year after year. Whatever small doubts most listeners may once have had were gone now. Repugnance toward anything American was rife, especially among persons under thirty years of age. Thus, store clerks may have been rude to me because of fear of the omnipresent police and informers; but their hostility may have been equally due to a revulsion against association with an American.

So except for a few pleasant contacts with foreigners like Mrs. Schumann, our social isolation in Dairen was complete.

Books have been written about the great successes and failures of the plethora of intelligence agencies of the major nations, which now operate, apparently, in every corner of our hyperactive planet. Usually the books emphasize that most of these superagencies live on a steady ingestion of innumerable bits and pieces of information, for which a network of informers is only one of several sources. However, there always comes the time when the flow of new information is turned off and a list of "data" must be typed up. Some gifted person in a cloistered office, today with the help of a computer, neatly selects a small percentage of worthwhile items and says, in an irrevocable pronouncement: "Now this is what is happening." Then he nonchalantly turns away and leaves it to the action people in another branch of the government to decide what has to be done about the whole messy thing.

Information gathering abroad is a beautifully structured organism, effiently designed for "the right people" to know exactly what "the wrong people" are up to.

Beautifully structured, yes, but, like a brontosaurus, it is so often vacuous at the top, the brain part. It is easy enough, generally, to get the pieces of information flowing into the central office. But is there really that gifted person—plus computer—working away at collating and digesting the material? Or do the items merely pile up in a corner because he and his staff are too rushed to read them? Or if he does indeed read them seriously and thoughtfully, is he intelligent enough to understand their purport? And if he does make the right analysis and passes it along to the action officials elsewhere in the government, will they believe him or will they go off at a tangent because of some extraneous "gut feeling"?

These became important questions in relation to the work of the Dairen consulate and also the the Foreign Service as a whole as it was then operating in China.

For, while informers were informing the Russians and Chinese Communists about us, we were reporting also to Washington about what was going on in Dairen.

There is no difference some persons may say, between the spy or informer acting in secret and the diplomat describing openly and legally what he sees or hears or reads in the press. To me, however—and I dare say to most professional diplomats—there is a great difference. In Dairen I was not a spy; I was a diplomat reporting to the State Department those data which I thought would be of use to its policy makers—data about this unique Russian-Chinese Communist microcosm. I soon came to regard these day-to-day observations as the primary reason for the consulate's existence.

Because of his knowledge of Chinese, Culver Gleysteen's chief job, (and it was almost a full-time job) was to read the local Chinese-language newspapers and periodicals and then to send to the Department a resumé of the material. Nearly every diplomatic and consular post does this in some form, usually as a weekly report sent by pouch through a courier, or sometimes as a daily telegram sent "in clear" (i.e., not coded). Because our courier service was too haphazard, a report would have little value; so we sent all such data by telegram.

There were four Dairen Chinese-language newspapers (the only Russian-language paper was published by the Kommandatura and was not available to us). Each was published by a specific organization: the Kwantung

Administration, the Labor Union, the South Manchurian Communist party and, apparently, the Kommandatura. Also, newspapers from Harbin and, later, Mukden were available in the stores.

The press material we thus reported is hard to characterize. As a comparable current example I will say that today, in the American consulate general in Hong Kong, there is a large staff of readers who for years have scanned carefully all periodicals that come out of China. Their reports are so thorough that the end result is nearly as encyclopedic as *Who's Who* and the index of the *New York Times* combined—masses of names connected with the Communist party and with provincial and city governments, plus the bulk of news items both national and local. However, it is not up to these press readers to determine what is really important, although they must use a degree of selectivity. That is done by the gifted analysts in the back rooms of the consulate and in the State Department in Washington who fit the puzzle pieces together, developing a picture of what must be happening behind the Bamboo Curtain. In the American embassy in Moscow a similar staff of readers and analysts is scanning the Russian press. And in Washington, of course, the Soviet embassy has its own group concerned with the American press.

The Dairen papers overlapped considerably: all often carried the same story; and sometimes headlines were identical. Seldom were there editorials. The material in the papers consisted mostly of feature articles by local Communists and by Russian dogma authorities. The comparatively few news stories that were printed came from the Russian news agency (Tass) or the Chinese Communist party news agency (Hsin Hua She).

Interestingly, the Russian magazines and pamphlets printed in the Chinese language contained stronger and more bitter anti-American articles than the local Chinese Communist newspapers presented. However, it was a matter of degree: Either way, the United States was the Number One Enemy, and no distortion of the news nor fabrication of a lie was too raw for printing. One constant theme was that the United States was responsible for keeping the port of Dairen "closed." (Yet one would think that, if regarded as true, this fact would show up Russia as a weak power, certainly not the goal of that nation's propaganda.)

In the Russian press and periodicals, we spotted as a consistent theme the claim that Russia itself had defeated Japan, implying that neither the United States nor China did much of importance in the war against Japan. Because of the constant repetition of this line by the Soviet propaganda machine—unchanged even today—one finds that some Western historians and commentators give serious credit to Russia's "conquest" of Manchuria as a major factor in Japan's defeat. Inside the Russian empire, certainly, this is the proclaimed truth. Actually, of course, Soviet forces did not even enter Manchuria until the issue already had been decided by the atomic bomb.

To illustrate how the Communists were writing about the United States (and talked in their never-ending political-indoctrination lectures to the workers), I made a list of typical opprobriums applied to Americans or the United States or our allies. I selected the epithets in Dairen from articles in *New Times*, a Russian weekly political magazine then published in Moscow with editions in English and several other languages, but the terms were common throughout all the Russian press:

> Fascist Fiends;
> Hearst's Typewriter Coolies;
> Tools of World Reaction;
> Inveterate Theorists of Espionage and Spying;
> Extortionist Speculators;
> Servile Panegyrists of International Reaction;
> Imperialist Interlopers;
> Connivers of Democracy's Sabotage;
> Crude Casuistics of United States Law;
> Chief Anti-Soviet Buffoons;
> General Clay's Hitlerite Cadres;
> Political Adventurers;
> Apostles of Imperialism;
> Feudal Reactionaries;
> Recrudescence of Reactionary Intrigue;

Jesuitical Fountain Pen Gangsters;
Forgery and Deceit Compounded;
Atomic wine has gone to the head of these brutalized
lackeys of imperialism;
Bourgeois Inquisition;
Pseudo-Socialist Ilk
Diversionist Trotskyite Wreckers;
Vilest Henchmen;
Atomic Blackmailers
Pen Pirates
Servile Factotums of Wall Street;
Brazen Hypocrites;
Lauders of Hypocrisy;
International Warmongers Trust;
Shady Adventurers Fat on War Profits;
Foul Fabricaters;
Moribund Munich Plotters;
Running Dogs of Warmongers;
Gang of Splitters at Work

The date in the publications provided the source of a number
of reports which the consulate sent to the Department on
technical subjects and matters affecting the Chinese Communist
administration apparatus. As samples of the subjects covered,
here are titles of our reports, at present in the National
Archives:

"Four New Electric Power Sub-stations near Port
Arthur"
"Present Railroad Network in Manchuria," listing all
services, including new construction
"Provincial Boundary Changes in the Northeast
(Manchuria)"
"Census in Liao Ning Province, Manchuria"
"American Aid to China Criticized by a Chinese
Communist," reprint from *Trud*, a Moscow
periodical
"Government Organized for Manchuria" (with this
Culver included a detailed list of the names of
government departments and officials, both in
English and in the Chinese characters)
"Pensions for Workers in Communist Manchuria"

"Formation of North China Provisional Government"
"Electric Power in Port Arthur City"
"Communist Editorial Charges that Chiang Kai-shek Is Seeking the Support of Governor Dewey"
"List of Kwantung Officials as of September 30, 1948"
"Opening of Middle Highway Between Port Arthur and Dairen"
"Prohibition of Nationalist Currency in Manchuria"
"Industrial Development of Mutankiang, Manchuria" (on the Korean border)
"Industrial Development of Chouts'un, Shantung"

In addition to covering the press, the other things the consulate reported on were a miscellany of goings-on in town, mostly what one could see by walking around. Although the authorities no doubt worried about their local secrets, it was hard for me to see what concealments of value there might be in Dairen. A list of the Russian freighters and ships using the port and a record of the freight-car traffic with Manchuria would have been highly useful in the middle of a shooting war, but now the information would not be of great interest. For one thing, there was no "think tank" of personnel in Washington organized to dissect the import of such data, as there would have been in wartime. The same was true of the movements of the Russian naval vessels into Port Arthur, although that area was outside our orbit. On the other hand, it would have been valuable to know which important Communist officials, agents and other personnel were traveling through Dairen to the outside world or meeting there, and what amounts of gold and other financing were coming and going through here on their onward destinations. Such information, however, could have been obtained only by a professional spy system, which means acting undercover. And never were there more public figures than Culver and I in Dairen. Whether that type of agent was operating here for the Chinese Nationalists I never knew. I doubted it because the Nationalists were too preoccupied with their own disintegration.

Surprising, I had received no instructions at all from the State Department, when I was on my way to China, about the type of work the Dairen office should perform. The top officials with whom I talked seemed to consider the job merely one of keeping the consulate open because it was already there. One said my principal chore was "to show the flag." Their seemingly continuing lack of interest concerning the Dairen consulate was a discouraging factor throughout my stay. I excused it partly on the basis that with all China going up in flames it was wrong to expect special interest in Dairen, a rather hollow excuse for neglect, but occasionally helpful to me.

We knew that the coded data we were so carefully telegraphing to the Department (with copies to Nanking and Moscow) were important provided that they were analyzed and evaluated in Washington and meshed with the data arriving similarly from the other American posts in China, Korea, and a dozen other places. If so, the continued existence of the Dairen consulate and our work there were worthwhile, no matter how small the contribution of key information might be to the total picture. Otherwise, there was little reason for keeping the consulate open.

Only when I was back in Washington and met a number of the lower-echelon "China expert" officers there as well as ones from our posts in Shanghai, Nanking, and Moscow did I learn that our telegrams and reports had been highly rated and had actually played a timely role in their assessment of the activities and mores of the Chinese Communists and the Russians. These men had incorporated our Dairen material into their overall reports for China and in their analyses of worldwide Communist propaganda. On that basis alone our work had been effective and valuable.

We performed virtually none of the traditional consular work that is a normal feature of every other post, such as issuing passports, granting visas, registering American residents, recording the births and deaths of Americans abroad, validating shipping papers, stamping invoices, providing business information. No American ships were coming and going; no Americans were here with citizenship problems; no local residents were able to leave Dairen to travel to the United States. Neither did we have what is called "protection work," that is, getting Americans out of jail, helping them after an automobile accident, sending the bodies home, which in many ways can be the most exciting and varied job in the Foreign Service. My first job at my first post, Mexico City, was protection work, and never again was I involved in such a range of funny and tragic experiences. Or maybe it was that Americans elsewhere were never quite as emotional, improvident, or harum-scarum as the ones in Mexico during the 1930s.) In Dairen I would have been delighted to break from my daily pattern and go out in the middle of the night to arbitrate a fight between Americans already in jail or track down a millionaire who had gone native with a gang of guerrillas in the bush.

Our schedule soon was established; Culver spent almost all his time with his press reading, plus a continuing series of errands around town that made use of his fluency in Chinese. Meanwhile I reported news and problems to the Department, called on local officials (sometimes with Culver, sometimes alone) and dealt with a confusion of administrative work such as checking Ch'en's accounts, coping with the office and personnel problems, and, most tedious of all, doing the never-ending coding and decoding of communications to and from the outside, typing up the messages and keeping the files in order.

For each of us a workload of sixty-five hours a week was usual. There was also our chief extracurricular chore: conjugating Russian verbs and practicing reading Russian periodicals.

And yet . . . and yet. The physical isolation of the place, the lack of social contacts and the long working hours rarely bothered me. There was no place like Dairen. I never knew what perplexing or fascinating problems the morrow might bring; and

I liked having to confront them myself, whenever possible, without immediate recourse to advice from Washington. Washington was too far away.

CHAPTER VI

EXCURSIONS
AND DIVERSIONS
(LATE SUMMER 1948)

The Kwantung countryside beyond our Dairen enclave was unknown territory. No one in the consulate, even in Benninghoff's earliest days, had gone more than a mile or so outside the city. Culver and I decided to make an excursion there. But should we ask the Kommandant for permission? We decided to go without asking, for quite probably he would say no. And we felt like seeing something different for a change. After all, we told ourselves, we could use our diplomatic status which assured us free movement within the consular zone.

The city boundary of Dairen, however, was a moot point. The 1945 treaty between Nationalist China and the Soviet Union had not spelled it out; China apparently assumed it would be the line long established under the Japanese administration. However, the Russians, upon their arrival, had unilaterally fixed a new line that reduced the municipality to the smallest possible geographic size. The balance of the original Japanese urban region was placed under the jurisdiction of the Port Arthur Naval Base Area. Presumably, Russia did this in order to have the maximum land within its Naval Base Area in case it was forced to release Dairen as a free port (which of course had not happened).

As a further complication, the Russian military line was not the same as the boundary used by the Kwantung Administration for its subdivision called "Dairen city." Where this might be we had no idea—except that it was somewhere beyond the military line. We had gone swimming at a beach just outside the military line but no farther. Were there border-patrol men at the second line? Soldiers? Communist police? Or no barrier at all? We could not help but feel curious.

A well-known local tourist objective before the war was Iron Mountain, the highest point in Kwantung, twenty-five miles from the city and halfway to the northern boundary of the Port Arthur Naval Base Area. Even during the war, a favorite holiday for the people of Dairen had consisted of climbing to the top of Iron Mountain, hiking around its rugged gullies and cliffs and visiting the Chinese shrine there, Frog Temple. With the arrival of the Russians, however, the populace no longer had transportation or gasoline available for going there, as well as the necessary travel permits from their police stations.

For us Iron Mountain seemed a good place to have a Sunday picnic. Culver and I intentionally went about our plans openly. Several days in advance we invited Mrs. Schumann and her older daughter, Marlene. We had our cooks prepare lunches and told our chauffeur—almost certainly an informer—that we were going to drive to Iron Mountain.

On a fine late-summer day we left the city in our merry new Oldsmobile. We felt exhilarated to be on our first drive into the open country. Mrs. Schumann had been to Iron Mountain before, and the chauffeur said he had driven there, but both before the advent of the Russians. About three miles past the official military boundary of the city, a Russian soldier motioned us to slow down. When he saw our Dairen license plates, he waved us on. No barrier here. Shortly beyond came a barrier manned by Chinese police of the Kwantung Administration but here also we were motioned through.

Approaching Chinchow, we left the paved road and took a graveled road. There was another barrier—and about three hundred yards further was still another, this one with Russian soldiers. However, no one stopped us. We wondered whether barriers existed in similar profusion all over the Kwantung area. We also noticed that Chinese police were ubiquitous in the villages and at intersections, as they were in Dairen.

The paved road had been full of potholes; the graveled road was corrugated. Obviously, there had been no maintenance of the roads since the Russian occupation. We crossed streams on stone-paved fords; half the width had not been maintained, but the remaining half was passable. There was no traffic, only an occasional cart pulled by the typically diminuitive Manchurian pony. The countryside was nothing special; some small agricultural fields producing vegetables for the Dairen market. The farmhouses were small and neat; people working in the field did not even interrupt their work to look up at us.

Driving along the graveled road, we somehow deviated and became lost in a maze of small dirt lanes. The steep, partly forested mountain, was always in view. But no matter which road we took, we ended up in a slightly new direction. It was frustrating; yet merely to be wandering around was pleasant. Rather soon, the terrain became a large flat plain, used as farm land at one time but now abandoned. The few times we saw someone we would stop and ask how to get to Frog Temple, but the directions never led us to the right road. As we bounced along in the late morning, enjoying the outing and knowing that eventually we would find our temple, we went over a slight rise. Our road came to a dead end at a dry irrigation ditch—and we found ourselves in the middle of a Russian army unit on a training exercise.

The commanding officer directly in front of us with his staff was as flabbergasted as we were. Several hundred soldiers and a few artillery pieces and anti-aircraft guns were scattered over the plain, all in motion. There were many jeeps and trucks too, and several were stuck in the mud, surrounded by soldiers sweating to get them out. Parked off to one side was a group of trucks, their rear platforms carrying soldiers sitting side by side on benches—all incongruously wearing gas masks—sitting there like macabre spectators watching the soldiers in action out on the plain.

It took a long moment before anyone stirred. My diplomatic training made me react in terms of protocol. After I made a gesture to Culver, he opened the door, took a few steps and said in English that we were trying to reach the temple at Iron Mountain and were lost. The commanding officer came back to life and nodded to an aide who came over to the car. Mrs. Schumann now explained in Russian what the situation was. The aide returned to the group of officers; shortly another one came over to give us precise instructions. We thanked him, turned the car around and reached our objective in three-quarters of an hour. All very formal. No smiles through the Curtain.

And that was that. I can report that Russians on their military exercises look as bored and lackadaisical as those of any other army. Later in the day we heard shooting from this direction and saw groups of planes flying, There was nothing new in this, however. In Dairen heavy gunfire was often heard in the distance, and military planes always were flying over the city.

The temple turned out to be a simple wooden building in a grove of huge pines, tranquil and harmonious, with a slight breeze rustling the pine needles. If only every picnic lunch could be enjoyed in such a felicitous setting. Afterwards, we climbed up the mountain, admiring the splendid wildflowers as we went. We arrived back at the car at six o'clock pleasantly exhausted.

On the return, the road was easy to follow. We were rolling along when we rounded a curve outside Chinchow and found two determined Russian soldiers blocking our way. They said we would have to go to the local Kommandatura. Without further ado, they forced their way inside the car, jamming their rifles into everyone's ribs.

At the Kommandatura, a ramshackle wooden building, I went inside while the others stayed in the car. Fortunately, the commanding officer spoke English. He asked where we had been. I told him, to the temple. Did I have my travel permit from the "authorities"? I said I had not known one was required, due to my diplomatic status. He said that this matter was outside his jurisdiction, that he would have to telephone Dairen for instructions in order to obtain authorization for us to continue back to the city. I said I understood.

He made the call on an army field phone, cranking at it vigorously. The delay in getting an answer and the renewed cranking were the same as at any field post I have ever visited. When someone was finally roused, the officer's explanation was short and pat. There was no doubt now that "Dairen" already knew about our being here.

We now sat back, waiting for the return call. It was getting dark. An orderly came in and went over to an enormous safe. It was far finer, I noticed, than the ones we had at the consulate. As the two big doors swung open, the safe was revealed as completely empty except for one electric light bulb. Without comment the orderly took it out, gravely screwed it into the empty socket hanging above us and turned on the switch. The surrealist touch of the lone bulb in that huge safe somewhat unnerved me.

The officer, about forty, was intelligent-looking and trim. His uniform, oddly, displayed no insignia of rank. We talked about this small thing and that. I told about the places I had visited in Moscow—the ballet, the Red Army Chorus and the rest. He was delighted to talk about Moscow, where he once had lived; but when I made some comments about the ballet and symphony in New York, he was clearly bored and let the subject drop. He seemed equally uninterested when I told about my being delayed for several days at the airport of Stalingrad (today renamed Volgograd) only a few months after the great German defeat there—a unique experience for me because of the mountains of war debris as far as the eye could see. He also showed no interest in the seven-day train trip I had made from Moscow through Central Asia to the Afghanistan border.

But every time I mentioned something about Moscow his eyes would light up, and the conversation would come back to life. It reminded me of the times I had talked about Paris with French officers on duty in the back desert of Morocco or on a bus between Damascus and Baghdad. They could not get enough, remembrances about Paris—but anything else lay outside a civilized man's interest.

Meanwhile, I kept wondering what a superior officer like this was doing in such an out-of-the-way village. At first I assumed he had been rushed out from Dairen during the day to deal with us. Then I realized this was not the case, since his living quarters were in an adjoining room. The orderly brought tea.

When the call from Dairen came in forty-five minutes, the officer told me we could leave. He scribbled a pass for us to show at the barriers and asked the orderly to take me to the car. We shook hands and the incident was closed.

The trip back to town was uneventful. But this time at the barriers the soldiers stood diligently at attention and carefully examined the pass.

The next day I sent a note to the Kommandant stating that my vice-consul and I, accompanied by a friend and her daughter, had been stopped by Russian soldiers while returning from a pleasure drive and that the officer in charge had said I needed a travel permit, even though we had passed through the various barriers earlier without being questioned.

A few days later (presumably after the Kommandant had received his instructions from Moscow) his office telephoned, saying I was consul only in Dairen; and thus my diplomatic status did not extend outside the city, that is, it was not pertinent to my travelling elsewhere in Kwantung. To enter the Port Arthur Naval Base Area I would need to apply in advance for permission.

Anyway, several weeks later—just to see what would happen—I applied for a permit to go again to the temple at Iron Mountain. Not surprisingly, there was no reply. I did not try again. We had had our one and only excursion outside the city of Dairen.

We never could fathom why the soldiers had not stopped us at the barriers on our trip out of Dairen or sometime during the day. (For surely our household informers must have alerted the authorities to our impending excursion.) Was it all a game of pretense, to make us think that we did not have spies in our entourage? Or, more probably, were the intermediaries between the informers and the action officials too slow and bureaucratic?

In any case, after our one-day fling at geographic freedom, we felt more circumscribed than ever. And the news events from the world outside Dairen could only give us a growing uneasiness in our precarious post.

China, from Dairen, seemed rather quiet during the late summer and early fall of 1948. But it was a false picture of the whole scene. In the relentless civil war troops were marching, cities lay under siege, and soldiers switched allegiances. The different fronts—if they were even stable enough to be called fronts—constantly shifted.

And around the world, the cold war was still being fought harshly and without respite. The Berlin Blockade had settled into a vicious stalemate that would last eleven months. To train pilots for winter air-lift duty the United States Air Force set up a special base at Great Falls, Montana, providing a facsimile of the German flight corridors.

The news broadcasts from Shanghai alerted us to other cold war happenings. Separate governments for North and South Korea were established. Yugoslavia broke away from Moscow. Russia succeeded in eliminating non-Communist countries from the Danube River Conference, thus ending the river's status of free, international navigation. Communist guerrillas fought on in Greece, Malaya, Philippines, Vietnam, and Java. The State Department charged that the Communists had launched a "drive for power" in Southeast Asia under cover of nationalist movements; in France and Italy strikes and riots continued in most cities as the Communist parties tried to wreck the aid program of the Marshall Plan, now getting under way; Britain extended by three months the service of men due for release from the armed forces, and also doubled the production of fighter planes as a defense against possible Russian attack.

In a speech Winston Churchill said the West should "bring matters to a head" with the Soviet Union before it got the atomic bomb. "Nothing stands between Europe today and complete subjugation to communist tyranny but the atomic bomb in American possession," were his words. He also called on Russia to free more than a million German and Japanese prisoners of war.

This period was, in retrospect, a high-water mark for the success of Russian plans. With Western Europe dazed and disunited from the war, and economically still stagnant, it looked as if very little could tip it into Russia's hands. Czechoslovakia had been incorporated firmly into the Soviet sphere since the Communist take-over in the preceding February; Finland was expected soon to be handled similarly. In Italy the Communist and left Socialist parties were given an even chance to win the election the following spring, removing that country from the Western orbit. In France and Austria the Communists were intensely active and had hopes of gaining the dominant influence over these governments.

Communism as both ideology and military force was indeed in full spate. The Chinese Communists now were about to consolidate all Manchuria under their rule, then lead their troops to the capture of Peking and afterwards all China—which would be accepted as Russia's greatest cold war success.

The first step was the destruction of Nationalist troops in Manchuria, perhaps Chiang's best forces and well-equipped with American-supplied armament. Unfortunately, they were commanded by scandalously incompetent generals whose primary qualification was that they belonged to Chiang's personal clique.

Up to now Mao Tse-tung had not instigated within the Chinese Communist party any purge on the Stalin scale. The Party still contained many of the old-line Chinese who formerly had been merely reformist in outlook or simply members of the military. They tolerated the excesses of the Communists against the middle class and against the propertied farmers in the areas they were conquering.

The educated Chinese knew of the convoluted early history of Communism in Russia, which led to the prison camps of Stalin. So there were certainly many fearful people among the Communists who, like our alleged agent of the last chapter, might have defected if they could have reached a safe haven like

South Korea. But once caught inside the Communist areas, there was no place where they could go to escape.

At the Dairen consulate we took careful, even anxious, note of the military situation in China at the end of summer 1948. The cities of Changchun, the capital of Manchuria, and Mukden, its chief industrial center, had been under siege for nearly a year, with the Nationalist troops receiving supplies by air. The condition of the semi-starving populace of nearly a million was desperate. Other air-lifts enabled the Nationalist forces to fight on in the similarly isolated cities of Chengteh, capital of Jehol province, Tsinan, capital of Shantung, and Taiyuan (now Yangku), capital of Shansi province. In the coastal area of Manchuria the Nationalists had harvested the best crop in years and were flying food into the beleaguered cities. However, in mid-September the Communists captured the area, gaining supplies for their winter offensives. On September first the Communists formed a North China People's Government, announced as the forerunner of an All-China People's Government.

* * *

Meanwhile, Culver and I underwent a series of irritating incidents with the police and frustrating arguments with officials during August and September. We thought each one was a temporary complication. Gradually, we realized the incidents were forming a pattern of ever-tighter surveillance over us by the police, closer restrictions in our movements around town, deeper isolation from the local people. The Kommandant was beginning to claim he did not have jurisdiction over the American consulate, saying all our dealings must be with the "civilian" Kwantung Administration. This position I consistently refused to accept, pointing out that the Administration was in fact subordinate to his office.

I summed up this new situation in a telegram sent to the Department in early September. I was replying to a message in which the Department had implied the possibility of closing the consulate because of the difficulties of getting a courier to us now that the Vladivostok consulate was closed.

> Gleysteen and I are eager to remain here, despite the isolation, because we consider the post to have strategic value as the only U.S. agency in Communist China. Communist subservience to Russia is highlighted here. Kwantung is now the transit link between Manchuria and Shantung province and is the outfitting center for the Communists in Shantung. Also, it is the exit point for Communists going abroad. Sporadic opportunities do occur to obtain pertinent information, largely due to Gleysteen's fluency in Chinese, such as data of value from local press and casual conversations. It is evident that mere existence of an American consulate here is good propaganda for U.S. The irritation of Russians and Chinese Communists at the presence of the consulate (because it is able to refute their propaganda and to observe their activities regarding local population) is emphasized by their constant efforts to restrict our movements. I now realize departure of Vice-Consul Patch has been used as opportunity to initiate new restrictions. Russian Kommandant now refuses to receive letters from the Consulate. Chinese officials in the Kwantung Administration usually refuse to let me call on them. The Consulate is forced generally to negotiate only with the Russian Consul General, but whatever request is made he claims it is not his "competency." He blandly insists all local population is free to go to my house any time for any purpose, whereas, in fact, they are frightened to have any contact. Although curfew is at eleven o'clock, it is almost impossible to drive Consulate auto after dark due to the police constantly stopping it, resulting in long, sometimes unpleasant delays; other automobiles not stopped. On bright side is fact our residence is comfortable. We have succeeded in acquiring full winter's supply of coal for both house and office. Although food costs are enormous for people here, they are low for us due to our dollar exchange rate for local currency. Thus, no hardship physically. In summary, I firmly believe difficulties regarding

servicing of this post are not themselves sufficient to close the office.

(Actually, food costs were exorbitant for those not employed by a state trust or institution, who were either Russian or Chinese. The workers in these government organizations received food as part of their wages, or, more exactly, their rations. It is likely that only a few of these bought food on the open market.)

The Department replied it did not intend to close the consulate, but added a qualifying "at least at this time."

The Russians showed how well pleased they were with themselves in Kwantung by publishing, for the August 14th anniversary of the signing of the 1945 Sino-Soviet Treaty and Agreements, three articles defending the treaty. These obviously expressed the official Russian position. The first article claimed that "reactionaries" were agitating for the treaty's abrogation, but that this was done at the instigation of the Americans and members of the Kuomintang (Nationalists) who were "conniving" to bring Japanese troops back into Manchuria to attack Russia and the Mongolian People's Republic. The second warned against the danger of future Japanese expansion in Manchuria and drew a distinction between the 1945 Treaty and the old "unequal treaties": "There is absolutely nothing in common between this Treaty of Alliance and those Chinese naval bases formerly seized or leased by the imperialists. . . . The Sino-Soviet Treaty is intended to protect the security of both countries on an equal basis." And the third emphasized that the entry of Russia into the Pacific War was decisive in securing an early victory over Japan, that Russia was protecting China from renewed Japanese aggression organized under American auspices, that Russia had fulfilled its obligations in the treaty and that the Russian refusal to permit Nationalist troops into Kwantung was based on stipulations of the treaty. It closed, "The Soviet Union is for world peace, for protecting, respecting and fulfilling international agreements and treaties.

For this, the Soviet Union will tenaciously wage war."

The Russian intention to wage war to maintain peace was a startling concept, but at least it had the refreshing sound of honesty.

All this, however, did not jibe with the U.S. State Department's view. It bluntly maintained that Russian unilateral action had formed the Chinese-staffed Kwantung Administration and that, therefore, this civilian government was a puppet of the Russian military. An illustration of this dependency was the military's arbitrarily assigning certain powers to the Administration and withholding others: for instance, jurisdiction over the Chinese population but not over the miscellaneous foreigners. Also, there were continuing instances when the Kommandant in Dairen overruled the Administration's officials.

This point of jurisdiction was important for the consulate because the Kommandant had now begun to claim that the Kwantung Administration had sole responsibility for all actions of its police in the continuing series of harrassments of consular personnel. It also was to be responsible for the issuing of exit visas—even, it now began to appear, for non-Chinese. In my notes to the Kommandant I always carefully denied our acceptance of such claims.

The matter was never resolved. The Kommandant continued to adhere to his new position that the Kwantung Administration was independent of him, and I kept to mine, namely that it was subordinate to him. As it worked out, each serious incident as it occurred was somehow settled by itself, but usually only when my letters to the Kommandant became quite strident.

Actually, the Kommandant's refusal to receive my letters turned out to be a shifting policy on his part. Possibly, it resulted from uncertainty among the local military and MVD police authorities as to their competence to handle documents with legal significance concerning international matters. A simpler explanation could have been that Dairen was a long way from Moscow, and in Moscow those in charge of Dairen were a long way from contact with Stalin, normally the only one who decided matters of long-range foreign significance.

The question of who actually ruled Dairen can be considered in the perspective of two terms which are common phrases in the world of diplomacy: *de jure* and *de facto*. Roughly translated, *de jure* refers to actions carried out legally by a ruling government. *De facto* refers to actions carried out by a government in physical control of an area. It has the power to operate a local government, even though its actions are not supported by any juridical authority, such as a treaty or other international agreement.

The maintenance of Russian troops in the Kwantung peninsula provided a good illustration of the two terms. In the Port Arthur Naval Base Area (all of Kwantung except Dairen) the troops were there *de jure* because Nationalist China as the sovereign power had agreed to this in the 1945 treaty. However, in Dairen the troops were certainly there *de facto*. China (Nationalist China, of course, at this time) as the sovereign power claimed they were there without its permission. (Russia, of course, asserted it had the right to keep them in Dairen "while in a state of war with Japan," whereas China denied that interpretation.)

Despite the questionable legitimacy of its rule, a *de facto* government takes upon itself the responsibility to maintain law and order and to carry on the basic duties of a normal local government. Yet Russia was now backing out of this by claiming that the Kwantung Administration was the legal civilian government for both Dairen and the rest of the peninsula—not the Russian military government. By now asserting that the Administration had been formed "spontaneously" by the local citizens, the Soviet Union tried to side-step certain *de facto* responsibilities.

This, then, was the paradoxical position in which our consulate was trapped. The Russians had essentially caused our difficulties; yet our only protection from the Kwantung administration's Chinese Communist police was for the Russians to retain their control over Dairen and to continue their official policy of "correctness" in relation to Nationalist China. Thus our embassy in Moscow pressed the Soviet Foreign Office to fulfill its *de facto* responsibilities in Dairen—at least its responsibilities for the protection of the American consulate. We knew that if Russia's *de facto* jurisdiction were ended by military withdrawal from Dairen or by the shifting of diplomatic recognition from the Chinese Nationalists to a Chinese Communist government (which could then grant permission to Russia to keep its troops in Dairen), the Kwantung Administration would gain *de jure* jurisdiction over our consulate. There would be no way for the State Department to bring pressure on our behalf to protect us. That precarious, even dangerous situation would continue until such time as the United States also shifted its diplomatic recognition from the Nationalists to the Chinese Communists: an unlikely event, surely, during this period of time.

* * *

In the telegram to the Department concerning whether or not to keep the Dairen post open, I reported that our quarters were "comfortable" and that we were suffering "no hardships physically." That was a subjective nicety. Here is a more exact picture that includes the warts, pimples and blisters.

All State Department foreign missions must prepare annually a "Post Report." Its specific purpose is to describe each post so exactly that new personnel assigned to it will know what sort of living conditions to expect, which items to bring and which are not necessities because they can be purchased locally. For the larger missions the report can be nearly a hundred pages long. Our Dairen report took twenty-eight pages, with these items as highlights:

> — The present staff fortunately has been in good
> health. Thus, it has not been necessary to put to the
> test if adequate medical attention is available. Russian
> doctors normally can be seen by the public only after
> an elaborate procedure of obtaining the required

permits. In case of serious emergency, presumably any of the local population would be admitted to the hospital, but this would apply only to those able to get there. If it would become required for a doctor to come to the Consulate residence, it frankly is not known how long it would take to arrange such a visit.

— No uncooked vegetables of any kind can be eaten. Fruit must be peeled, pork thoroughly cooked, water boiled.

— No spices of any kind are available except salt.

— The best items we can buy are the excellent sea food; there are many kinds of fish, also prawns, shrimps, crabs, oysters, and sea slugs.

— The American officers are allowed to use the highest ranking of the Russian spetstorgs (like PX commissaries). However, the Russian products are of such poor quality there is little temptation to buy much as long as our present supplies hold out. All that is currently purchased there is cheese, fresh butter, rice, sugar. These are not always available, however. The trend is definitely toward austerity. Products formerly available, such as Caucasus wine, fresh meat and canned crab, have disappeared. The Siberian "spirit" sold in the spetstorg is ninety-five percent alcohol and is almost undrinkable in any form (vodka is not available).

— Water pressure is often weak and at times no water is received for several days. Fortunately, each half of our house has a large tank and thus usually there is little inconvenience. Only occasionally is there no water in the house for more than a day. However, for one month this fall the pressure was so weak it was difficult to get enough water for a bath.

— The heating of water for baths is done by a trick arrangement with the kitchen stove. The ordinary use of the stove heats a tank of water placed over it. The tank is large enough for all normal hot water needs during the day. Since the same fuel is thus used for cooking as for heating the water, money is saved. However, because coal itself is difficult to obtain and expensive, efforts are made to cook on electric plates as much as possible. This then results in no hot water. The plates often cannot be used due to the weak current.

— Regarding electricity, it often has not been possible to read in the evenings except with a sixty-watt bulb placed a foot away from the book. Periodically, the current is cut off and candles must be used. Electric heaters cannot be used because they blow out the fuses. Restrictions on the use of current by the municipal authorities are increasing; it is likely the current may be cut off during daytime.

(This Post Report did not provide an explanation for why our house had electricity most of the time. In the rest of the city the power was rationed during the winter, taking the sections in turn in the course of a week. Thus, each section had no electricity two or three evenings a week. However, our block of eight houses—"Millionaires' Row—was seldom affected. One story in town ascribed this to the presence of the consular residence, which was obviously not the reason. On the other hand, the director of the electric light trust and the head of the MVD police lived in the Row. Either one had the clout to pull the electrical strings. But the two together! No wonder we had electricity. As for the brown-outs and black-outs affecting the rest of the city, the major source of electricity, the Kanchingtzu Steam Power Plant, had had a minimum capacity of 58,000 kwh during the Japanese regime. The Russians had shipped away most of its machinery. Now semi-repaired, it was operating with a capacity of 15,000 kwh, "for short periods.")

As an integral part of my life in Dairen, an assortment of police generally followed me in my daily rounds. This business of someone tagging along when I walked between the office and the house or took a walk around town started during the fall of 1948. At first, a young man dressed in a blue cotton suit, visor cap and tennis shoes would pursue me. Then he started riding a bicycle; perhaps I had been walking too fast for him.

I noticed too that whenever I was in the consulate car I acquired a Ford as my shadow. A most ancient and fragile touring car, the poor thing hardly could go over twenty miles an hour. (But then my own car seldom went faster, in order to avoid "incidents.") Inside were three, sometimes four, men in mufti. At first it had moved discreetly a hundred yards or so behind, but then, bored, it moved in to ten yards. A rather expensive operation to check on my comings and goings.

On the other hand, Culver was not shadowed consistently in this fashion, although it did sometimes happen.

Most ostentatious of all, however, were the plainclothesmen, and occasionally policemen in uniform, who at times followed us into stores and stood obnoxiously at our elbows, breathing heavily and glowering to frighten the clerks.

In the American Foreign Service each post has ready for immediate use a "Plan for Emergency Action." In September I brought up to date the Dairen plan originally written by Benninghoff. Here is a summary of the part of my data that points up some of the conditions confronting us at the consulate.

— A special incinerator has been installed for destroying all confidential files and material within twenty minutes. All unnecessary items already have been destroyed. The incinerator is kept permanently outside the window of the security room. Depending on emergency conditions, the material can be handed out through the window for burning, or the incinerator can be brought inside, although then, of course, the smoke might become overpowering. The Department is requested to send us a chemical which could destroy papers safely without removing them from the safe. It is deemed inadvisable to pack for storage the non-confidential files and supplies not in current use; to pack them now would create tension among the Chinese staff. However, packing boxes and materials have been assembled and are ready for use.

— Effort is made to have the accounts finished two days after the end of each month. This policy is due to the ever-present possibility that the office may be closed with little warning by either the Department or the Russians.

— The local authorities have refused continually to give the consular officers night passes; to be exact, they have not answered our requests for the passes. Our consequent inability to come to the office in the late evening or during the night will be a restriction of major importance in a time of emergency. Curfew is officially at eleven o'clock, but the consulate car is stopped constantly by the police before that hour. The result is that we sleep at the Consulate when we work in the evening.

— In the event of war with Russia, it is not known whether the occupation of our office and house will be carried out by Russian soldiers or the Chinese police of the Kwantung Administration. If it is by the latter, then our internment possibly would involve the two American officers in all the difficulties and uncertainties which already have faced many foreigners held by the Chinese Communists. If by the former, note that the Russian Government has been consistent in giving lip service to Chinese sovereignty over Dairen and in recognizing that this sovereignty is held by the Nationalist Government. Thus, even in the event of war between the United States and Russia there is a slight possibility the American officers might not be interned in the normal sense of the word unless the Nationalist government itself enters into the war.

— The round trip of a courier from Shanghai to Dairen and return to Shanghai averages three months. The service was always irregular but has stopped now entirely since the closing of the Vladivostok consulate; we do not know how or when it will be reinaugurated. Any new emergency conditions cannot make the service more tenuous than it is now.

— It is impossible to get money here by cashing drafts drawn on the Department. We operate entirely on the supply of dollar bills we brought upon our arrival; this was to have been replenished via the courier trips. The bills are exchanged for local currency about once a week. In the event of internment it is planned for the principal officer to carry this money with him personally; otherwise, there could be no funds to supplement the financing of living expenses during the internment, if such action is, in fact, allowed.

By the fall of 1948 we had begun to prepare ourselves for either a sudden departure or an unpleasantly long stay. We were bound to encounter problems, whether leaving or remaining in Dairen.

CHAPTER VII
MANCHURIAN FALL
(AUTUMN 1948)

The Dairen consulate, occupying a unique position within the Communist orbit, could closely observe the propaganda themes and related activities of both the Chinese Communists and the Russians. The several Dairen bookstores carried a full stock of books, magazines, newspapers and maps published by the Chinese Communists. We were the only American post where such a collection of publications was available.

Beginning in September, we noticed that the Chinese Communists were shifting the emphasis of their propaganda, at least in the Dairen and Manchurian press. Less space was now given to maligning the Nationalists and more to emphasizing the positive aspects of the Communist regime for "substantial" people, such as members of the bureaucracy, those with technical skills and even the propertied class.

During the summer and now during the harvesting season, the fighting had been relatively stabilized. When the winter offensives began, this new type of propaganda might make the progress of the Communists easier. The press emphasized Mao Tse-tung's one-time statement that China must experience a further period of capitalism before full communization would be possible. It said that, in the future, following the capture of the big cities all people would be protected except members of the Kuomintang (the dominant Nationalist party) and their property.

Furthermore, the farmers of north China were being assured

that no changes would be made after an initial land reform. Harbin was cited as a successful example of this policy. (Without outside, unbiased observers in Harbin, however, it was impossible to know the real situation there.) When Tsinan, the capital of Shantung, was captured in early October, it was also held up as an example where, the Communist press insisted, no drastic changes had been made. (In rebuttal, I point out that, in the historical record, for a few months only did the Communists, after seizing control of an area, allow even a remnant of capitalism to remain. For a similarly short time the Communists adhered to their other propaganda "promises.")

* * *

After a heavy three-day battle, the Nationalists lost Changchung, the capital of Manchuria, on October 20, 1948. Chiang Kai-shek's troops had once numbered 200,000, but during the long siege they had been cut down by fighting and desertions to 50,000.

Ten days later Mukden was captured. The Communists now controlled all Manchuria, although the Nationalists did regain the coastal area for a short while. Despite determined Nationalist resistance, Tsinan, the capital of Shantung Province, also fell. And then Chefoo, the chief Shantung port, directly opposite Dairen. The large Nationalist forces in all these areas lost their stocks of military supplies to the enemy. Peking was soon reduced to an enclave, supplied either by air or through the port of Tientsin. The American embassy, located in Nanking, now advised all Americans to leave Peking and, on November 5, it told American citizens to depart from Nanking, the Nationalist capital, because of the approach of the Red Army. On November 17 the U.S. State Department warned Americans that they were unsafe throughout mainland China, except in the extreme south. American army planes flew evacuees to Shanghai for embarkation to the United States on military transport vessels.

In the United States many politicians and statesmen urged a

step-up of economic and military assistance to Chiang Kai-shek. However, President Truman reported to Congress (four days after his reelection in an upset victory over Dewey) that there were many difficulties in supplying aid to China. It must be closely supervised, he said, by Americans on the spot. (Translated, this meant that corruption among Nationalist leaders was so great the aid could be effective only when administered by Americans.)

The criticisms of the fighting abilities and of the morale of the Nationalist troops made by foreign observers, American and otherwise, both during the war and afterwards, were almost uniformly harsh, even virulent. Thus, one wondered how, if such evaluations were indeed correct, the Nationalist cause managed to field any troops at all, let alone keep them combating the enemy. Yet the bulk of the soldiers and line officers stayed on at the front, fighting. The ideology and the assurances of the Communists for a better life, so loudly trumpeted, apparently were not enough to win many of them over—at least not until they realized their cause was lost. Was it their fault that their leaders had proven to be inept and greedy?

As historians have since written, the Chiang Kai-shek clique that controlled the Nationalist government became ridden with corruption during World War II. Worse, it was badly out of touch with the mass of Chinese citizens. After the war the decay and remoteness increased. Although the United States gave great amounts of money and supplies to the Nationalists, Chiang Kai-shek succeeded in organizing a viable government for China within the framework of his Kuomintang party. The greed and incompetency of his chosen generals contaminated almost every military unit. The administrative officials were little better.

As good a summary of the fatal influence of Chiang Kai-shek on the collapse of the Nationalists as any I have come across is in the *Enclyclopedia Britannica* (1966 edition, Vol. 5, p. 478). While acknowledging his earlier strengths and his key role during a chaotic period of transition in Chinese history, it states:

Among the reasons for Chiang's defeat, one frequently cited, is the corruption he countenanced in his government. But corruption is not a mortal disease, or few governments would live long. Nor can Chiang's downfall be ascribed to personal failings alone. Insofar as these contributed, however, none proved more fatal than his loss of flexibility in dealing with changing conditions. Growing more rigid, he became less responsive to popular sentiment and less tolerant of subordinates venturing novel ideas. He came to prize loyalty more than competence and to rely more on personal ties than on ties of organization. His growing dependence on a trusted clique also showed in his army, in which he favored narrow traditionalists over many an abler officer.

A telegram from the State Department ten days after the fall of Mukden informed us that the American consul at Mukden, Angus Ward, had remained at his post and, so far, had received courteous and considerate treatment from the Communist authorities. In fact, it said, the response from the Communists to exploratory remarks regarding a courier service into Mukden was "not unencouraging." And if service into Mukden were arranged, then possibly it could be extended from there to Dairen.

Ward may have been receiving "courteous and considerate treatment" at that particular moment, but in a matter of days his optimistic expectations for such things as courier service were terminated by an abrupt silence—as if they had all been dropped down a deep well. Presumably, Ward and his staff were under the tight seclusion of house arrest. No further messages came from him. No one knew what was happening. I kept sending him telegrams, but never knew at all whether he received them.

An amazing round of telegrams with the Department, Moscow, Shanghai, and Nanking had begun. First there was the hope of establishing a courier service through Mukden to Dairen. Later, we tried to arrange for passes for Culver to travel overland to Mukden to find out what was happening to Ward.

(The early plans, hatched before our Dairen arrival, for me to go to Mukden periodically had of course died long ago.) Because he was the junior officer and also fluent in Chinese, Culver was the proper person to pick for a pioneer trip into the Communist netherworld.

In my telegrams I kept emphasizing that any plans to obtain Russian road passes enabling Culver to travel across the peninsula and obtain Chinese Communist passes for travel from the boundary to Mukden would have to be formulated in Moscow. It was true that Communist officials were dominant in the Kwantung Administration and the few civilians going to Mukden did receive their passes there. As for Culver, however, it was certain that the Administration officials would not, in fact, could not, accept his application without specific approval from the Kommandant, who could not give this without special authorization from Moscow. The Department instructed the Moscow embassy to make an effort to get the passes granted. They also told us to keep trying to get them in Dairen. Neither endeavor had the least chance of success. Why should the Russians allow American couriers to travel between Mukden and Dairen or permit Culver to go to Mukden to contact the unfortunate, incommunicado Consul Ward? (Assuming, of course, that the Chinese Communists themselves were willing to receive him, a chimerical matter by itself.) However, we all kept trying . . .

Meanwhile, a new element had surfaced: the radically singular attitude of the Chinese Communists toward foreign diplomats. The world's foreign ministries would become acutely aware of this in the following year, after the occupation of Peking and Hankow.

Heretofore, diplomats everywhere in the world usually had floated above physical hardships and dangers during wartime and rioting, unless war between the home and host countries was specifically declared, when they were then interned. The Communist officials throughout the conquered areas in China promptly displayed the unheard-of policy of simply ignoring the internationally respected rights of diplomats, giving them no assistance and often refusing even to receive them. (At least, they usually acted this way toward the diplomats of Western Europe and the United States.)

Previously, when a group seized power in any country, it craved, as proof that it was the new legal controlling force, the immediate diplomatic approval and recognition of other countries. Recognition was usually granted to the de facto government that was in control and maintaining order. Whether to grant this recognition has recently been established as a major weapon in diplomacy (for instance, by President Woodrow Wilson in Latin America). The group coming to power was itself so anxious to be recognized that, to secure recognition it would make all sorts of promises to other nations, like guaranteeing the foreign debts of the previous regime. Although the value of this entire issue of diplomatic recognition remains a matter of contention among students of international law, no one disputes the right of any country to withhold recognition for policy reasons for as long as it sees fit.

Now, without warning, the Chinese Communists made no effort to gain foreign recognition. Certainly they were not offering to guarantee property and other rights of foreigners under their jurisdiction. Later on, when the Communists controlled most of China, the representatives of several countries, such as India, the United Kingdom, the Netherlands and Sweden, granted diplomatic recognition after a period of bargaining. They usually did this because of national self-interest (Britain was obliged to protect its colony, Hong Kong) or for economic reasons, or as with India, for a combination of these plus sympathetic ideological affinity.)

Possibly, this attitude of the Chinese Communists, which seemed so arrogant and unexpected on the international scene, had its roots in a justifiable reaction to Western antagonism and support of Chiang Kai-shek as well as in the centuries-old tradition of the Chinese: they occupied the center of the civilized universe and all others were barbarians. In the past, when envoys came from foreign places they were treated as vassals bringing tribute—even ambassadors from the European powers in the nineteenth century. For the Communists to withdraw into that tradition must have been a natural reflex. Anyway, they used this tactic of indifference quite effectively.

The first Western diplomat to suffer from this emergent policy of the Chinese Communists was Consul General Angus Ward at Mukden. Instead of recognizing his traditional immunity, they sealed him off from the rest of the world by placing him under house arrest. Similar troubles, although not so drastic, would afflict other diplomats, especially the hated Americans, as the Communists occupied the cities in northern and central China. By the time their forces reached southern China nearly every Western nation, including the United States, closed its posts and evacuated their personnel in order to escape such harrassment.

In November, I reported to the Department that the anti-American articles in the Dairen press and in the Chinese Communist press were more numerous and rabid than at any time since our arrival.

Mao Tse-tung himself wrote an article that was printed in the Dairen papers. Presumably, it was published throughout Communist China. Its conclusion made strong and telling statements:

> The estimate of victory in the Second World War is incorrect. American imperialist running dogs have taken the place of Fascist Germans, Italians, and Japanese, and they are preparing frantically a new world war. This reflects the fear of capitalism in its final decadence.

> The enemy still has strength. Therefore, revolutionary forces of all countries must unite under Soviet Union leadership. Because of its internal weaknesses the enemy can be defeated in war.

> The duties of the Chinese Communist Party are to overthrow American imperialism and the Chinese Nationalist reaction and to build a democratic people's republic.

* * *

All the while, our consulate was going bankrupt. In October I telegraphed the Department to say that the cash on hand was $2800. Monthly expenses could be kept to a minimum of $1000. By mid-January our funds would be exhausted. We needed cash . . .American money. Only by cashing our American bills in the local money-exchange market could we obtain local currency; Dairen had no banking facilities. Our impending insolvency was the one factor that broke up the logjam of courier difficulties. The State Department was now forced to stand up to Russian procrastinations. Somehow, they assured us, they would get couriers to us soon.

We kept up our spirits. On November 11 Princeton beat Yale at football, 20-14. Culver, as the loser, had to organize an especially fine dinner. Our surrogate family—Mrs. Schumann and her children—enjoyed the event with us, even though they were all hazy as to what sort of fisticuffs comprised American football.

Then, on November 15, all Kwantung collapsed financially, sorely affecting at least the Chinese portion of the population. Overnight, the Russians canceled the old Kwantung paper yuan currency (issued by the Kwantung administration) and had the administration put out new yuan bills under ruthless rules of exchange.

The first indication of the crisis had come two days earlier, when the Russians suddenly raised the prices on the government-controlled grain market. Flour went up 50 percent, corn and kaoliang 100 percent and gold 70 percent. Other commodities followed. Perishables like fish rose 500 percent. A panic ensued, and by the night of the 14th business was at a standstill. The merchants refused to sell most things except at fantastic prices; the cost of some manufactured articles and curios, however, remained steady.

The new currency decree stated that workers could exchange 5000 of the old yuan for 5000 of the new; sums over that could be exchanged at the rate of ten old yuan for one new yuan. (In actuality, this promise often was not honored.) If you were not a worker, such as a housewife or student, no exchange at all was ordinarily allowed.

Since a loaf of bread cost 600 yuan, with other prices in proportion, there was little cash left in most households. For if a man had had 20,000 of the old yuan, he immediately took a loss of nearly 75 percent. No one had savings in reserve after this day. The remaining small, independent merchants were the hardest hit, and many now closed their shops.

Russian citizens, however, exchanged their old currency through their factories or government organizations, apparently without limitations on the amount they could present. Anyway, 80 percent of their income was in the form of commodities and services, so cash usually was of little importance to them. Non-Russian workers in the state factories received an extra 5000 yuan, and the Russian-controlled companies also received a variety of other exchange compensations.

By no standard was it a fair law, certainly not from the Chinese point of view. We speculated over how it was affecting the present current of Sino-Soviet relations in Kwantung, and what such a grossly discriminatory act could mean in future attitudes toward continued Russian control of the area. A rather comparable cancellation of an old currency took place at a few American bases concerning PX script during or soon after the war. Then, however, the purpose was to cancel PX bills that had been accumulated illegally by the local non-American people, and this illegality was well known to them.

The members of the consulate staff had received their biweekly salaries the day before the decree issuing the new yuan money; the Department authorized me to reimburse them for their losses. Fortunately, the consulate did not have much yuan on hand, including the staff's currency. Nevertheless, it took prolonged negotiations to get even that exchanged.

Within a few weeks of the devaluation, the rate on our dollar bills at the foreign exchange market decreased to about half what it had been. Thus, the cost of operating the consulate doubled.

We received one dividend from the currency reform. During the long negotiations to exchange our money, we had more contact with the Chinese Communist officials of the Kwantung Administration than at any other time during our stay. When we were able to arrange interviews with them in advance—giving the front men time to prepare for the ordeal of meeting us—we were received with tea and courtesy. If we went directly to them without an appointment, we were treated harshly, in fact, in a hostile matter that was downright rude. Long waits in the anterooms and corridors of the Administration's building gave us the opportunity to observe the clerks. Offices were obviously overstaffed and themselves inefficient by Western standards, but there was noticeably a definite air of enthusiasm and self-confidence. Here, at least, the Chinese considered themselves in charge of their own city's affairs—in their first opportunity for self-government in a half-century. Alas, it was also apparent that the anti-American indoctrination was all-pervasive, even among the lower levels of personnel.

The foreign-exchange market where we sold our American bills for Kwantung yuan continued to operate after the currency reform just as before. There, about thirty stalls ranged around the sides of a large room on the second floor of a business building, looking something like the booths of vegetable dealers at old-time American farmers' markets. To obtain operating funds, as for paying salaries, Culver would go to this exchange market once a week or so. Selling our American money, usually in twenty or hundred dollar bills, for Kwantung yuan, he would go from dealer to dealer to get the best price. The dealer paid a tax on each transaction. Each proprietor sat behind a glass case that contained a scattering of old coins, some also sold nondescript jewelry. But their primary business was the buying and selling of foreign currencies and gold bullion. The gold sold here was in the form of "bars," each bar about the volume of two cigarettes. The price of gold and of the currencies varied each day, sometimes widely.

This capitalist market was a most peculiar institution to find in a Communist stronghold. In all the Communist world, from Vladivostok to East Berlin, probably no place like this existed; normally one of the first things a Communist government does is to eliminate free trade in foreign currencies. This market probably played a necessary part in the flow of Chinese Communist money into and out of Dairen port, so it served the regime's purposes to allow it to remain open. The market remained in existence all the time we were in Dairen, but, toward the end, the number of dealers had decreased by half.

The dealers were certainly a nervous group, for they perpetually feared that the market would suddenly be closed and that they might be accused of some sort of malfeasance. They worried constantly about their contacts with the American consulate; they worried too that the authorities would bring retroactive charges of some kind against them. Rumors sprang up regularly that the police were going to "crack down." However, they did not decrease transactions with us. Despite everything, the temptation to stay in business remained. They must have been turning a good profit.

The old coins displayed in the glass cases formed an extraordinary array. In no sense were they intended for collectors; they were merely for the local people who wanted to buy a little piece of silver or gold to hoard. Here were coins that through the years, centuries, had found their way to China and to Dairen: Mexican silver pesos, a former standard medium of exchange in the Far East, Austrian Maria Theresa thalers, a medium of exchange for centuries in the Gulf of Arabia, and above all the Imperial Russian coins. Most of the European and Asiatic currencies of the past century were represented, plus coins dating from the reigns of Charles II of England, Frederick the Great of Prussia, Catherine the Great of Russia. None were in the mint condition prized by coin collectors. They had been traded decade after decade, or perhaps hidden for a century in a peasant's house. Usually, they were sold merely by weight.

I had never been interested in coins, but gradually I started buying these Dairen offerings, at first those the size of a United States silver dollar, and then the smaller silver ones. I found a book that pictured most of the types; thus I knew something about what I was buying. Two years later, in London, I sold my small coins to Spinks, a well-known dealer; there were no rarities in the lot. The most unexpected items in my collection were a dozen different Chinese pieces larger than a U.S. dollar, beautifully designed, crafted almost like medals. Spinks said they had never been issued as money but had been manufactured in Shanghai during the 1930s to sell to gullible tourists as "coins from the days of the Manchus." There had even been a technical book written about them, called *Coins That Never Were.* I kept these as mementoes of the Communist exchange market.

Wandering around the Dairen shopping area occasionally inspired other collecting projects. In one place, almost a hole-in-the-wall, I saw secondhand phonograph records that cost about ten cents each. All were prewar and, of course, 78 rpm's. In retrospect, I guess I spent most of my free time in Dairen winding the blasted old phonograph. The recordings of classical music were mostly Japanese repressings of European issues. Since my knowledge of the classics was admittedly superficial, I often did not know opus and sonata numbers and even many symphony numbers. Also, since many of the Japanese labels did not have translations under the titles printed in ideographs, it became an intriguing grab-bag each time as to what I was actually buying. When I kept going back to the record store, the owner did not protest my visits to him: after all, I was his best cash customer, and for that he would risk police scoldings.

(On my return to the United States I tried to buy new records of my favorites, but many of the works were so out of the ordinary they were unavailable. I had bought a Japanese set of *Don Giovanni:* ninety-six sides!—I had never seen the opera, but I knew the general plot and enjoyed the tempestuous music dramatizing what I thought were duels and rapes and murders. When I finally saw the opera performed, it was a shock to discover that poor Don Juan never laid hands on a female on-stage, in fact, could hardly be classified either as a lover or a fighter.)

Another hole-in-the-wall shop I found sold tropical fish. I bought a tank and a supply of the little creatures, including—for rather a high price—a large goldfish, beautifully coal-black, lush as rich velvet. After a few weeks it became an ugly, mottled thing as sections of its skin turned a sickly oyster color. The shopkeeper had failed to tell me to keep it in a deep dark tank. *Caveat emptor.*

One day when I was at the Kwantung administration regarding the changing of our old yuan into the new currency, I had a long conversation with the head of the East China Bureau of the Chinese Communists without ever understanding how it came about. Also, the "Commissar of Art Objects," told me that Communists had found few antiques in Mukden. Those persons who could escape the city during the siege, such as by plane, had bought up all the gold metal available as a way to take out their capital; when the gold was gone, they had bought antiques and curios. He said the Communists were now "collecting" (i.e., confiscating) art objects throughout Manchuria to use in projected museums or to export to the United States for foreign exchange.

I was reminded then of an odd happening a few months before, when Culver and I began purchasing some Oriental objets d'art. Not long after our arrival in Dairen, while making conversation during one of my few calls on the "chief of state" of the Kwantung administration, I commented how sorry I was that no store in town sold the sort of antiquities which were available in any major Chinese city. I asked if this was the situation in all areas under Communist control. For some reason the question confused him mightily (which was not my intention), and he assured me that small, private-enterprise stores could carry on in Dairen the same as elsewhere, but that there was no normal market for antiques here—probably true enough.

A few days later a man appeared at the office and invited Culver and me to come to his shop. It turned out to be on the second floor at the rear of an old building, and so far as we could judge, had been hastily turned into a "store" just for the two of us.

Scattered around on the floor and on a few counters were a miscellany of dishes, paintings, bronzes, carvings. The "shopkeeper" glibly gave the dynasty of each: so glibly, in fact, that we did not believe him. Nevertheless, because of our favorable rate of exchange, the prices were temptingly low. Most of them cost about five U.S. dollars, a few ten. Whatever the dynasties really were (and the man turned out to be wrong in most cases), the objects were undeniably old. This and later purchases from the man were the most delightful shopping I have ever done. The element of price played no part. Here were these beautiful objects before me, and I could choose the ones I liked solely on the basis of their appeal to me. (Always, in the outside world, if one item costs more than another, that presumably proves its greater esthetic value or age. For example, a poorly executed ceramic of the Sung Dynasty is often priced higher than a similar, good example of the Ch'ing Dynasty.)

When we left the "store" we asked the man to bring his next lot of goods to our house. This he did several times. Eventually, we decided these must be the cheaper items the Communists had acquired in Manchuria, who knows how, for forwarding via underground channels to Peking (which was still in Nationalist hands and visited by foreign buyers). Presumably, they were carrying on this trade with Peking to get foreign exchange. Getting our money was as good as acquiring the dollars in Peking and more convenient.

I bought some attractive rough pottery with a deep green glaze because it was the same color and shape as a type of crude dishes sold today in the bazaars of Afghanistan. (Back in the United States, I had these pieces examined by a museum expert. They came from the Liao Dynasty, about 1000 A.D., which had originated in Manchuria.) My most interesting item was a Japanese painting dating from the sixteenth century. (The "shopkeeper" said it was Mongolian, showing how wrong he was about almost everything.) This would have been valuable except for someone's attempt to "renovate" it with crude brushstrokes. Nevertheless, it is a picture I still enjoy.

Whenever the man came, Culver and I each bought about a dozen items. Then he never appeared again. Perhaps the

Communists had no further need of our money, we thought
—rather disappointed in the termination of such pleasant
antique-shopping at my own house. But I began to wonder
whether the Communists were beginning to recognize the
intrinsic value of such antiquities and wished to hold on to
them.

As with so many other events and circumstances in Dairen,
we pondered this matter and, came up with at least several
reasonable explanations—but never a satisfactory one. Gradually
we learned to accept the fact that events could happen suddenly,
for better or for worse, and we might never know why. For
example, in November Culver and I received night passes from
the Russian Kommandatura. We had applied for them last June.
Why they were given so unexpectedly now, we did not know.
However, to avoid the chance of unpleasant stops by the police,
we continued to sleep at the consulate office whenever we
worked in the evenings.

In the fall of 1948, as Manchuria fell to the Red Army,
Dairen experienced a "population registration," later extended
to cities and countrysides in northern China. Carried out by the
police of the Kwantung administration, it involved thoroughly
investigating everyone in the entire Chinese population above
the age of fourteen. In addition to the identification passports
each had been carrying, household certificates were now issued.
Periodically, the police made rounds at night, checking up on
the households to see that everybody was in place.

Ever since the fall of Mukden on October 30, Dairen had
been awash with rumors that its political status would be
changed—all of which I duly reported to the Department. Mao
Tse-tung, Chu Teh and five other members of the Chinese
Communist Central Committee were said to have arrived in
Dairen from Harbin. One rumor said they were planning to
negotiate the withdrawal of the Russians from Kwantung and
the annexation of the peninsula to Communist China. Another
said they wanted merely to arrange for Russian diplomatic
recognition of the Communists as the real government of China.
Still another claimed that they had come to set up the

Communist style of land reform here.

Nothing happened in any of these matters. But the possibility of formal Russian recognition of the Chinese Communists always hung over our heads like the sword of Damocles, for if that happened, the Kwantung civil administration would be turned over openly to the Chinese Communists, and the present pretense that this area was a separate entity might be eliminated. Dealing with the Russians was frustrating enough, but at least we were legally under their protection. Living directly under the aegis of the Chinese Communists would be far worse, as our Mukden consulate was currently finding out.

There were also rumors that the port of Dairen would be "opened up" for normal commercial world trade. Of course, Russian freighters often went directly to and from other countries, although their shipping papers, carefully prepared for foreign officials, read that they had come from or were going to some port in Siberia, instead of Dairen. As evidence, Russian sailors in Dairen traded articles like fresh American or British cigarettes.

Now that the railroad connection into Mukden was being repaired, it was natural to assume that these plans might really be serious. For instance, it was said the Chinese Communists were particularly anxious to trade their Manchurian soybeans for vitally needed medicines and manufactured articles. However. the status of the port regarding foreign freighters remained unchanged until the following summer. So much for the veracity of rumors.

To our vast joy and relief, a pair of couriers reached us shortly before Christmas. They brought twenty-eight pouches of office supplies, personal mail, accumulated magazines—and gifts from home. Celebrating the Christmas holiday season in a place where we were social outcasts was an odd experience, but somehow the isolation forged closer bonds and heightened our feelings.

On New Year's Eve we invited Mrs. Schumann and an elderly Italian named Policello, who had been unable to leave Dairen, for dinner and bridge. The four of us felt elegant and civilized:

Mrs. Schumann wore a prewar evening dress and the men wore black tie. The cooks outdid themselves with fine dishes. At midnight we drank a bottle of sparkling burgundy which Mrs. Schumann had brought; she said it was the custom in her husband's native East Prussia to drink this wine at midnight on New Year's Eve. We toasted her Edmund somewhere in Siberia; we toasted the cooks; we toasted the brand-new year of 1949.

And next New Year's Eve? Where would each of us be? The bridge game with its set of rigid rules gave us a feeling of snug security away from the troubles of the outside world. We played bridge all night—partly because the guests could not leave until dawn due to the curfew, but equally we all felt reluctant to end this intimate yet festive party.

NOTE: In Russia, the secret police has been an arm of the government since czarist days. To sort out all the initials of the various agencies under the Soviet regime, we start with the Cheka, established December 1917, and abolished by decree in 1922, when it was superseded by the GPU (a part of the People's Commissariat for Internal Affairs—NKVD) later the OGPU, and in 1934 absorbed by the NKVD.

January 31, 1941, the NKVD was divided into the NKGB (to deal with state security) and Ministry of Interior (MVD), both agencies headed by Beria. In March 1954, it was again divided and, as the KGB (Committee for State Security) the secret police was downgraded to a committee. On January 13, 1960, the central MVD was abolished and the organization of the secret police remained under the KGB.

CHAPTER VIII

STARTING
A NEW YEAR
(WINTER 1949)

In January the Dairen authorities focused an unwelcome attention on the White Russians. How many now lived in the city it was hard to say. Of the eight hundred or so there at the end of the war nearly all still remained. Then the Russians brought in at least a thousand from Harbin and probably more from elsewhere in Manchuria. Apparently, they were needed as technicians and for clerical help; perhaps they also wanted to concentrate them in one locality, where they could be controlled better. We heard that the newcomers were glad to be in Dairen because they felt safer under the Russian military than under the Chinese Communists.

Although the White Russians were given jobs in the state-run trading organizations and trusts, they were not on the same footing with the "Real Russians" from the Soviet Union. They received lower wages and lived under tighter police surveillance and restrictions. For one thing, White Russians were not allowed to marry Real Russians.

The White Russians were classified in groups, and were sometimes known euphemistically as "New Soviets." At the beginning of the Russian occupation, those who spoke Japanese—probably a rather large percentage—were (to repeat the word one foreign resident used) "enslaved" by the KGB (MVD) police. This meant that they were compelled to work as translators in various KGB work, "various" being an interestingly vague term characterizing the activities of that infamous organization. (See note on facing page.)

Now, without warning, these KGB employees were being sent off to Vladivostok— not necessarily as prisoners— yet certainly ·they were forced to go. As part of the procedure, the head of a family had to write a letter asking to be allowed to return to the "fatherland", a typical touch of hypocrisy. Formerly, the few White Russians who had been repatriated could not take their families; now entire families were going. In Vladivostok they would be told where they would be sent within the vast Russian land mass.

One possible reason for this action regarding the KGB employees may have been to bring into Russia all those who could speak Japanese because of the declining need for them in Dairen. More likely, the KGB had decided it did not want anyone outside Russia familiar with any portion of its affairs.

A significant recruiting technique of the KGB and presumably of similar police forces in other dictatorship countries involves forcing nice, normal persons to become informers through various threats, often against their families. Once thus involved, they cannot hope to escape from the organization. Possibly, this situation applied to the White Russians working as translators for the KGB. They had little hope of transferring into some other governmental body; they knew too much about how the KGB carried on its business.

Another group of White Russians were those who, in the early days of the Soviet occupation, had applied for Russian passports (like those in Shanghai mentioned earlier). These applications implied the desire to "return home." In Dairen many had applied, either from enthusiasm or fear, but the authorities had consistently refused to let them leave. Now they were suddenly told they must go with their families, although many reportedly had changed their minds. At the Russian consulate general they were informed they could choose the city in which they intended to reside, but at the Kommandatura they were told that after their arrival in Vladivostok they would learn where they would be sent—obviously a frightening discrepancy. Those White Russians who had never asked to be repatriated now feared they would also be removed.

An unhappy footnote in this repatriation of the White Russians was that in the thirty years since the Revolution many had acquired families with complex nationality variations through marriage. Now they learned that those without "pure" Russian blood might not be allowed to accompany the other members of their family. Thus, many White Russian families were tragically broken up.

In January this exodus of White Russians had ostensibly been "voluntary." In February the police began to arrest a number of White Russians, sometimes at their homes, sometimes on the streets. These were the first large-scale arrests among them since immediately after the Soviet occupation. Significantly, all of those taken were young, mostly men.

The rumors were that of roughly half of the remaining White Russian families at least one member had been seized and deported to Siberia. Often this was the husband, leaving the wife alone with the children and with no money; friends often were afraid to help for fear of implication in the "cause" of the arrest.

Further repatriations or deportations or arrests—whichever was the right word—continued intermittently thereafter. By the time we left, there were almost no White Russians remaining in Dairen.

As for the others trapped in Dairen—the Germans, East Europeans and miscellaneous foreigners—nothing had changed. No more ships were available, and no exit visas. Occasionally though, a few Poles and Czechs were reported to leave for Siberia and then home. The rest survived, one way or another, in a drab and dreary existence.

* * *

Ch'en, our accounting clerk (who we always suspected was an informer) went to jail in February. The incident confused everyone on our highly nervous staff, who jumped to the conclusion that this was another pressure on the consulate. However, it may have been a legitimate police action. A female relative of Ch'en who lived in his house had died from poisoning. Ch'en, telling me about this, said it was suicide. The police who questioned him periodically, seemed to agree. Then both he and his wife were arrested. As the facts in the case gradually surfaced, it appeared there had been considerable turmoil in the household. It was rumored that an autopsy revealed that the girl had died of a different poison than would be allowed by the original suicide theory.

Culver called several times on the local police, asking for permission to see Ch'en in order to clear up certain matters about the accounts, but his request was always refused. In typical Communist police fashion, Culver's calls were met with the usual discourtesy and abrasiveness: they would not even admit knowledge of Ch'en. Ch'en's three children were taken in by a neighbor. With the Department's approval, I retained his salary, giving enough to the neighbor for the children's upkeep. Eventually, I placed Ch'en on "Leave Without Pay" status. Two months later the wife was released and called at the office to receive the salary due Ch'en. During a heated interview, in which she demanded great sums of money, she admitted that Ch'en had indeed been an informer during his employment at the consulate. The police ordered her and the children to leave Dairen. When she succeeded in reaching Tientsin, I warned the consulate there to have no relations with her. As for Ch'en himself, he remained in prison all the rest of the time we were in Dairen.

Meanwhile, not even attempting the hopeless task of finding a new accountant, I added the preparation of the monthly government accounts to my other chores. The official regulations concerning these, I sadly point out, are excessively complex and intricate and comprehensive and murky for reasons known only to the accounting bureaucracy in Washington. Yet small errors can lead to trouble. Fortunately, all my accounts were eventually cleared, perhaps because Washington never could fathom our money-exchange procedures.

Since all our local currency was obtained by selling American bills in the exchange market, each courier brought us a new supply of money. Then when the couriers were inevitably delayed, our cash supply would become dangerously small.

In mid-winter of 1949 we were again in a financial crisis. By some fluke I was suddenly able to sell the consulate's dejected Willys Jeep for $883.34. This would have been an extraordinarily high price back home, but in Dairen it was an indication of the scarcity of cars. I was never told who bought it although I would have liked to know who had command of that much cash. The protracted negotiations were carried out through a go-between. Since the car was not seen again in Dairen, it must have gone to some military gentleman in Port Arthur.

With this cash windfall we bought a year's supply of coal, so that this vital commodity, at least, would be on hand. It cost $250 for the office, $750 for the residence.) By next fall it was possible that the consulate would somehow be prevented from obtaining coal. Consequently, with this surplus on hand, we probably had the only warm office quarters in town and, except for the very highest officials, about the only warm house.

By now, troubles with the Russian and Chinese authorities which in the fall we had sanguinely shrugged off as unimportant or even, hopefully, temporary aberrations, had by now become constant. The occasional questioning of our office staff by the police as to why they were working for the "enemy" Americans became a steady and threatening practice. Head Clerk Chao, their chief target, began to sleep at the consulate rather than go to his home. In fact, by spring he seldom went outside the office. Whenever he did, the police invariably stopped him and asked why he was fighting the Chinese people by working for the Americans. When I suggested that he resign, he said that it would actually increase the danger of his arrest. At my request, the Department formally transferred him to our post in Taiwan, but neither the Kommandatura nor the Kwantung administration would acknowledge his application for an exit visa nor answer the consulate's many communications on the subject.

The same pressures plagued Radio Operator Chao. For him I felt particularly contrite: he was still in Dairen due to the Department's recreant failure to keep its promise that his assignment in Dairen would last for only six months. I pressured the Department to send in a replacement for him, but, so far as I could judge, that remote organization made no real effort in his behalf. It was apparent too that that when a replacement came, it would be extremely difficult to obtain an exit visa enabling Chao to leave.

As for Culver and me, we were still settled in rather regular patterns. In the mornings each of us had an individual Russian lesson with Mrs. Schumann. During the day we followed different schedules, as walking alone the mile to the office and home again for lunch. We usually left the office about six o'clock. Culver then would hike up the steep hill in front of our mutual residence with his dog, a lively mongrel named "Angry" which he had inherited from Patch. Meanwhile, I took a walk around town, always followed by my man on the bicycle. (The Ford continued as a faithful shadow when I was in the Oldsmobile.) Afterwards, if the winter sun was shining the two of us would have a drink in the garden and play gin rummy. Most evenings we had dinner separately. Then homework studies on the laborious Russian grammar and vocabulary. Once or twice a week we would invite the two Chaos for dinner, bringing them from the office in the Oldsmobile. They would spend the night in the two small bedrooms in the attic. Two or three times a week either Culver or I would sleep at the consulate, depending on the pile-up of work, such as the coding and decoding of telegrams, doing the accounts, reporting on the Communist press.

The pattern was seldom interrupted, and then usually because the police would stop the car to harangue us over some fancied traffic violation. Whether this scene took a half-hour or two hours depended on whether or not we had to go to the police station.

Ever since Culver had moved at the end of the summer from Patch's house into the other half of my double house, that building had remained empty. In February I suggested that Mrs. Schumann move into it, rather than leave it unoccupied and vulnerable to vandalism. We wanted to keep this house located a half-mile from ours, and not let the municipal building authority "repossess" it. The Department had finally assigned a third American, a clerk, to Dairen, and this would be his residence. In the meantime, he was standing by in Shanghai, waiting either for a Russian transit visa via Vladivostok or for the equally elusive pass for travel via Mukden. So, for now, Mrs. Schumann and her family could enjoy their first comfortable quarters since the end of the war.

The restrictions against this new clerk's entry in Dairen also applied to the men assigned as replacements for Culver and me. Our eight-month assignment period at the Dairen post, designated by the Department, was coming to an end. Realistically, I could not expect the new men to arrive soon, as they were stuck at posts in areas now occupied by the Chinese Communists. Also, I was sure that they would never get into Dairen unless the Department did something more decisive and drastic than just wait passively for Russian documentation and/or visas.

We rarely had guests. Occasionally we socialized with a few of the remaining foreigners, usually members of the German group. The biggest entertainment event would be when one of the Schumann children had a birthday; then the family came to our house to celebrate in style.

We never saw the Russians socially aside from their attending our Fourth of July function and our going to the Russian consul general's reception in honor of the Day of the Revolution. Also, two months after my arrival in Dairen, I had invited the Russian consular staff for dinner. But there was no chance thereafter for a repeat; relations simply became too strained. Socializing with the Chinese officials, of course, was even less possible.

Sometimes on the street or in a store I would pass officials I had met in the Kommandatura or the Kwantung Administration. Almost always they seemed highly embarrassed at the prospect of having to greet me publicly. So whenever possible, they looked the other way or turned aside entirely, as if they had not seen me. Obviously, they were afraid an informer might say they had met me or conversed with me. I always felt sorry for them. To have to operate in the world under such tight social restrictions seemed abhorrent to me, or, at least, absurd. If our eyes met, I would cooperate by doing nothing more than nod.

I often encountered the Russian officials when stopping at the *spetstorg*—the Russian word for "commissary." For those unfamiliar with the way "equality" is practiced in the Communist world, it is helpful to explain about the different levels of their commissaries. When stationed in Moscow during the war, I was told there were seventeen levels of *spetstorgs*, with every citizen assigned to a specific one in accordance with his rank and occupation. This assignment of rank was of vital importance because the range of selections and the quality and quantity of goods lessened drastically as one went down the social ladder. Thus, in wartime Russia the families of generals and admirals and equivalent civilians went to a commissary where they had a relatively wide choice of items in adequate amounts. The lower ranks and the civilian clerks, however, found in their own commissaries very few things.

This sort of uneven procedure also operated in the Dairen *spetstorgs*. In Moscow the foreign ambassadors were assigned to the commissary of the generals and admirals. Since in Dairen a similar privileged position had been arranged for my predecessor, Benninghoff, it remained unchanged for me. I would go shopping there every other week or so, but it was a rather dismal exercise, because about all I ever bought were staples like flour and sugar, cheese and Siberian "spirit."

By now, Culver and I had run out of our original stock of civilized liquor. (The near-lethal liquor sold in town shops were a raw Chinese rice wine and some "twenty-year-old brandy" from Chefoo, across the straits in Shantung, apparently concocted the night before the smuggler sailed.)

The spirit from the *spetstorg* was 95 percent alcohol and had a sour taste. Culver had learned how to treat this brew from a

Hungarian chemist—one of the foreigners stranded in Dairen. He bought carbon black and permanganate in town. The first step was to dissolve several permanganate crystals in a bottle of the spirit. After twenty-four hours a large gray mass of impurities had settled at the bottom; these he drained out through a fine cloth. Then he filtered the spirit several times through carbon powder. Last, he diluted it with water and flavored it with whatever happened to strike the imagination. By now the Siberian liquor was not undrinkable. In an attempt to capture the flavor of gin, we used berries and needles of cryptomeria trees, but, for sure, they will never take the place of juniper. Dried orange peel was best at cutting the still unpleasant taste. Culver also worked out a sort of cocktail combining the spirit and Vermont maple syrup at about ten to one, plus the plentiful canned lemon juice that had come to us in two cases which proved especially good in covering up bad liquor.

Rumors of plans for serious Russian economic expansion never ended. The early 1949 batch concerned representatives of the big Russian combines, said to be coming to Dairen on frequent trips from Siberia. Even the famous Anastas Mikoyan, a member of the Russian Politburo and Minister of Foreign Trade, was reported to have been in town, supposedly resulting in a big shake-up of many top executives in the local trusts, who were replaced by new men from Russia.

We also heard that 105 Russian engineers just out of universities were arriving in Dairen. Because they were mostly bachelors, and also because of the many unmarried military personnel around, it was said that "several hundred" Russian girls were coming here to work. Whatever truth there may have been in this, it did appear that the Russian population in Dairen and Kwantung was on the increase, either to replace the Japanese technicians or due to plans for trade and manufacturing expansion.

We reported to the Department that ever since its initial occupation of Kwantung, Russia had followed the classical colonial policy of economic exploitation:

— The Russians removed to Siberia great amounts of capital equipment in 1945, especially machinery. The plants left in operation—really semi-operation—were those that could carry on with local raw materials and labor and also be able to turn out products needed in Russia. These plants were taken over by large Russian trusts, such as Dalienerga (paint, dyes, firebricks, glass, cement), Kwantung Riba (fish, salt, canning glass), Export Khleb (grain, soybeans), etc.

— Plants not kept under Russian control had been stripped of equipment and then turned over one by one of the Kwantung Administration to be operated, or repaired, if at all possible, by the Chinese Communists, or, rather, by their front organizations, in order to get some sort of output underway. To achieve even a semblance of production took super-human efforts. In that respect, the Chinese managers could be sincerely complimented.

— The prices at which the goods from the Russian trusts were sold when shipped to Russia were considerably lower than when the same goods were sold to the local Chinese population. The stories of this practice, though often exaggerated, were a constant irritant among the Chinese.

— A preferential system controlled the paying of salaries in the Russian trusts and, more important, the distributing of food rations to the workers. The scale was "Real Russians" at the top, then the "New Soviets" (White Russians), other Europeans, Japanese and, down at the bottom, with the lowest wages and smallest rations, the Chinese themselves. (It was interesting to consider how much this economic discrimination must have rankled among the rightful residents of Kwantung.)

In his nearly year and a half of closely reading the press, Culver never once encountered any mention of Russia's removal of machinery from Manchuria or from Dairen. Yet surely it was no secret to the townspeople. After all, the coolies and dock workers were well aware the equipment had been loaded on ships leaving for Siberia. But it had happened over three years earlier, and it was interesting to note the propaganda technique used to erase this memory from the populace. In typically totalitarian fashion, it involved a counterattack with semi-truths and outright untruths. When explaining why the formerly great Manchurian industrial complex in Dairen, a mainstay of the Japanese economy and war effort, was now in such bad shape, the press kept repeating that part of the machinery was destroyed by the Japanese before their surrender and another part destroyed by "wreckers and spies." To explain why the economy was not reviving, a major theme was to accuse the Chinese Nationalists and the United States of blockading the port of Dairen.

As an example, here is an excerpt from the *Dairen Daily* (published by the local General Labor Union and accepted as a mouthpiece of the Chinese Communist Party):

> The industrial foundation left in Port Arthur-Dairen by the defeated Japanese Imperialism three years ago was deficient and paralytic. At that time, the people who had just been liberated were subjected to the economic blockade of American Imperialism and Kuomintang Reaction. They were in an empty-handed, starving and half-starving condition. Under such circumstances many people said that to restore and expand industry was recognizably almost impossible or would be difficult to believe. However, with the help of the local Russian Army and under the leadership of the Communist Party the working class of Port Arthur-Dairen firmly supported the factories. Furthermore, they displayed a spirit of self-sacrifice of a high degree and a most heroic deportment; advancing along a road beset with every kind of difficulty, they rebuilt and expanded the industry of Port Arthur-Dairen.

Thus, although many factories were still empty shells and production in nearly every field was only a fraction of previous levels, the newspapers consistently talked as though output had been restored and even increased.

Oddly, some private industry still did exist in Dairen, limited to plants employing less than twenty workers. The owners were shackled by government interference and subjected to unpredictable levies. They produced small quantities of consumer goods, such as soap, candles, glassware, leather goods, and fish nets.

The Kwantung Administration published a detailed outline in the local press of its "1949-1950 Two-Year Economic Plan" (which excluded the production of the Russian trusts). This was a most unusual happening; normally the press contained only percentages of increase or decrease, but what they were percentages of always remained a mystery. (This practice is standard for most economic articles in the press of Communist countries.) However, here suddenly, were firm figures about the Kwantung economy and about production plans.

Although the administration's goals were modest, it was obviously going to be difficult to meet them due to the earlier dismantlement of machinery. There was a lack of trained technicians; also, the administrative offices in all plants were vastly overstaffed. Further strains on these Chinese-operated factories were caused by attempts to pattern their management system on Russian models and by the low morale among the unskilled, laboring class.

Nevertheless, because the region no longer was war-torn and transportation was resumed, trade into and out of Manchuria was gradually beginning to revive; soon it might develop significantly. A full-scale effort was being made to restore the once-impressive Manchurian railroad system to its previous efficiency.

At the time of the currency reform in November, the Russians promised to reduce consumer prices in Dairen by 30 percent, but this had been done with only a few staples like grain and sugar. Now a real effort to lower prices was started by bringing in supplies from Manchuria. Fourteen hundred tons of pork were reported to have arrived in Dairen, reducing the price by a third. A greater variety of foodstuffs and grain was seen in the markets.

A new department store, owned by the Kwantung administration, also opened with unusually cheap prices; the cost of its sugar undercut the Russian outlet by 40 percent. Since the store was large and clean, I wondered how those Russians who had been in Moscow reacted to what was a rather embarrassing contrast to the shabby department stores there.

The newspaper publicity announced that the store was opened "for the masses" and that it was not like the former capitalist stores, which served "the slaves of foreign goods." Maybe so, but a large proportion of the goods displayed were strictly for the new Communist elite, such as the comparatively well-paid police force and the office managers. Although in public statements the officials urged that foreign exchange be husbanded, this store generously offered a variety of items imported from Hong Kong, such as British cloth, American cosmetics, drugs, vitamins, light bulbs, automatic pencils and also clocks and watches. The only really new item to Dairen, however, was aluminum kitchenware.

The new store carried, of course, that great status symbol seen throughout Asia immediately after the war: Parker 51 pens and, equally important, the caps of Parker 51 pens. Men would clip the cap onto the handkerchief pocket of their coats, to make it look as if they had been able to afford the full pen. If ever there was a symbolic bit of capitalistic nonsense and social sham, it was the widespread wearing of these pen caps. (This was no more amusing than the similar ridiculous pretenses of Americans and all other nationalities. Blame it on human nature.) Ironically, here in Dairen were the Communists indulging in the same pen-cap foible as did the "bourgeois" people they so castigated in Hong Kong, Manila, Bombay.

To illustrate the level of local income, a typical wage for a dock worker (surely a genuine member of the masses) was 800 yuan a week plus food rations. The complete Parker pen sold for 35,000 yuan, or 44 weeks of his wages. Yet the store's stock was sold out regularly. Rather often I saw a bureaucrat or policeman sporting one of the pens—and not just the cap.

News of the world outside, came to us still from the Shanghai broadcasts. The Berlin airlift was continuing its dramatic flights. Communist guerrillas were fighting in Greece, Vietnam, Burma, Philippines, Malaya. In Hungary, Cardinal Mindszenty was arrested for "political activities" and sentenced to life imprisonment. The North Atlantic Treaty Organization (NATO) was established. The leading labor union organizations in many Western countries, including Great Britain and the United States, resigned from the United Nations-sponsored World Federation of Trade Unions, charging that it had become a Communist tool. The leaders of the Communist parties in France and Italy, and later of several other countries, announced that their parties would side with Russia in the event of a East-West shoot-out war.

In China the city of Tientsin had fallen to the Chinese Communists in January, its popluation of two million increased by a million refugees. The Red Army then took Peking. Nearly all of north China above the Yangtze River was now firmly in Communist hands. Tragic stories of defeated soldiers and roads full of refugees filled the news. Six thousand were killed when a Nationalist Army evacuation ship exploded off the coast of Kwantung. To us the worst tragedy involved the millions of people now trapped behind Communist lines, with no chance of escape if they wished to.

The continued isolation of American Consul General Ward at Mukden had become a major international news story. Every rumor would revive interest in it. Yet the only firm fact was that the State Department did not know what was happening to him and to his staff and it had been unable to contact him since last November.

Technically, perhaps the Chinese Communists should not be faulted too harshly on this matter. In fact, the Communists had not yet even formed a national government; and, as the CCP and the United States had not exchanged diplomatic representatives, they considered us to be the chief prop and ally of their enemies, the Nationalists.

The unusual news angle of the Ward case lay in the

Communists' violation of traditional diplomatic immunity.

The back and forth telegrams continued to and from Washington concerning the efforts to get passes for Culver to go to Mukden and try to learn what was happening to Ward, and also regarding efforts to have couriers reach Mukden through Communist China and then onward to Dairen. Looking on both projects as hopeless, I was wryly entertained by the Department's bemusement with them. Nevertheless, I kept on pressing the Kommandant for the passes while continuing to stress to the Department that the real decision would come from Moscow not Dairen.

In February, unexpectedly, I did receive a telephoned reply from the Kommandatura, refusing to give Culver a pass to go to the Kwantung border. When I demanded a written reply—since I had sent several communications about this matter—a letter did come.

I regarded it as a major event, for it was the *first* written communication any Russian or Chinese official had sent to the consulate since I had arrived in Dairen, seven months before. To me it was evidence that a decision had indeed been made in Moscow.

The telegrams, however, continued.

In one message to the Department I summarized the consulate's difficulties arising from the peculiar political status of Dairen. On the one hand was the Russian interpretation of their rights here and the United States' acquiescence to that interpretation, such as conforming to the Russian refusal to allow an American ship to come here with couriers. On the other hand was the fact that the Kwantung government was dual by nature: that is, it was both a Russian "puppet" and an extension of the Chinese Communist command centered at Harbin and Peking.

I pointed out that until recently both the Russians and Chinese Communists were sensitive concerning the 1945 Sino-Soviet Treaty which, among other matters called for a Chinese civil administration in Dairen. Both of them implied this stipulation had been fulfilled by the organization of the

"People's Democratic Government" (the Kwantung administration) after the "refusal" of the Chinese Nationalist government to cooperate in the civil administration in Dairen in 1946. (Their failure to do so had, of course, been due to Russian interdiction.) Dating from the fall of Mukden, this sensitivity had rapidly disappeared. We could now expect that whenever the Russians recognized diplomatically the still-unorganized Chinese Communist government for all China, the present "temporary" arrangements in Dairen would be confirmed. (There were constant rumors that such recognition would take place "soon.")

In another telegram I said that neither the Department nor our embassy in Nanking had ever given the Dairen consulate a directive on how to deal formally with the Russsian occupation authorities and with the Kwantung government: "Although the Consulate obviously is not able to dispute the legality of Soviet-Chinese composition here and although every effort is made to comply quietly with the many irritating restrictions, there is still a sphere where the Consulate is doubtful how to act."

The Department thereupon sent such a directive, which I quote almost entirely because it is a key document—even though it repeats several points I have stressed earlier. Here was what the Department called its "views":

> The status of the Soviets at the Port Arthur Naval Base Area and at Dairen is determined by an Agreement accompanying the Sino-Soviet Treaty of 1945. The Soviets contend that Dairen is subject to military supervision or control established in the Port Arthur Naval Base areas pending the formal termination of war with Japan. The Nationalist Government of China does not agree that such is the meaning and intent of the Agreement. It is palpably absurd to maintain that other than a fictitious state of war exists after the unconditional surrender and occupation of Japan. The United States, of course, was not party to this Agreement of the Sino-Soviet Treaty. This Government has taken formal cognizance of the undesirable situation at Dairen in

notes to the Soviet and Nationalist Governments in January 1947, urging prompt consideration by those governments regarding the current unsatisfactory situation at Dairen, with the view to implementing the pertinent provisions of the Sino-Soviet agreements regarding Dairen and adding that the United States Government perceives no reason for further delay in re-opening the port to international commerce under Chinese administration as contemplated in the Agreements.

In a note to the Soviet Government on August 14, 1947, the United States reiterated these views and expressed hope that the Soviet and Chinese Governments would soon be able to reconcile their differing views and added that in the interim the Soviet Government should be held responsible for the treatment accorded to American interests in Dairen. This latter responsibility the Soviets categorically rejected. Thus, each case of American interests in the area must be handled with the Soviets and Chinese as and how the occasion arises.

From the standpoint of practical operating procedure it is recognized the Soviets exercise *de facto* control at Dairen and you will have to deal with them. In such dealings you should try to treat them as a military authority exercising *de facto* control in the area without attempting to pass on the legality of that control.

Notwithstanding special concessions to the Soviets in this area, the sovereignty over Kwantung remains Chinese. The Kwantung Administration has existed in defiance of the Government of China recognized by the United States and should be treated as an unrecognized authority. The continued functioning of the Consulate in an area under control of unrecognized authorities or the dispatch of consular officers to such a territory does not itself imply recognition, but in any course of action it is most important to leave no doubt that recognition by this Government is not implied and the Consul is acting entirely in his consular capacity.

Relations with the unrecognized local officials should be maintained insofar as possible on an informal and impersonal basis. Social invitations of a private nature may be accepted in the discretion of the principal officer, but acceptance should be in his personal and not his official capacity. In general, invitations to social functions of an official nature should be filed without formal acknowledgement and such functions should not be attended. The foregoing applies to the Kwantung Administration or to any successor which is not established by the Government of China recognized by the United States.

American policy with respect to Dairen has been directed toward the establishment of a Chinese civil administration responsible to the Nationalist Government of China and a free port open to the commerce and shipping of all nations, as provided in the Sino-Soviet Agreements. While it is unrealistic to expect that the Nationalist Government under present circumstances can establish a civil administration in Dairen, the implementation of the free port provision remains the United States objective.

Furthermore, the Department considers the continued maintenance of the Consulate at Dairen to be highly desirable from the standpoint of American interests in the area and believes the importance of the office will increase with the cessation of hostilities in Manchuria, re-establishment of communications and general reconstruction.

It may be possible to work out an agreement whereby personnel at Dairen and Mukden are interchangeable.

Whatever may be the legal basis of the present control and administration at Dairen, the Department realizes that the control by the Soviets and the Kwantung Civil Administration is a reality and must be accepted as such in working out practical operating procedures at Dairen.

A later telegram added:

The Department realizes it is inevitable that you have to apply to the Kwantung authorities from time to time, and does not consider your application to the Chinese police as such is a form of recognition of the Kwantung Administration. To avoid any possibility of misunderstanding in this connection, you should, when possible, direct your requests to the appropriate official by name without title, or to the appropriate official by title without name, viz., to "Chief of Police, Dairen."

For historians and students of diplomacy and international law this may be an interesting document. It hardly changed things for me at Dairen. All the variables mentioned were irrelevant, such as "social invitations" from the officials of the Kwantung Administration, for I never received any. So my empiricism had to remain, to "play it by ear" as a succession of incidents mounted.

CHAPTER IX

SPRINGTIME IN DAIREN (SPRING 1949)

The long winter drew to a close. The weather had been similar to the weather in Washington, a few light snowfalls and a lot of drizzle, but without as much sunshine.

A courier arrived on April 1, having begun his three-month round-trip journey from Shanghai via Vladivostok in February. We realized that this courier would be the last to reach us out of the already doomed Shanghai. The Department now hoped to establish a regular service from Moscow via Vladivostok.

What an April Fool's Day: the courier had not brought us enough money!

Several months before, we had requested the Department (informing the consulate as well) to send us five thousand dollars in gold bars as part of the regular shipment of cash. Gold, actively traded at the money market, was an often-used medium of exchange, and its value was steadily rising. Although exchange rates varied between the money dealers, the rate on our dollar bills had been kept generally rather static by a single, behind-the-scenes buyer, the Kwantung Administration. Actually, rates over a three-month period averaged about the same, but serious fluctuations could take place during that period. Since we anticipated a future emergency if our dollar bills were arbitratily refused or greatly discounted, we wanted the gold on hand. We also planned to start exchanging the gold in advance of any emergency to make this an accepted practice by the consulate.

Our request for gold bars must have been a startling event in Washington but it was honored. Via the United States Treasury, they were sent to Shanghai. Alas, the glittering metal arrived the day after the courier left. And since the consulate general in Shanghai did not make up the difference, a serious cash crisis for us would be sure to arise.

The courier was John Koval, who was making his second trip to Dairen. A lively extrovert who spoke a Russian dialect (his parents had emigrated from eastern Europe), he was able to cope with any bureaucratic snafus in Vladivostok and elsewhere. With exuberance and skill he bluffed or blustered or sweet-talked his way across the Communist boundaries. By now, of course, we looked upon him as an old friend.

I sent out twenty-six pouches with the couriers. The bulkiest item was the accumulation of Russian and Chinese Communist books, magazines, and newspapers for the Department and for the Library of Congress. I also sent the consulate archives dating from its opening in 1904 to 1941, when it was closed after Pearl Harbor. The future of the post was too uncertain to warrant keeping them here; anyway, conditions were now so different from those days that we never referred to the old volumes.

We also returned the personal mail for the American staff at Mukden. The previous couriers had brought the mail and left it with us because there had been hope then that Culver would be able to get through to that isolated group from Dairen. Now it was obvious that was not going to happen.

Following the capture of Peking, the Communists had spent the balance of the winter consolidating their forces throughout most of the territory north of the Yangtze River. They were now approaching Nanking and Shanghai. As the Communists threatened the Nationalists' capital, the embassy at Nanking sent its biographical files to the Department and confined its reporting in that field to minimum spot coverage. The Department now asked us to increase our own biographical reporting from the Dairen and Chinese Communist press: we were not to concern ourselves about possible duplication from other posts. This activity, carried out in every embassy and consulate, involves amassing from the press and other sources bits of information that enable the Department's research staff to build up complete biographical data on all important personnel of a foreign government—or, in this case, of the Chinese Communist Party.

Along with the greening of spring, we watched the CCP in Dairen come out into the open. The Communist military successes gave confidence to the local Communists and Russians to "regularize"—if that is the right word—the Kwantung Administration. No more hiding behind puppet, top-titled officials in the Kwantung Administration and behind the facade of Russia's policy of "correctness" regarding the Chinese Nationalists on the international scene. Police controls over the populace became even stricter. Anti-American propaganda intensified.

My telegrams reported the successive steps in the changes in Dairen and in the Kwantung Administration:

> — March 19, 1949. A preparatory Committee of New Democratic Youth Corps is formed in Dairen in accordance with a resolution of the Central Committee of the CCP [presumably then based in Peking]. This is the first public admission by a Chinese body in Kwantung of any Communist connection, and it hints the CCP may soon emerge here.

> — March 31. The daily newspaper of the General Labor Union, the *Dairen Daily*, announces it will cease publication. The consulate had accepted this as the leading front paper of the CCP, and the final issue confirmed that it had "propagated all along the policies of the CCP." Responsibility for the "labor press" is transferred to a new newspaper for the Port Arthur-Dairen area called the *People's Daily*, The *Kwantung Daily*, press organ of the Kwantung administration is now changed to a weekly gazette. The Kwantung News Agency becomes the Dairen branch of the New China News Agency, which is the official news-gathering organization of the Chinese Communist government [roughly similar to Associated Press, United Press

International and Tass]. In summary, the media here is now openly an integral part of the Chinese Communist propaganda machine.

— April 1. The local branch of the CCP officially emerges from underground and announces it is subordinate to the Northeast Bureau (Manchuria) of the CCP. Various front agencies have changed their names or admitted Communist connections. The Regional CCP Secretary made a long, programmatic report at an "activists meeting," saying the CCP endorsed the Sino-Soviet Treaty of 1945 and that the Russian military occupation of Dairen would continue until the Japanese peace treaty is signed. Until today the Chinese Nationalist and Russian flags had flown over public buildings together, as a token of Russia's "correct" policy. Now the Chinese Communist flag replaces the Nationlist flag. Parades of various front organizations, government employees, factory workers and police are held in honor of the official emergence of the CCP.

— April 12. The puppet mayor of Dairen, Hsu Hsien-chai, is granted a "long" leave of absence and is replaced by his deputy Mao Ta-sun. This is the first sign of personnel changes within the Kwantung Administration itself.

— April 22. The puppet chairman of the Kwantung Administration, Ch'ih Tzu-hsieng, announces his resignation and is replaced by his deputy, Han Kuang. The vice-chairman and leaders of "democratic groups" (all now admitting their CCP affiliations) call for a People's Republic Conference in Dairen to elect a new chairman and officers.

— April 25. "Elections" to the conference are held. Only "democratic organs" are allowed to vote and these are controlled by the CCP. (Note: Despite constant propaganda that the delegates had been elected by the "masses" and the "workers" in "democratic, popular elections," and that all actions at the sessions were taken in their names, this definitely was not the situation. No elections were held;

the delegates were selected by the Communist leaders already in charge. The propaganda, however, never changed its rote).

— April 27. The three-day conference begins. The hotel where the delegates are lodged and the Hall of Culture where the sessions meet are both heavily guarded by the police. In no sense is the public allowed to be present. The conference changes the name of the Kwantung Administration to Port Arthur-Dairen executive administration. [I continued, however, to use the old name, Kwantung Administration anyway, the local population kept on using it.] In a keynote speech, the Regional Secretary of the CCP states that Port Arthur and Dairen are part of a CCP-liberated area. He indicates the Russians will remain in the Port Arthur Naval Base Area but avoids any reference to Russian-occupied Dairen.

In the weeks following the conference the resignations of various factory managers and bureau and office chiefs were announced. Those who resigned were the puppets; those who replaced them, usually their assistants, were CCP men.

Newspaper articles on local political and economic subjects in the Dairen press now became almost indistinguishable in vocabulary and general content from the Mukden-published newspapers.

In my interpretation to the Department concerning these governmental developments I emphasized that the day-to-day relations between the CCP and the Russians appeared unchanged. The continued use of the term "Administration" again pointed up the traditional separateness of Kwantung from the rest of China; the CCP's regular term for such a political organization was "Executive Committee." Although CCP officials spoke of the Port Arthur Naval Base area, they remained significantly silent on the special status of Dairen. The CCP affirmed that the Sino-Soviet Treaty of 1945 continued to be the governing document for the area, thus adhering to the Russian interpretation that nothing should change until Russia, sometime in the future, signed a peace treaty with Japan.

This left the question: Why did the CCP and the Russians make the governmental changes at this time?

From the point of view of the CCP the reason apparently was that it wished to emerge openly so it could then take credit for the economic accomplishments it expected the Kwantung Administration to achieve as soon as trade was reestablished with Manchuria.

As for the Russians, allowing the public appearance of the CCP constituted a dramatic departure from their "correct" policy, to which they had carefully adhered since the end of World War II in order to mask the active support which they were covertly giving the CCP. At least, that was what most commentators in the world press thought was behind the "correct" policy. Our embassy in Nanking suggested the Russians, in now abandoning that policy, must have obtained from the CCP an important *quid pro quo.* If so, the "this-for-that" remained a secret. I myself wondered why the Chinese Nationalist government did not break off diplomatic relations with the Soviet Union after the "correct" policy was abandoned, for it seemed to have nothing to lose by expelling the Russian diplomats from the remaining Nationalist territory. As it was, however, the Russians officially closed their posts in areas taken over by the Communists (although the staffs were probably retained) and kept open the ones in the Nationalist sections. (I am often left with the conclusion that nothing in that vague terrain called "diplomacy" is ever simple!)

The Central Committee of the CCP did not seem to take the Kwantung CCP officially into its fold, but actually we had no way of knowing whether it had or not. The local CCP's announcement that it was subordinate to the Northeast Bureau of the CCP did not necessarily mean it was a full-fledged member of the CCP. This may seem a quibbling item, but matters of status or protocol are extremely important in a communist hierarchy. In this case, it must have meant that Russia was not yet ready for the full incorporation of the civil administration of Kwantung into the CCP of Manchuria.

Certainly, whenever the Kommandant wished, his word still overruled the Kwantung administration officials.

Up until now it was our observation at the consulate that in aspects of communization—such as economic planning based on Communist dogma and the use of Russian industrial-management techniques—the Port Arthur-Dairen area had gone much farther than other "liberated area" in China proper. On the other hand, Kwantung lagged behind the Manchurian hinterland in the CCP's propagandized program of "new democratization," for instance, land reform. Due to the Russian policy of "correctness," no publicized land reform had been carried out in Kwantung although the Communists had already doubtless pushed through what they ominously called "settling accounts in the villages." And in Dairen most property owners by now had been dispossessed of their holdings through heavy taxation and enforced contributions.

To the already-established means of police control over the population, such as passports which individuals older than fourteen had to carry at all times and house certificates enabling the police to verify at night that all residents were inside, now were added block chiefs, each one "representing" a group of residents in a small area. This type of "group responsibility" prodded people to report any criticisms of the regime by their neighbors; it also punished everyone in a group for any anti-regime action by a member.

This block-chief system closely resembled the notorious *pao chia* system used in Chiang Kai-shek's own form of police state which made neighbors responsible for each other's behavior. Mao Tse-tung had constantly attacked this practice, making it a major theme in Communist propaganda. Yet his own police quickly installed the same controls as soon as feasible after taking over an area. Actually, throughout all the Soviet empire under Stalin a similar population-control system was used.

Whatever clique of the faction-ridden CCP in China was now in control in Dairen, it was certain the representatives here were thoroughly pro-Russian in their political outlook: in fact, ultra Russian. In a speech, the Chinese Communist Regional Secretary, referring to the Russian occupation of Kwantung, said the Russians would be here for thirty years in order "to prevent the United States from seizing the area."

During this time of political change a new name surfaced in the newspapers that was previously unknown to the consulate. Ou-yang Ch'in had the title of Secretary of the Port Arthur-Dairen Committee of the CCP. Although he remained in the news the rest of the time we were in Dairen, he never held any governmental position. He appeared regularly at important functions, making speeches which established changes in the official policy "'line"—speeches that were then parroted for weeks by lesser men in order to drive home the new policy. Later, in February 1950, when a new treaty was signed between Russia and the new Communist Chinese government, our embassy in Moscow noted that the Russian press reported Ou-yang among the dozen distinguished Chinese present at the ceremony. Thus, he can be assumed to have been the key Chinese Communist in Dairen, at least from the spring of 1949 onward. Only by such piecing together of data are the facts usually learned about Communist officials, whether Chinese or Russian. This illustrates the value of biographical reporting, a chore of all Foreign Service posts.

I did not understand then, nor do I understand now, why Russia turned over the civil administration of Kwantung to the Chinese Communists, first tentatively in 1946 and then definitely reaffirming it in 1949. As an occupation force first forecast in the Yalta Agreement, Russia could have continued to rule as a military power, at least outside Dairen, without concern about civil administration niceties. In the beginning, Russia did worry about possible Chinese Nationalist interference and about world opinion. Yet, it set up the 1946 predecessor of the Kwantung administration presumably for political advantages of the moment with the Chinese Cummunists. Russia thereby let the Chinese Communists staff the civil administration, which in 1949, for the first time, was publicly displayed. Even though Russia still remained in control—or as far as I could observe, the Chinese Communists, when forced to do so, always acceded to Russian orders—surely it was obvious that the situation would alter radically once Mao Tse-tung governed all of China. Did Russia actually believe that Mao would let it retain its special position in Kwantung and remain in Dairen indefinitely until a peace treaty was signed with Japan? (One theory is that Stalin never expected or wanted Mao really to win his fight against the Nationalists, but figured that the civil war would conclude with Mao holding only the northern sections.) Russia, like the Western powers, makes errors in interational politics, and its handling of Kwantung during these years would seem to be one of them, the proof being that today the region is not under its control. Would this be the situation if Russia had treated Kwantung from the beginning purely as a military camp and had never allowed entry to the Chinese Communist personnel? It's anybody's guess.

A specific change included in the new governmental developments was that the Kommandant in Dairen now said the miscellaneous foreigners were entirely subject to the Kwantung administration, thus shifting them out of the jurisdiction of the Kommandatura. The Russian military, however, retained control over the White Russians.

Perhaps as a warning of things to come in Dairen and elsewhere, the press reported on May 5 that in Kirin, a major provincial capital in Manchuria, a special CCP "re-registration" committee had been formed in March, its function to reregister all Kirin members of the Party. Some names were given in a way which indicated that a purge of Party members was definitely underway. The press said the committee claimed to have apprehended several spies and traitors who were accused of "anti-Russian, anti-CCP, anti-people activities and of organizing reactionary theatrical plays."

On International "Red" Day, May 1, processions of various kinds organized by the CCP marched around the streets of Dairen. Groups of Chinese dressed as American soldiers carrying an atom bomb, as British soldiers pulling a tank, and as Japanese sailors were followed and prodded down the street by Chinese dressed as Russian soldiers with bayonets.

We estimated that 35,000 marched around the city for six hours. The day ended with a torchlight procession lasting until midnight. The police graciously allowed curfew to be a little late that night.

* * *

Painting slogans over the facades of buildings and blank walls seems to be an ingrained obsession of Communists. These are not the graffiti and advertising posters found in the rest of the world, but formal messages put up by organizations, government units, and similar groups. In the last few years slogans had covered the majority of the principal buildings in Dairen, but never, oddly, those occupied by the Russians. (Yet in Russia itself the same sort of slogan-painting was widespread.)

During the May Day celebrations some one or some organization applied Communist slogans on the garden walls of the British consulate. The wording was not anti-British, but the principle of the deed was offensive. I suggested to the Department it might wish to inform London about this, pointing out that if the action should go uncorrected, it might serve as a precedent for the Kwantung administration to take further liberties with the British consulate building. I said that the only way the signs could be removed would be for the British to protest directly to the Russian Foreign Office in Moscow. The caretaker was afraid to remove the slogans himself, and certainly I could not have hired anyone to do so. However, no word came from the British, so the signs stayed.

.Occasionally I transferred my worrying to the British consulate although technically I was not—to use the diplomatic term—"representing British interests." I had inherited from my predecessor, Benninghoff, the chore of paying the salaries of the caretaker and gardener from funds periodically supplied from

London. Presumably, the responsibility had originated when Benninghoff did this as a favor after the British were unable to open their own consulate in 1946.

One day in late spring, an official of the Kwantung administration pounded at the gate of the British consulate, threateningly demanding to be shown the building. The caretaker told him that the key was at the American consulate. (I had asked him to send over to me anyone who might call.) However, the official never did return, leaving us to wonder what *that* visitation had been about. I informed the Department I had no instructions either from them or the British to serve as a basis for forceful efforts to protect both the building and the 122 boxes of personal effects of British officers stored there (which dated from Pearl Harbor days, when the British staff had been interned). Although this too was reported to London, no instructions came.

Later, when two Russian army officers and one Chinese police officer of the Kwantung administration called at the British consulate, they said "they" had received a telegram from the British government asking them to "look after the building." The caretaker was not there, but the gardener admitted them. They examined the building thoroughly and made a detailed inventory. This was probably the first time Russian officers had been inside. Perhaps the British Foreign Office had approached the Russians about the removal of the slogans, which they used as an excuse to inspect the premises. Anyway, the signs stayed untouched.

When a bad storm damaged the roof of the British consulate, I was unwilling to get involved in its repair without an official directive. (The caretaker was afraid to ask the Russians for help unless definitely instructed to do so.) This finally did prod the British to telegraph me. They appreciated the American consulate's efforts, they said, but realized little could be done if the local authorities demanded or forced entry into the building. I was instructed to take no action except to report developments and to continue to pay salaries to the caretaker and the gardener. By picking out a phrase here and there from the hazily worded telegram, I was able to write a letter which the caretaker took to the Kommandatura, thereby obtaining authorization for workmen to repair the roof.

The storm that hurt the British consulate building was the tail end of a typhoon that caused great destruction on the island of Okinawa. In Kwantung it blew down several thousand trees, broke windows, caused minor damage to many buildings, and downed electric and telephone wires. Crops were flattened and fruit trees destroyed. Even this partial loss of current produce was serious for the local economy. Grim stories circulated around town. In several large factories, the machinery was crippled by backed-up drainage water; it took at least a month before work could be resumed fully. Sea water had flooded the wharves, damaging the goods stored in the godowns. Many fishing junks broke their moorings and some were lost. A group of fifty Russian "Studebakers" was seriously damaged. (During the war "Studebaker" became the common name in Russia for big trucks because of the large numbers of that now-vanished American brand which had been shipped under Lend-Lease.) Port Arthur reportedly was as badly hit by the storm as Dairen.

The next morning, as I walked around the city, sidestepping the fallen trees that filled nearly every street, I was amazed to see the Chinese full of animation and laughter. They even smiled at me as I passed. Until now the entire population had been glum and quiet; almost never had I seen people laughing or even congregating in little groups to gossip. Now the excitement of the storm had stirred them into a semblance of their normal Chinese exuberance. When I was in Shanghai and Peking, under the Nationalists the people had been vivacious; always there was the clangor of talk and shouting and street noises. But except for this one time, not in Dairen, ever. This unusual liveliness lasted all day; then the city went back to the perpetually sullen, grim, subdued mood which, in my observation, typified those Communist areas where I had lived or traveled.

I have a theory that I could be dropped by parachute in an anonymous place and in a few hours tell if the country were

Communist-governed by the lack of animation of the people in the streets and by the bored, dispirited look on the faces of the Communist-ruled population.

* * *

Our continuing series of incidents with the Chinese traffic police of the Kwantung administration were becoming more frequent and more blatant. These actions were discriminatory; we never saw the occupants of other cars questioned. Of course, there were, practically speaking, no private automobiles in Dairen; they all belonged in title to some unit of the government. Anyone who might own a private car was probably a very high official indeed, so no policeman would dare to challenge him. The consulate, however, was fair game. And there was no question about our identity. The American flag was always flown on the fender of the Oldsmobile unless the chauffeur was alone in the car.

In the past, these troubles would become serious and then die down for a while. In the spring a new wave of incidents was more awkward and intense than at any time before. The policeman would harangue the chauffeur, while leering at me, or at Culver if he were the passenger, as the inevitable crowd of Chinese gathered. This gave him his chance to repeat the derogatory epithets about "American running dogs" that had been pounded into him at his indoctrination meetings. Sometimes he let off the chauffeur after a stern warning. At other times, the chauffeur had to drive to the police station, where he would be questioned perdurably and ranted at while I sat outside.

The reasons given for stopping the car were so picayune that we realized the police had received specific instructions to step up their program of annoyances. In early April, I had written the Kommandant asking for an interview in order to discuss these actions of the police but, as usual, got no reply. In a telegram to the Department I said I was now reporting this new program of unwarranted discourtesy and discrimination merely for its background information, in case some serious incident might occur.

Our troubles with the traffic police did not stop all the time we were in Dairen. When we left the house, we would never know how much time we might lose in a useless confrontation with the police. We always feared that one of these affairs might suddenly flare up into something really bad.

Here are a few typical happenings.

One day, a policeman stopped the car at a corner between my house and the office, that is, on the street I traveled every day. I was the only passenger. The policeman subjected the chauffeur to a long scolding while a group of Chinese gathered to watch the sport. Eventually, it developed the traffic rule which the chauffeur was supposed to have violated had not been published as yet (and never was published).

Another time, at a downtown corner, the traffic policeman motioned the consular car—with Culver, the only passenger—to proceed straight ahead; when another car suddenly cut in, the chauffeur stopped to avoid hitting it. Two policemen on the curb thereupon came over and gave the usual prolonged discourse telling the driver he had stopped in the wrong place in order to make a turn. Culver was suspicious because traffic was so nearly nonexistent in Dairen that one would often see only one car traveling down the main street. It looked to him like a set-up. The chauffeur, usually meek and patient during these incidents, now refused to admit he had done anything wrong. The police summarily ordered him to drive to the local branch police station, and without asking Culver's permission they pushed into the car—a diplomatic affront in any other country. At the station Culver stayed in the car. When the chauffeur finally came out, he merely shrugged and said he had agreed with the policemen.

Then there were the times when a policeman would yell at the chauffeur, claiming he had parked in the wrong place. Later another policeman would shout because he had parked where the first one had told him to!

During these occasions the policemen in the Ford that always followed me would sit impassively and unconcerned, twenty feet away.

A more serious and complicated incident occurred early one evening. There was still an hour and a half of daylight left when Culver and a German girl drove in the consulate's jeep to a small point of land in the Rokotan area of Dairen, above a beach where Culver and I had gone swimming during the previous summer. (In fact, we had enjoyed several picnics at this little park.)

In a few minutes two Chinese policemen and two Russian soldiers ran up and asked to see Culver's documents. This was the first time anyone in Dairen had asked to see such papers. Although we had requested identification cards from the Kommandatura like those which everyone else carried, our letters were never answered. We had received night passes the previous November, but we kept them in the Oldsmobile so they would be at hand in case some emergency in the middle of the night required our going to the office. Nor had any sort of registration been issued for either the Oldsmobile or the jeep.

Culver's failure now to produce identification papers may or may not have caused the ensuing confusion. When he offered to drive away, one of the policemen refused to let him, climbing into the back of the jeep and thrusting an automatic rifle into the small of his back. The whole group now drove to a Chinese police post, but Culver refused to get out, insisting he would deal only with the Russian Kommandatura in Dairen. An odd sort of odyssey now took place as Culver and the German girl were taken first to a nearby Russian tank park, then to a garrison in quite a different part of Dairen and finally to the Dairen Kommandatura. At each stop the personnel of the "guard" changed. At one stage six Chinese and Russians, two armed with machine guns, were crowded in the rear of the jeep. At another time Culver was ordered to follow a Russian jeep full of soldiers.

At the Kommandatura he was turned over to a colonel whom he had previously met during an official visit. Thus, his identity as the American vice-consul was established. However, he was kept in a room for over an hour that was so cold he did push-ups to keep warm. When another officer, never identified, came in, Culver assumed he was a member of the KGB police. He accused Culver of signaling out to sea with the jeep's lights to contact spies, although at no time earlier had anyone made this statement. Culver pointed out that his jeep was parked facing inland, and also that his headlights were not even on because it was still daylight. Finally, the officer accepted Culver's statements, relaxed and tried to turn the conversation into a social affair. When he said Culver could go, he assured him most seriously the police had been protecting him "from being thrown into the sea by bandits."

This burlesque tag line made a fitting climax to the strange incident. During all this time, some five hours, Culver had been trying to get permission to telephone me, but was always forbidden, in itself a breach of diplomatic rights.

Naturally, I sent the usual note of protest to the Kommandant and even managed to have an interview with him. I also reported the affair to the Department and to our embassies in Nanking and Moscow. The Department agreed that this had been an arrant violation of the consulate's diplomatic immunity and asked the Moscow embassy to make a formal protest to the Russian Foreign Office. Before doing so, however, a dozen or more telegrams went back and forth to pinpoint the facts.

This is how the messages went. Yes, the jeep had been parked facing inland. No, the headlights were not on in the daylight. Yes, the Kommandant when I met with him claimed that Rokotan was a military area; when I inquired for how long he said a couple of weeks; when I said there had been no notice in the press he did not answer. No, there were no military barriers anywhere and no guards stationed there. Yes, Rokotan is an integral part of the built-up area of the city but somewhat farther along the coast from the main part. No, Port Arthur Naval Base area begins at the city limits and the only way to get to it from Rokotan is through the city; so if the Russians are implying that Rokotan is a part of the Naval Base area, which they seem to be doing, then it is an arbitrary, unilateral, unannounced extension of the area, further reducing the city limits of Dairen. Yes, during the previous summer Culver and I were swimming several times at Rokotan and also went there on picnics, but we had not gone during the winter. No, Culver did not have any identification with him because our repeated requests to the Kommandatura for such documents were never answered. Yes, Culver had been under armed guard throughout the incident until he was delivered eventually to the Dairen Kommandatura. Yes, he was detained at the Kommandatura for three hours. Yes, in my opinion he was treated as if he were under arrest.

The Russian Foreign Office's reply to the Moscow embassy's note I shall quote verbatim:

> On evening of April 12, 1949, at oncoming darkness in a forbidden zone of the Naval Base of Port Arthur there was detained by Soviet military authorities guarding this base a stranger who from shore was making light signals with the headlights of his automobile. The detainee did not present documents establishing his identity and did not present a pass for the automobile. In the Military Kommandatura where the violator of the regulations of the forbidden zone was brought it was established that this person was American Vice-Consul in Dairen, Culver Gleysteen. Upon establishment of his identity Mr. Gleysteen was released. The [Russian Foreign] Minister will be grateful to the American Embassy for assurances that such actions of Mr. Gleysteen will not be repeated.

There were still more communications . . . but why carry on such an absurd tale? Dealing with the Russian Foreign Office's messages in Stalin's time was like reading the Russian press; They both formed intriguingly vacuous arcana. What the Russians said in print did not necessarily relate to the facts; one quickly adjusted to this practice. The goal was to determine why the Russians made the statements at all—and why they made them then, and not last month or next month. If one dug deeply enough, he would usually find out the "why," even though the underlying facts of the case might remain forever buried.

As for Culver's arrest, the Department decided that the initial incident with the soldiers was probably unplanned and happened by chance. However, the peculiar note of the Russian Foreign Minister, in which he repeated the false accusation of signaling with the headlights, must have been intended to reemphasize the vulnerability of our consulate personnel in Dairen and perhaps to make the American government more impatient with the constant troubles of keeping the consulate open.

Although the Kommandant assured me that identification cards and driving licenses would be issued, Culver and I continued without them. But we did get new night passes for use after curfew. When the old ones expired, I had made the proper application for renewal, but nothing had happened. At least the incident prodded them loose for us, and the very next day, too.

Three weeks after Culver's misadventure the two of us went to the park at Rokotan for a picnic at noon, just to see what would happen. The police quickly took us to the nearest station. We did not go again. Apparently, this part of Dairen city had been summarily transferred into the Port Arthur Naval Base area; yet news of the action was never published in the press. Actually, when the Russians first established the boundaries of the Naval Base area, they had arbitrarily included sections which had been integral parts of the city of Dairen under the Japanese. For the local population—if not for us—there was no real difference in the administration between the Naval Base area and Dairen.

(The traffic ordeals would continue. By midsummer Culver and I were virtually prevented from going outside a small triangle bounded by our house, the office, and the chief corner in the downtown shopping area—each leg of the triangle a little over a mile in length. Although we continued to have incidents inside the triangle, they were always more serious and prolonged whenever we ventured outside that circumscribed area.)

* * *

Due to the pressure of these traffic annoyances and, more importantly, to the continued police harassment of the two Chaos living in the consulate building, I decided on a drastic change in our work quarters.

The Chaos continued to be so hectored by the police that they seldom left the consulate. Radio Operator Chao was now afraid to go outside even in the middle of the day; Head Clerk Chao would leave only for a rare visit to his family. In March the police had warned shopkeepers in the neighborhood near the consulate against dealing with them, which made it difficult for them to buy food. I told my cook to buy their supplies which the chauffeur then delivered to the office. (The police did not lean quite so hard on the shops which our household staff used; in their minds there must have been a distinction between employees of the American government and personal servants.) When alone in the office, as at night, both men were extremely vulnerable. Should they disappear, I would never be able to learn what actually had happened to them.

Furthermore, the consulate's confidential files and coding material were also unprotected—accessible to any half-determined agent.

We now planned to remove the two Chaos and all the confidential work of the consulate to the double house that Culver and I occupied. Once we worked the details out, the projected move seemed surprisingly sensible for solving our problems. Culver's dining room would make an excellent security room for the files and codes. After we added some locks, his attic could be turned over to the two men where each could have his own bedroom and share a small kitchen. It would be simple enough to move the radio equipment into Radio

Operator Chao's room; he could receive the incoming telegrams there as clearly as at the office. With such a well-populated house I need not worry about outsiders breaking into the security room. At night, too, Culver's mongrel, "Angry," could sleep in the security room. She was a sure-fire barker.

The tricky thing was the logistics in moving the files, the radio equipment, one safe, the two Chaos and their belongings to the house without any incident, such as being stopped by the police. The solution, of course, was to do it suddenly and without advance notice to our household staff or the chauffeur.

On our Day of Exodus, we first loaded the Oldsmobile with closed cartons containing our confidential files and codes—actually rather a small amount in bulk—and took them over to our new security room. Neither the chauffeur nor the servants were suspicious of what was in the cartons. Then I had the chauffeur take the two Chaos and Culver to the house, as if for lunch, a common enough procedure for we had been inviting them to meals several times a week, each time driving them in this same guarded fashion. Then Culver hired four coolies and two pushcarts at the nearby port area. The safe and radio equipment were loaded onto the carts, which were then pushed along the street to our house, with Culver and me riding in the Oldsmobile directly behind them all the way. At the house the coolies carried the safe into the security room and the radio equipment was installed in Chao's room. And that was that. It all took less than two hours. The chauffeur had remained in our sight all the time. The office messenger, the only other employee at the consulate, learned that something was taking place only when the coolies appeared; I had him accompany the carts to the house, ostensibly to help out. The household staff found out about the move only when the carts appeared at the front door. Thus, no presumed informer had had the opportunity to alert the police and thereby enable them to halt us en route. A true *fait accompli.*

Immediately, I wrote a formal note to the Kommandant: " . . .drawing your attention to a rearrangement of the American consulate that I am effecting today. I have decided it is more convenient and efficient for the consular officers not to have to come downtown in the afternoons. Accordingly, I am moving part of the office to my residence. Any communications you may have for the American consulate I would appreciate your sending to the old address in the mornings and to the residence in the afternoons. Thus, the consular office is now located in both buildings."

I wondered if the Kommandant was aware of the implicit irony in my directions about sending messages to the consulate: forsooth, since my arrival I had received only one written communication from him.

The move proved to be a great benefit to all of us. Culver and I no longer had to work nights at the office (which included our sleeping there too, rather than driving back to the house and chancing a confrontation with the police). I continued to do the accounts at the office, usually in the mornings, and Culver did part of his press work there. Thus, we maintained the appearance of carrying on work in the consular building.

The two Chaos were almost in tears with relief; they knew they were much safer now, living in the official residence of the American consul, where I could stand physically between them and the police.

Residents in our double house now were: In the basement on my side—the consulate's messenger, my Number One Boy, his wife, and his infant son; in the basement on Culver's side—his cook; in the attic on Culver's side—the two Chaos.

Out of fear for both them and him, Head Clerk Chao stopped visiting his family, and they seldom, if ever, came to the consular residence. One of the household staff would take Chao's salary to them.

Surprisingly, each in his own fashion, all of the varied inhabitants in the house managed to get along together, at least I did not notice tensions between them. Perhaps it was because everyone realized that there was nothing permanent about our life in Dairen. We all seemed to develop a common philosophy: Be comfortable for the moment, for who knows what changes the morrow may bring.

Obviously, the Chaos "safety" with us would be only of degree. Two weeks after they moved into the house, four Chinese policemen came to the front door at ten o'clock at night. They said they had come to "investigate the population, i.e., interrogate the Chinese staff. I told them that I would not allow such irregular nocturnal visits. (As is well-known throughout dictatorship countries, it is standard procedure for the police to make their calls at night; fear of the midnight knock is a most effective psychological control method.) The police said they would not enter the house by force, but soon reinforcements totaling fourteen men had surrounded the building.

Eventually, a rather high-ranking Chinese officer arrived. After a lengthy debate I agreed that the police could come in the daytime to interrogate the Chinese staff, but they were to enter only their private bedrooms, not the rest of the house. The police withdrew at two o'clock.

As a result the police would now be permitted to come into the consulate residence anytime during the day, even when Culver and I were not there. I firmly told the officer that the residence was also now officially a part of the consulate office. I pointed out that over the door into the security room I had placed a large round metal shield displaying the coat of arms of the United States, the same insignia as is found over the entrance of our official missions around the world. As such, most of our rooms had to be respected as definitely "off limits" to Communist police penetration and inspection.

CHAPTER X

FIRST YANK
AT THE NOOSE
(LATE SPRING 1949)

The Chinese Communists' big thrusts against the Nationalist forces came fast and heavy in the spring. They occupied Nanking on April 24, Hankow (the "Chicago" of China) on May 17, and Shanghai itself on May 25. By late spring their drive into south China was well under way.

Understandably, the American consul and vice-consul in Dairen were becoming increasingly uneasy about their own situation. Kwantung was geographically a part of China. The Russian hold on the area was probably temporary, but our own safety would become precarious should the Soviet Union suddenly turn the rule of Dairen totally over to the Chinese Communists, whose hatred for us as Americans was abundantly shown.

We began a long and arduous campaign to get out, somehow.

One of my typically ignored notes to the Russian consul general informed him that I had been transferred from Dairen and would leave as soon as my successor arrived. (The personnel branch of the State Department had decided that a formal message might help to obtain the visa from the Foreign Office in Moscow.) I did not mention in my useless note the key fact that my replacement was stuck in Nanking and could not leave until allowed to by the Chinese Communists.

In my note I also applied for a transit visa for myself via Vladivostok, together with a laissez-passer. (Culver had asked for a transit visa sometime earlier.) I added that an American clerk had been assigned to the consulate and that he was now in Shanghai awaiting his Russian transit visa. I furthermore pointed out that the consulate had made application for a transit visa for Radio Operator Chao on February 25 but had received no reply.

None of us ever received a visa. To quote from one of my telegrams: "The one consistent factor in Russian policy is to reply by inaction and silence."

A telegram I sent to the Department in mid-May fills in the background of our problems:

> After three months my replacement still has not received his transit visa and there is no indication he ever will. Yet even if he should, he is now bottled up in Nanking. Ditto re Gleysteen's replacement stuck in Peking and also the new clerk in Shanghai. The most important problem is a replacement for Radio Operator Chao; as I have emphasized before, an American is the only solution. Also, I repeat again that his assignment as originally promised him ended last December and he should have been replaced then.
>
> On the basis of current attempts to send in replacements, it is apparent Gleysteen and I shall be here until fall or even winter. Unless Department has reason to believe Russian visas for all personnel are equally affected and will be issued soon, and this I personally doubt, I suggest entire problem of Dairen replacements be tackled from some new point of view. My own drastic proposal is:
>
> 1. Cancel the assignments of the three men now assigned here.
> 2. Assign new principal officer, clerk and American radio operator from the staff of Moscow Embassy.
> 3. If they do not receive transit visas through Vladivostok within one month, cancel their assignments.
> 4. Assign new unit from staff of Seoul Embassy.
> 5. Instruct it to charter Korean flag vessel to come to Dairen.

6. If Russia obstructs the ship, the isolation of Consulate same as now. Except for disruption to new personnel and expense of abortive plans to get them here, it would seem no harm done.
7. This does not solve problem of getting a Chinese language officer here; whoever is assigned must come from outside Communist China, not isolated in our posts there.
8. Safety of Radio Operator Chao is my principal concern. He can be assigned to whatever post he may reach after departure. Due to developments of past month I now doubt he will be able to leave Dairen unless a special ship is sent here, such as a Korean flag vessel with the unit from Seoul.

The Department did consider sending a vessel from South Korea or Hong Kong, but political and military events in China were breaking fast, and all the Far East was in a state of suspension waiting for the Communist conquest of the rest of mainland China. After the experience of Ward at Mukden and the enforced isolation of the American staffs in Nanking, Shanghai, and other posts in north China, the Department was now closing each consulate in south China before the arrival of the Chinese Communists and withdrawing the staffs to safety. Obviously, to them the Dairen personnel problems were a minor matter. Perhaps we actually received more attention than was due us during such a time of crises.

A major difficulty for Head Clerk Chao was that he did not have a passport. Although our Nanking embassy had obtained Chinese Nationalist passports for him and his family, we would not receive them until couriers should succeed in getting through to us, and this, of course, remained as uncertain as ever. No matter how our other personnel problems might be resolved, it was obviously going to take considerable diplomatic force to get him out of Dairen. In June he learned that his nineteen-year-old son had been arrested and held in prison for three weeks. Pressured to give information about his father's work at the consulate and told that unless he confessed all he knew about his father's "spying activities" he would suffer serious consequences, the young man broke down mentally. Chao heard the news with great alarm: His worst fears were being realized as his family began to suffer because of his connection with the Americans.

Both Chaos remained in the consulate residence, never leaving unless some special demand of the Chinese police made it advisable to go to the local station, usually in the consulate car while Culver waited outside in the car.

As compensation for their problems, the Department proposed promotions and salary increases for the Chaos. I replied that all the staff already were receiving wages above the highest local rates and that any promotion would merely accentuate their exposed position.

One night the consulate's chauffeur was taken from his house by five Chinese plainclothes men and driven into the countryside. They interrogated him regarding his role in "spying" for us and asked whether any other Chinese on the consulate staff were involved; also whether he had seen any secret movements of the consulate's officers. The police released him at midnight but warned that they were not "through with him." Because I had assumed that the chauffeur was a police informer, I did not know what to make of this incident when he told me about it. Perhaps a rival clique in the police force had taken him. Certainly he was undergoing strong tensions and pressures in our behalf, not only in this incident but during our constant troubles with the traffic police. A very quiet and stoic man, I never saw him lose his temper, nor did he ever complain to me about his problems.

Oddly, the month of May provided a lull in our local harassments. The Chinese police did not return to the house until the middle of summer. And there were no confrontations with the traffic police, for a while at least. We could not discern the reason for this relative peace. Perhaps it resulted as an aftermath of the several communications both in Dairen and Moscow about Culver's arrest at Rokotan.

* * *

In May the first non-Russian, non-North Korean vessel, other than the small Chinese coastal junks, to come to Dairen since the Norwegian *Nortuna* nearly a year ago was a 10,000-ton freighter said to be flying the Egyptian flag. It was an unusually large ship compared to the Russian vessels using the port.

I made determined efforts to meet the captain because I wanted to send out some boxes of excess office equipment which the consulate did not need; I could address them to the American consulate in whatever city the freighter next called at. However, the Kommandatura denied permission for me even to enter the port area.

In June another 10,000-ton freighter, reported to be Danish, arrived. I tried to visit this captain as well, but found that a new Chinese police barrier (put up by the Kwantung administration) had been set up on the street leading to the port, which made it impossible even to get to the office of the harbormaster who issued the permits to enter the port area. (In the 1945 Sino-Soviet Treaty the only special right granted to Russia in Dairen was the provision that the harbormaster would be a Russian national. By sealing him off behind a police barrier, even this minor article of the Treaty was arbitrarily annulled.) I needed a pass from the Kwantung administration to go through the police barrier, but efforts to get it met with the usual procrastination, both from Chinese officials and from the Kommandant.

Attempting to buck the Communist system, as in asking for passes we would never get, became a sort of game for us. We could not win—but trying to kept us on our toes.

To complete the dead-end circle regarding the two ships: their captains were not ever allowed ashore, and the Kommandatura said there was no local shipping agent acting for them.

When I asked the Department whether there was any legal basis for my insisting on visiting a foreign ship in harbor, it unequivocally answered "No."

Later on in May, a French ship arrived. We learned about it only when one of the sailors was taken to the local hospital. Our attic view of the harbor yielded only a partial faraway perspective. We could sometimes see vessels entering or leaving port, and only some of the wide pier area was visible to us. Denied entry to the harbor area itself, we had to rely on our eyes and on secondhand information to find out what was going on there.

Although we reported to the Department whatever information appeared in the press about exports through Dairen, the news items were scarce; anyway, trade was still unimportant. If goods from Manchuria were really coming into the port by now, the quantity did not amount to much.

But this situation would gradually change during the summer as more and more produce from Manchuria, mostly soybeans, was brought into Dairen after the railroad system was restored.

During the summer the harbor came back to life, reviving some of its once-bustling activity. An average of three Russian freighters came every two weeks, some in ballast for repairs at the shipyard. A passenger ship, usually one called the *Gogol*, would make a monthly trip from Vladivostok. Even our old friend, the *Smolny*, appeared two or three times. And there were many coastal junks on minor commercial errands.

Yet for a port that formerly, with Shanghai and Hong Kong, was one of the three major shipping points in East Asia and that had docking facilities in Japanese days large enough to accommodate forty to fifty medium-size ships at a time, this amount of shipping was, obviously, minor. But of course the Russians had looted so much of the dock equipment that now it would take great sums and effort to restore the port to its old cargo-handling capacity. Still, the change must have cheered the Chinese residents dependent on commerce for their livelihoods.

In June we also heard of a three-masted sailing ship in the Diaren dockyard, supposedly owned by the Vladivostok office of the Kwantung Fishing Company, a Russian trust. It left for Port Arthur and then came back to Dairen, went to Port Arthur and again returned. It was reported that the captain had said that his ship had had a complete overhaul and was now outfitted for polar waters: it received the fuel oil which two warships had expected to get, delaying the warships for some time. This mystery sailing ship, called the *Zvesda*, caused many fascinating rumors in Dairen—but where it sailed to we, and the public, never learned.

At this same time the first Japanese repatriation ship since last summer arrived. I could not find out how many people it took on board or how many were still held in Dairen by the Russians. I suggested to the Department and the Allied Command in Japan (SCAP) that if information was wanted about the economy of Kwantung and about the local police controls, the repatriated Japanese should be systematically interviewed upon their arrival. Having worked in almost all the Russian and Chinese economic units throughout Kwantung, they could, as a group, give a thorough overall report on the place. Hereafter, such data would only be fragmentary, regardless of the sources used.

The few hapless foreigners left in Dairen kept on trying, month after month, to get their exit visas so that they might leave on some future ship. The repatriation of the German group for a while had remained as uncertain as ever. But in June the American consulate was appointed the "agent" for the Germans' repatriation. Heretofore, my telegrams regarding them had been sent informally, partly out of sympathy, and partly because once I started to do this it was hard to stop: After all, the group had no other way to get messages to the authorities in West Germany about their plight. These messages at last opened up a channel of communication whereby the consulate could officially approach the Kommandant on their behalf.

The administration of the American-British-French zones of West Germany had agreed formally to arrange the repatriation of all refugee Germans from any part of the world. For those in China, the French embassy in Nanking was to function as the liaison office. Now the consulate was named the representative of the French embassy for Dairen. In that capacity I was able to obtain from SCAP the clearances necessary for the Germans to enter Japan en route to Germany. This development, however, did not move the Russians to let the Germans leave on the foreign freighters that were now appearing in Dairen nor on the Japanese repatriation ship. I never could understand why. One would have thought the Russians would be happy to get this group out of the way; their departure would cost them nothing.

In early July, though, one did go away, the first of the German group to leave postwar Dairen; in fact, the first foreigner to do so since last summer, except for the Poles and Czechs who had returned home through Russia. I will give the story in detail, for her experiences in receiving her exit visa and then boarding the ship illustrated the tribulations and fears affecting all the foreigners.

Mrs. Aza Schmidt was actually a White Russian married to an Austrian businessman, her husband had been among the Germans whom the Russians deported to Siberia shortly after their occupation of Kwantung. (This was because he had a German passport, due to the absorption of Austria into Germany in 1938.) Fortunately, she had a brother-in-law in the British diplomatic service and thus had someone on the outside actively working in her behalf. In addition, she had kept her old passport, which classified her as an Austrian national.

In the previous October Mrs. Schmidt had received clearance to leave when the Kommandatura accepted her application for an exit visa. However, the officer said there was no need to give her the visa at that time because no ship was available. In the middle of May, when the Chinese Communists openly took over the Kwantung administration, she was told she must now apply to the Chinese police for her exit visa; the Kommandatura henceforth disclaimed all responsibility for issuing such papers. She made the new application to the police but never received a reply.

On July 2 the consulate received a request from the British mission in Tokyo to urge the local authorities to give Mrs. Schmidt permission to leave on a British freighter due shortly in Dairen. With this authorization I was able to write a strong communication to the Kommandant that reviewed her past efforts to get a visa, pointing out that it had once been granted. I also questioned the right of the Kommandant to refuse to handle her application now. In the following five days she went many times to both the Kommandatura and the Chinese police, but the Russians continued to say they had no jurisdiction, and the police refused to give a reply.

Then, suddenly, her visa was granted—with only six hours left to go on board. In the excitement she accidentally learned that, beyond a doubt, the visa had come through on the direct order of the Kommandant to the Chinese police. This episode showed again, if proof were needed, who really was boss in Dairen.

There was an extra bit of annoying red tape for the foreigners. Although the Chinese police now issued the exit visas, it still was necessary to obtain a permit to board the ship, and this was issued by the Russian port authorities. Fortunately for Mrs. Schmidt, she also received this document now—which of course gave further evidence of the arbitrariness of the Russians in their relations to the "independent" Kwantung administration. On matters that were not of importance to them, such as exit visas to the foreigners, the responsibility was given to the Chinese; on important matters, such as the security of the port area, they kept the reins firmly in their own hands.

Mrs. Schmidt, an ebullient, sociable woman, had picked up somewhere a cheap paperback book entitled *How to Tell Fortunes with Cards.* To pass the time after the internment of her husband, she memorized the rules and as a sort of parlor game started to tell her friends' fortunes. She gradually began to realize that many of the future events she had jokingly predicted were really taking place. After a while, she refused to tell any more fortunes; in Dairen, she said, there was never good news in the cards, only bad news, and she did not want to know about it. When I asked her once to tell my fortune she declined, explaining that she was afraid her cards would forecast that the American consulate would be closed before the Germans and the other foreigners could leave Dairen—and if that happened there was no hope for anyone. In her case this would have been true enough. Without an American consulate which the British mission in Tokyo could ask to intercede in her behalf, she certainly would not have been able to leave, at least that soon.

A large number of friends accompanied Mrs. Schmidt to the dock. There the Chinese customs inspectors spent four hours slowly and carefully examining her small amount of personal and household effects. The men were rude and their chief was drunk. Some money was stolen and several items willfully seized. She vainly tried to have the confiscated articles given to a friend. The Chinese ordered her friends to leave, but some insisted on remaining. Grouped on the other side of the customs barrier, they were convinced that only their presence in the lonely shed saved most of her possessions from being stolen and perhaps prevented even more serious troubles.

A Russian official, known to have been a customs inspector at the departure time of other foreigners the year before, entered the shed from time to time. Although he emphasized that the customs work was now strictly a Chinese affair, at his direct order Mrs. Schmidt's friends were allowed to remain. He also ordered that all Mrs. Schmidt's documents, including her passport, which the Chinese had confiscated, be returned to her. Each time, the Chinese inspectors obeyed his orders in bad grace, and became even ruder after he left.

But she did get away.

Two weeks after Mrs. Schmidt's departure, the small number of Europeans who periodically called at our house was reduced by one. Martin Roth—about sixty years old, a native of Ruthenia at the eastern tip of Czechoslovakia—suddenly was arrested.

In the 1930s Roth had been a minor businessman in Dairen; then, as is the way with wars, he became rather wealthy by Dairen standards. According to local gossip, he had done nothing illegal; he simply had the knack of buying and selling in a war-shortage market. He put his profits into antiques, jade and other valued objects: his house was overflowing with them. The previous summer, when foreigners were being evacuated, he had received the necessary SCAP clearance and the coveted

Russian exit visa. Just as important, he possessed an American immigration visa and was planning to join his wife in the United States. He packed all of his cherished antiques and objects of art in cases. Ready to go aboard with the others, at the last minute he panicked and would not go; he was afraid the Russians would not let him take his things. (Ironically, the Russians probably would have made no trouble; they did not with any of the others.)

Now, by remaining, Roth made himself especially vulnerable to difficulties with the authorities. At the end of the war, when the boundaries of Eastern Europe were redrawn, Russia took away from Czechoslovakia the eastern half of Ruthenia, including the town of his origin. Thus Roth technically became a national of Russia, or at least would be presumed so in lieu of other documentation.

Although we all tell ourselves that we would never place our physical possessions before our personal safety or happiness, how would we really act when put to the test? As Roth did, or not? Apparently he had made a tragic decision. For now the police suddenly had taken him and there was no word as to what was happening to him. At first, it had been merely rumored he had been arrested. Friends who called at his house were turned away by the police without explanation. Now someone heard he was back in the house and the police were gone. I asked Culver to go there, as if on a social call, to determine what the situation was. The Chinese police, however, were still on hand. They led him into the living room and then took away his identification paper.

(I must interpolate here: Our night passes for the curfew were still the only official identification issued to Culver and me. We had decided not to carry our passports with us, for that document was too precious to lose. All the time, however, each of us now carried an official-looking paper that I had prepared on the consulate stationery. It stated our titles in both Chinese and Russian and was loaded with red ribbons and wax seals. This was an old trick of the Foreign Service throughout the world. The paper of course had no legal standing. It was—to use the sometimes gross jargon of our profession—a "dago dazzler," intended to "dazzle" low-ranking officials, who may be unable to read, with the obvious importance of anyone with such a flashy document.)

Only with great difficulty did Culver retrieve this paper. He was then taken under guard to the district police station, where he was treated insultingly. The police refused to recognize his official position, referring to him simply as an "overseas American." They also would not let him telephone me. Fortunately, within fifteen minutes some superior telephoned instructions to release him.

Once more I wrote the Kommandant to protest this surly treatment of an American diplomat by the Chinese police—whom I again referred to as "police agents of the Russian authorities." No response; but I did not expect any.

I never heard what really had happened to Martin Roth—nor what the specific reason was for his arrest, if any. Reportedly, his effects remained in his house unmolested, but no one ventured there again to verify this.

The Roth case became a famous incident locally, and it created further tension for the consulate. The others who came to our house had been warned periodically by the police that any business or social relations with us could cause troubles. But they continued to come now and then, as they believed we were their only hope in arranging SCAP clearances and Russian exit visas. Yet some of the small businessmen now asked Culver and me not to call at their shops because more than ever they were afraid of the police.

CHAPTER XI

OUR
SECOND SUMMER
(SUMMER 1949)

In Mukden on June 18, 1949, the American Consul General Angus Ward and his staff, after six months of isolation during house arrest, were formally charged by the Communists with espionage. Five days later Ward met with a Communist official and telegraphed the State Department, the first message he had been able to send out. He said he was arranging for the staff's departure. Maybe so at that moment; but nothing happened, and the consulate's silence resumed.

Now an intense barrage of Communist propaganda began about the spying in Mukden which, so the Communists said, the consulate general had conducted. Since no one was able to visit Ward, it was impossible to determine what was actually going on. As for the spying, the entire staff had been under house arrest since November 20, a few weeks after the Communist capture of Mukden. Before that the city had been in Nationalist hands. Thus, it was hard to understand when the alleged spying could have occurred. Nevertheless, the propaganda about that "nest of spies" was constant in the Communist press throughout China, including Dairen, where the Mukden story was stressed week after week at the political studies classes which the workers of all ranks had to attend.

In Dairen everyone was warned more blatantly than ever to avoid contact with the American consulate.

Featured prominently in the Russian bookstore at this time too was a book by Annabelle Bucar entitled *The Truth About*

American Diplomats. An American who had been a clerk in the embassy in Moscow, she fell in love with a Russian opera tenor, defected and then wrote this book. Its claim that senior officers of the American embassy in Moscow at that period were spies made it a major Russian propaganda tool for several years. In Moscow a play based on the book became a hit of the theater season.

Three days before the Communists made their public charges in Mukden, the Kwantung administration bestowed upon the Dairen populace a deceptive and rigorous new regulation, apparently already widely used in Manchuria. This timing suggested (at least in retrospect), a connection with the Mukden/Ward affair, as part of what seemed to be a carefully organized propaganda campaign to warn the people throughout the Communist world of the dangers of having contact with foreigners or with foreign-connected institutions.

The Kwantung administration announced that all "anti-people" and "anti-democratic" individuals, elements, and organizations must register with the police within one month; at the same time they had to surrender their documents, member lists, correspondence, codes, weapons, funds, etc. Persons who formerly were members of such organizations but were not now must also register. "Ample rewards" were promised to informers who reported those failing to register.

Since the guilty organizations were not named, it was thus slyly left to each individual to determine whether he was then, or had been, a member of an "anti-people" organization. It was indeed a tricky regulation. Obviously, anyone who did come forward and confess to being a "reactionary"—another epithet for supposedly "anti-people" people—would be branded as such for life. So almost no one did.

The press initiated an intensive propaganda campaign that was both threatening and cajoling. It urged the reactionaries to report voluntarily, promising lenient treatment. At the same time the administration claimed to have received from other cities material incriminating the "hidden reactionaries" of Dairen, but it was using this voluntary method of registration, instead of direct arrest, in order to adhere to the exemplary policy of the Chinese Communist Party that encouraged people to save themselves through confession. The press also claimed that the present regime in Dairen had liquidated the underground spies of the Kuomintang Party of the Chinese Nationalists. It warned that individual reactionaries now had no opportunity to flee or to continue their "wrecking efforts" and the spreading of rumors. The tone of the articles became so strident it was evident the registration campaign was producing few confessions.

Whatever may have been the other purposes of the new regulation, it was successful in increasing the population's fear of arbitrary arrest at any time. Also, the fact that these registration methods now were used publicly illustrated the degree to which the local Chinese Communists had been freed from the restraints of Russia's "correct" policy.

The consulate's chauffeur was a Catholic. He said that members of his church were under pressure to register on the grounds the Catholic Church was a "worldwide, anti-people and espionage apparatus."

All the staff and servants were told to register, but they refused, realizing it would be against their safety.

A month after the regulation was published, Radio Operator Chao was compelled to be present at a police "meeting." I wrote a memorandum about this, and quote most of it here to demonstrate how the Communists handle these affairs.

> This morning a policeman came to the front door and requested Radio Operator Chao to go to the local police station. At first, Chao protested he had work to do. However, the authorities sent for him several times. At ten o'clock he decided he could not avoid going and I agreed. When he reached the station, he was told to go to a meeting in a house opposite. Eleven persons were there, including four girls. As soon as he arrived the meeting opened. A police official explained the purpose of the present Registration of Reactionaries. After an hour of this the official asked several of the persons there to give

their opinions about the regulation. They rose and said they were members of this or that Nationalist Kuomintang organization and how they had registered to take advantage of the "generous" policy of the government. One said he had undergone a similar experience in Mukden where he had registered as a reactionary but the government had released him and permitted him to resume work. Later, he came to Kwantung. When registration started here, he was told to re-register as this was a special area and although he now approved of the Communist Party in the rest of the liberated areas that might not mean he approved of everything in this special area; therefore, he would be kept on probation for a short time until he made his loyalty clear to the local authorities.

After three-quarters of an hour of these "confessions" the official indirectly addressed himself to Chao, and said, "I know there is one Kuomintang agent here among you who was sent to this area especially. I want him to give his opinions." Although Chao knew this meant him, he said nothing. The official went on to say that not only must Kuomintang and the Three Peoples Principles Youth Corps members register, but also "American spies" and "running dogs of imperialism." He said the policy of the Government here is a lenient one, that after the people had registered the Government would have plenty of work for them to do. "The Government needs people who can write and know figures." Chao said the language of the official then became abusive and there was no doubt at all it was directed at him.

The meeting stopped promptly at one o'clock. The official warned everyone that only a short time remained before the end of the registration period. Therefore, all reactionaries in the categories described should register immediately if they did not wish to be arrested. Chao said his impression was that the other persons at the meeting were there solely for his benefit, that most already had registered or were tools of the police.

Chao told me it would be senseless for him to register

inasmuch as this would be the opening for which the police were looking. He added he did not know if one or two of our staff would be able to withstand the pressure and if anyone of our staff did register he thought the matter would end badly.

In another development Radio Operator Chao was ordered to attend the district meetings of Chinese residents at which Communist laws and propaganda were expounded. The hour happened to be the same as when Chao received the Department's telegrams and news bulletins. Although I could have requested our broadcasting unit to change the hour for Dairen's telegrams, this actually was a good protection for him; accordingly he did not have to go to the meetings. At the few which he did attend the police proclaimed their vengeance on all those who did not voluntarily register as reactionaries.

At this time too the wife of Head Clerk Chao was questioned for four hours by the police. She was told to report on her husband's "spying" on behalf of the American consulate and was ordered to bring her husband to the police headquarters for all Kwantung on the following Sunday. When he went, he was questioned for an hour and a half about his work at the consulate. The interrogator was rude; he pounded the table and used vile epithets. However, by now this accusation about his being a spy and a reactionary was an old familiar line to Chao. Nothing new developed except he was ordered to arrange for a friend to act as guarantor that he was not spying, which he did. Although the police had called regularly at his house the past few years, on one recent midnight visit they had broken down the front door and searched the house for three hours.

On the Fourth of July 1949 I received from the embassy in Nanking the longest telegram sent to the consulate up to that time. It would take nearly a day to decode. The message was a wrap-up about all our personnel and replacement problems. I had only begun to decode it when I had to stop for my official National Day reception.

This year no Chinese officials came, but the Kommandant and the Russian consul general and his staff were at hand. Also present were the same few Europeans who maintained social relations with us and a half-dozen Germans. A total of nineteen—in contrast to last year's forty-five. The same Russian faces and the same Europeans—as if time had stood still in Dairen, waiting for events to happen elsewhere that would bring back to life the individuals, the personalities, in this inlet isolated from the mainstream of world affairs.

Whatever the tensions underneath, the social function went off pleasantly enough. This year, however, we had no exotic American beer or whiskey to serve: only the Siberian "spirit" from the Russian *spetstorg*. Our fruit punch, well-laced with it, was an adequate success. But this time there were no fireworks afterwards. I had learned not to do anything to provoke the police always outside my door.

All during the party I was itching to get back to the Nanking telegram. It was obviously an important message. The opening sentence read, "We have racked our brains for solutions to the problems of communications, supplies, and personnel which beset our consulate in Dairen, but must confess we still find no answers."

The long telegram, when at last decoded, summarized the current problems as well as the value of the Dairen post:

> It is doubtful the Japanese repatriation ship scheduled for later this summer can be used to bring couriers and new personnel to Dairen because Russians may refuse clearance. Little hope of reestablishing courier service soon. Last year it was difficult and expensive to carry out this service from Shanghai via Vladivostok. Now Russian vessels have ceased to operate between Vladivostok and Chinese ports.

> Although telegraphic communication with Dairen is still open, there are, of course, no assurances this will continue indefinitely.

Dairen is running low on commissary and official supplies (also dollar exchange and fresh codes). Our only suggestion is to try and have U.S. establishments in Far East learn of the sailing of some foreign vessel to Dairen sufficiently in advance to arrange to ship new supplies. However, our establishments in Communist-occupied areas of China have few supplies to spare even if direct shipping from Shanghai or Tientsin were available. Whether such supplies would be allowed duty-free entry into Dairen is a moot question.

Only four ways by which personnel replacements could travel to Dairen:

1. From Shanghai by Chinese vessel across Yellow Sea or by rail through Manchuria. The Chinese Communists already have refused cooperation on such a project because of absence of diplomatic relations. We add that it is unlikely they will have diplomatic relations with U.S. before next year.

2. From Hong Kong (or Shanghai if port re-opens) to Vladivostok for transshipment to Dairen. In this the Russians refuse to cooperate by failure to act on applications for transit visas.

3. From Japan by an unarmed LCI or other small U.S. Navy vessel, unarmed plane or chartered vessel. Russians already have shown reluctance to assist in this when last December they preferred for couriers to travel via Vladivostok rather than permit such transportation to enter Dairen directly. Presumably, Chinese Communists, now that they have theoretically taken over responsibility of Dairen administration area, would also object to such entry on grounds they have no diplomatic relations with U.S.

4. Reassignment of an entire new staff from U.S. or Europe who would travel across Russia to Vladivostok and thence to Dairen on a Russian

ship. This seems the most promising since replacements now assigned to Dairen are all immobilized in Communist-occupied areas of China (and Clerk Colling presumably has acquired a bad name with the Chinese Communist Party as a result of his persecution on trumped-up charges of brutality toward a disgruntled former Chinese employee of Shanghai Consulate General). Anyway, the probability is that Russians also would refuse transit visas for trans-Siberian travel of new personnel.

We clearly perceive advantages of retaining our last toehold in Manchuria. Not least in this respect is that Dairen is an open port in which we are fully entitled to maintain a consular office. Also, Dairen is our only vantage point from which to observe day-to-day joint Russian-Chinese Communist Party administration. However, we reluctantly conclude that under present circumstances those advantages are outweighed by the struggle, expense, humiliation and danger involved in keeping post open. The indefinite continuance for the consulate in its present state is unfair to Paddock and Gleysteen who already have exceeded their anticipated tours of duty. American consular officers in Dairen are now hardly more than hostages awaiting Russian retaliation in some new crisis.

Due solely to Russian and Chinese Communist police pressure, Dairen Consulate for some time has been more productive in administration-personnel headaches than in political and economic reporting. Thus, we disagree with thesis expressed by Moscow Embassy that since Russians apparently want U.S. to close post we should try to keep it open. Rather, main issue is whether, under existing circumstances beyond our control, we ourselves stand to gain more than lose by maintaining it.

We fully endorse Dairen Consulate's statements to Department that "the Russians are still directly responsible for the city of Dairen and for the

Consulate's difficulties" and that "Russian control of Dairen is likely until Japanese treaty concluded."

Thus, unless Department and Moscow Embassy are finally convinced of futility of continuing our efforts regarding Dairen, we believe we should make one final approach to Russian Foreign Office, informing it that:

1. The Chinese Communist Party authorities have no facilities or inter-port regulations for travel to Dairen, thus forestalling possibility of Russians shifting the onus onto the CCP.
2. We therefore request the Russians promptly to issue transit visas for the men now assigned to Dairen for use on first available ship from China to Vladivostok or to authorize their entrance into Dairen on an unarmed U.S. Government carrier out of Japan when they are able to leave China, with simultaneous exit permits and visas for Paddock and Gleysteen.

If this approach meets with no success by August 15, we believe the Department should then proceed without delay to close the office, at same time giving maximum publicity to the Russian restrictions which forced us to take this step. The principal theme of such publicity should be that, paralleling the troubles of Mukden Consulate, the U.S. Government's experience in Dairen constitutes impressive evidence of Russian domination of Manchuria and of compliance by the Chinese Communist Party.

My reply, sent to the Department, was just as long. (I somewhat condense it here.)

Dairen Consulate seems to have failed to emphasize to Embassy a basic change in our problems. Until early spring Consulate's difficulties were primarily re couriers, supplies and replacements. Now chief question is whether Consulate is physically able to operate even when courier service is resumed and replacements arrive.

The protection of Head Clerk Chao and Radio Operator Chao is the most important problem. Consulate is anxious this not be neglected in midst of administrative problems of servicing or closing the post. As of now, Consulate is unable to assure them slightest help if seized. The two Chaos live in our residence and rarely leave. Yet the police are able to enter openly any time to arrest them and this event is expected to happen some time. Meanwhile, police are terrorizing family of Head Clerk Chao; his son's mind was affected after one course of police treatment. Department's attention is drawn again to Chao's service of twenty-seven years and his outstanding record, including continuing loyalty under Japanese police pressure and torture.

The urgency for the replacement of Radio Operator Chao is far more important than replacements for the Americans. He was promised departure from Dairen by last January 1. Since up to this spring conditions remained similar to those of last two years, Department could have kept its promise if it had then made proper arrangements to get his replacement here.

All plans should include utmost effort to arrange departure of the two Chaos when present Americans leave, regardless method of transportation used.

Other possible difficulties regarding Consulate's operation during next few months:

1. Exchange of dollars: The dealers already are so frightened to buy Consulate's dollars that getting local currency is a constant problem.
2. Access to press: For past two weeks Consulate has been unable to buy Gazette of Kwantung Administration. Delivery boy of one newspaper said two days ago he was forbidden to deliver it to Consulate (although he is still doing it). Such tactics are also open to other papers.
3. Purchase of food and other supplies: Fear of private merchants and enmity, or fear, of clerks in government-owned stores may soon make

such purchases irregular and perhaps impossible.

4. Insults: All ranks and classes have been trained to be rude to consular personnel or else they act that way for their self-protection. Our messenger has ceased to wear his consular uniform. Department should note that anti-American propaganda is definitely a success here.

5. Servants: So far they have not been unduly troubled by police, but there always is the latent threat they will become frightened and leave.

6. Social isolation: The half-dozen foreigners who still are willing to come to Consulate residence are trying desperately to leave Dairen. If they succeed, isolation of Consulate will be complete.

7. Exit visas: Russians now blandly claim Chinese police have sole jurisdiction over exit visas for foreigners. Consulate fears trouble regarding this at such time when couriers next arrive.

8. Some manufactured incident: If either Russians or Chinese should set up an artificial incident, as has happened apparently with our Consulate in Mukden, U.S. would then be on defensive when Consulate is closed.

9. Official contacts: There is no official, either Russian or Chinese, to whom Consulate has access. In a time of trouble Consulate would be unable to negotiate with, or channel its opinion to, any person of responsibility.

The importance of maintaining Consulate at this strategic point is obvious and Consulate sincerely hopes Department will be able to solve present difficulties. It is realized other posts in Communist China probably have parallel troubles or soon will, although various telegrams repeated here from Embassy seem to indicate exposed position of Dairen Consulate is unique.

However, Consulate is discouraged regarding present and future worth of this post. Its value can not be restored until Department is able to force Russians to allow workable conditions here, including physical protection to Chinese staff. Otherwise, it appears better to close Consulate on our own initiative with dignity, and then perhaps Chinese staff can be withdrawn.

Nevertheless, closing the post will still cause many problems: exit visas, Russian visas via Vladivostok, transportation on Russian vessels including freight charges at exorbitant cost and efforts to take out Chinese staff. Only efficient and cheap way to close Consulate is to send a special ship here to remove all staff and files.

But the Department did not want to close the Dairen post as yet. They assured us that even the lessened amount of reporting we were doing was worthwhile and should be continued. All told, it was an authentic commendation for Culver and me.

As samples of the sort of local information we were sending in our telegrams during these summer months:

— Russian aircraft are more active than usual over Dairen all week, but not yesterday or today. Dull explosions are heard day and night. Rattling of windows last for about a second each time. Small caliber artillery fire is heard, sounding about the same as the anti-aircraft fire practice I heard while in Vladivostok.

— A White Russian, recently returned from Mukden, said the United States flag is flying over the American consulate there and also over a large house opposite where all U.S. citizens are held. Police guards are stationed in front of both quarters. However, this is also true of the Russian consulate general, evidence, apparently, the Russians have kept their post there. The general condition of Mukden has "settled down," but some looting and robbery still going on in the outskirts. There is little evidence of Russian political activity. The railroad trip from Mukden to Dairen was made without changing trains at the Kwantung border, a new development.

— Last week Russian army soldiers dug emplacements at the top of the hill directly in front of consulate residence, a point that gives a fine view of entire city and port. It seemed to be an artillery observation post and was equipped with periscopes and radio telephones. At times up to thirty men were at the site. Field telephone wires were stretched along the hillside. Then it was abandoned after a week; thus, it was a training activity. Russian military training of various kinds is carried on inside Dairen city steadily.

— Chinese Communist soldiers in their regular gray "liberation" uniforms supervised the blasting of the post office annex building, now being dismantled. Russian authorities obviously worry less and less about their policy of "correctness" when they allow Chinese troops openly to wear their Communist uniforms here.

— Telegraph service between Dairen and Mukden is now open to private individuals. Yesterday Gleysteen tried to send plain language telegram to American consul general there. Telegraph office said it must be in Chinese language. Gleysteen translated it. When clerk realized Gleysteen was from American consulate he said a permit from Kommandatura necessary. There, the aide to the Kommandant said telegraph service is concern of the Chinese, not Russians. Thus, no telegram sent. This is a typical impasse often met by Consulate in day-to-day relations between the two sets of authorities.

— Chinese Communist newsreel in local cinema shows the completion ceremonies of repairing a long truss bridge over the Sungari (a major river in northern Manchuria). No foreigners, such as Russians, in film.

— Chien Hsien Corporation (machinery, chemicals, steel casting) is operated by CCP Northeast Bureau (Manchuria). It is rumored to manufacture armaments and explosives for Chinese Communist Army.

— Russian trust Dalenergo (units include glass, soda,

electric bulbs, ceramics, oil paint, cement and metals) failed to achieve its first quarter plan, despite press accounts that it had. According to rumor, the failure was ascribed to inadequacies of Soldatkin, the new manager.

— Story in Dairen is that former director of Dalenergo, Rokatien, who left here last year, had all his Dairen purchases confiscated on arrival in Vladivostok and is now in a minor post somewhere in Siberia.

— Dalenergo bookkeeper, wife of a lieutenant colonel who is Political Commissar of the Military Hospital here, has been accused of embezzlement. Twenty Russian citizens (not White Russians) are involved in the case which is up for trial. This is the second incident known to Consulate where Russians in local trusts have been accused of large-scale speculation. Such trials are held locally and the defendants, if guilty, are sent to Russia. More common than theft of office funds is the illegal sale by Russians of ration goods bought at reduced prices in their spetstorg commissaries. This practice is widespread, despite constant attempts to stop it by warnings and punishment of both Russians who sell and Chinese who buy. These Russians are not tried in court here but returned to Russia for administrative punishment.

— Electricity in Dairen went off last night at 6:40. Still off. Rumor says cause is at the North Korean power plant. Possibly, fighting going on there. Situation could become serious as without electricity no water.

— Austrian representative in Mukden sent a letter to a Dairen German saying two Germans are imprisoned with Ward and his staff. This supports former rumors reported by Consulate that Mukden consulate staff has been under formal house detention. Letter says economic conditions in Mukden very bad, three-quarters of year after Communist capture. All private enterprise stopped. Prices high. Austrians formerly were able to go to Vienna via Moscow, but not now. Most Poles are leaving Harbin end of this month for Poland via Moscow; this supports rumor several more Dairen Poles now leaving for Harbin. Only four or five Germans left in Mukden.

— Local German has received in a letter list of camps in Russia where the Germans collected from all Manchuria have been interned. Because uranium deposits are said to exist in Ferghana [Central Asia]. it is perhaps of interest that all Dairen Germans with chemical training are at Camp 7387 in Ferghana.

— One-year trade agreement signed by Russia and the "Manchurian People's Democratic Authorities" July 31. It provides for exchange of Russian industrial equipment, trucks and automobiles, oil products, textiles and other manufactures for Manchurian oil, soybeans, rice.

— Both Dairen and Mukden papers emphasize this new trade agreement was made to counteract effect of Chinese Nationalist blockade of Dairen "which was ordered by the U.S. imperialists." This theme long has been applied in Dairen as local papers insist this port was closed due to blockade by U.S. and Chinese Nationalists, but that the factories were able to operate because of Russian economic help and raw materials.

— Recent Voice of America broadcast (on its Far Eastern Service) regarding the new Russian-Manchuria Trade Pact is considered by consulate as effective in hitting at Russians and Chinese Communists where they themselves feel weakest. Only occasionally has there been a reference in local press during past year to disappearance of Manchurian industrial equipment, and then it is claimed part of it was destroyed by Japanese before surrender, part by Chinese Nationalists during civil war and balance by "wreckers." It is hoped this Voice of America feature, concerning Russian removal of the machinery, was broadcast in Chinese language and that this subject can be used often and expanded in detail.

— A vessel of the era of 1900 has been painted white with red band on stacks and was given a trial run in Dairen Bay, after which it was again put in drydock for repairs. Outfitting of this ancient ship (estimated 4000 tons) may illustrate the degree of stringency of Russian shipping.

— Workers are compelled to deposit in savings accounts 10 to 20 percent of their salaries. This is one of several indirect methods to relieve the workers of their wages.

— Article entitled *History of the Chinese Communist Party in Port Arthur-Dairen* in local press says Dairen Municipal Committee of CCP was formed 1924. The many incorrect statements throughout article are further evidence that propaganda aims are habitually placed above factual accuracy. For instance, it is claimed CCP protected local industrial property "from damage and loss" after defeat of Japan. Actually, that was the period when Russian army was dismantling such equipment for shipment to Russia and when other property was abandoned to wild looting by Chinese populace. The CCP, if it were here at all, was not in evidence, certainly not in trying to restrain Russians from taking away machinery. Why they now claim to have "protected" it "from damage and loss," when all the population knows the truth, is typical of the mystery behind so much Communist propaganda.

— Northeast (Manchuria) Political War College was moved some time ago to Hankow and its name changed to Central Political War College. Because it followed Lin Piao to central China this may indicate that most of the Northeast Armies were also shifted there. Of all the Communist forces, the Northeast Armies and training schools are probably most familiar with mechanized warfare and are the most pro-Russian in tactics.

— During a walk on the hill in the park facing consulate residence Gleysteen had a talk with a goatherd. He said he is forced to work as a stevedore on the docks because he is young and fit, working there six days a week and earning 800 yuan a week, plus meals, mostly corn, at job. He receives also a ration of 16-18 catties (about 24-27 pounds) of corn or kaoliang to take home each month. On his one day a week off he tends the family's sheep and goats. He has a wife, father, several brothers and sisters. Normally, the goats and sheep owned by family would be enough to keep him busy or to launch him in some personal agricultural or pastoral enterprise. However, he is obliged to work on the docks as a "proletarian." His chief objection to the Russians is that they sometimes refuse to pay the salaries to workers when latter are accused of "loafing." He said living conditions are more difficult than in Japanese times and the new system is more oppressive in other ways. However, he made it clear he has no respect, either, for the "little noses" (Japanese). He dislikes the Chinese Communists because "they force money out of anybody and everybody who happen to make a little or to save a little, and they beat people who do not obey them."

The goatherd's greatest complaint against the "system" was the compulsion to attend the never-ending police meetings of instructional classes in Communist doctrine for each block of houses and to comply with the incessant police demands for "cooperation" in this and that community project organized by the police. It is impossible for anyone outside the Communist sphere to realize the extraordinary amount of time involved merely in coping with police regulations and police-organized meetings. Foreign observers have said this is a calculated method to keep the populace so distracted they have no time for normal lives and, possibly, normal anti-regime thoughts.

* * *

One intriguing propaganda thrust was made in the local press as trade began to revive with Manchuria. It praised Russia for exchanging machinery and gasoline for Manchurian soybeans, in contrast to the "plastic belts and raincoats" which the Nationalist government had received from the United States for *its* soybeans.

In the summertime about one foreign ship a week, usually of the 6000-ton size, arrived at Dairen; by early fall there were perhaps three a week. The exports were mostly soybeans shipped by rail from Manchuria. Although ships left for a variety of Asian and other ports, Japan was the principal customer. Imports for the most part were cotton destined for Manchuria. At one time four tankers arrived. They berthed at a rather distant section of the harbor, indicating that the oil probably was to be transported by rail to Manchuria. The ships were of various flags and lines. The crews were not allowed ashore, not even the captains. Much effort was made to prepare the port for this new business, including cleaning the area and fixing up several buildings in the commercial section as offices for the Russsian organizations handling the trade.

I drew the Department's attention to the fact the majority of these ships called at ports in Japan, Korea, Hong Kong, and the Philippines, either before or after coming to Dairen, and that American missions in those countries might obtain pertinent data on this increased trade. I emphasized it was impossible for our consulate to learn details like names of ships, type of cargoes, itineraries.

I also pointed out that the Russians obviously were not asking the Nationalist government for permission for these ships to enter Dairen, despite the August 15, 1947, Nationalist decree closing the port and despite Russia's continuing to maintain diplomatic relations with it. This decree, mentioned earlier, had been a major excuse for Russia's policy of "correctness" in not allowing foreign ships to come to Dairen until this summer. Now, of course, as the Nationalists were ceasing to exist as a viable government on the mainland, the issue became academic.

Always separate within this subject of shipping was the trade with Communist North Korea, which apparently had continued steadily through the years of Russian occupation. Although the bulk of it was carried in Dairen-owned ships (mostly junks), some North Korean flag vessels did come. Trade with South Korea, if it ever existed at all, had stopped long before.

The summer ambled along, everyone at the consulate still waiting for events happening elsewhere to end or at least to alter our deadlock with the authorities. One such development would be how the final Communist conquest of the mainland would affect Big Power relationships. Another was what the Department would do about its several posts now isolated in Communist China—or, more specifically, what the Communists themselves were going to do about them. Did they want them open or closed? The Department could adjust its stance according to the type of relations the Communists wanted with the United States. Another development would be the timing of Russia's severing diplomatic relations with the Nationalists and recognizing formally a new Communist Government for all China (which, however, Mao Tse-tung had not yet organized).

We were concerned that we might have our last telephone cut off. The office and residence together had five telephones. For nearly a half-year three had been dead despite our many requests to the Telephone Bureau and the Kommandatura to "repair" them please. Instead, the Bureau had ordered us to pay a fine for not reporting they were "broken"—showing someone had a sense of humor. I refused to pay the fine, but I did keep paying the monthly bill for all five phones. The most prolonged and contrived squabble came over the Bureau's claim that we had moved a phone from one room to another, for which it had levied another fine. Since the change had been made by a telephone repair man and we had paid the service charge, I refused to pay the fine. Ergo, that phone had been cut two months ago. This left us with one phone at the residence and none at all at the office. (Culver and I joked that the police probably had only one wire tap available.) The worry was ever-present as to when "they" would kill off our last phone.

The rate charged for our telegrams was now radically increased. Although the costs were paid by the Moscow embassy, this was accepted as a further pressure on the consulate. I discontinued the weekly press telegrams on routine economic and political matters. Those items that were significant I sent as individual telegrams or in a monthly summary limited to three hundred words.

And the five thousand dollars we had received with the last couriers (on April 1) were dwindling away. Another financial crisis was imminent for us.

* * *

While we waited for the wheel to turn, in one direction or another, the cold war headlines were continuing.

When Communist espionage agents were caught in the Western countries, the Communist countries would, in retaliation, say that they, too, had seized so-and-so as a Western agent. Three major trials dragged on in the United States related to Communist espionage: the Alger Hiss case, the Judith Coplon case, and the trial of the leaders of the American Communist party. There were also several congressional inquiries, plus the flushing out of dozens of guilty or innocent people on charges of spying. (Canada and other nations had similar trials.) Congress made the Central Intelligence Agency (CIA) a permanent, rather than a temporary, government bureau. President Truman at a press conference said the current spy trials and loyalty checks had produced the same sort of nationwide hysteria which led to the Alien and Sedition Acts of 1798, but " . . .the United States didn't go to hell then and it would not now."

Russia accused Finland of staging an "aerial wolf hunt" that was a trick to let American and British agents get a look at the Russian border. The eleven-month-old Berlin Blockade had ended in May without Russia's gaining the slightest advantage. (It was a thorough defeat, no matter how the Russian propagandists phrased it.) The United States-controlled Berlin Radio charged that 80,000 persons had died in Russian concentration camps in East Germany during the last four years (out of a total of 180,000 who had been imprisoned in them). Russia announced that 95,000 Japanese prisoners remained in

Russia. Japan responded that Russia still held 390,000; another 60,000 were in Chinese Communist hands. The Vatican issued a world-wide excommunication of Communists and "fellow travelers," including members of Communist-led unions. This was said to be the most drastic decree issued by the Vatican in over three hundred years. In South Korea the last of the American army troops departed, leaving only a military mission to advise South Korea's army. (Note: almost to the year, North Korea thereupon invaded the South.) The United Nations stated that 700,000 persons were homeless due to the Greek Communist guerrillas. Elsewhere, Communist guerrillas were fighting in many countries.

In Shanghai, the Communists raised property taxes one hundred times above rates fixed by Nationalists for 1949 (another example of the Communist procedure of confiscation by taxation). Also in Shanghai a United States vice-consul was arrested by Chinese Communist police when his jeep came in the way of a parade; released three days later, the American consul general charged he had been "utterly, brutally beaten."

The State Department announced it had closed the Mukden consulate, but would keep open most of its other missions in Communist China for the time being. The Communists, however, still did not allow Angus Ward and the Mukden staff to leave; their isolation continued. Although they remained charged with espionage, they were not brought to trial nor was other action taken: they were simply left hanging in limbo.

On August 5 the State Department issued a most important document: the 1054-page White Paper reviewing the history of American support of the Chinese Nationalist cause. Although some details have been altered by later research—and also twisted by the personal opinions of historians and writers—the White Paper is still the jumping-off point for any factual discussion of this complex struggle which racked China for so many years.

Essentially, the White Paper recognized Nationalist China as a lost cause now and explained why the United States would not give it further aid. At this time, the Communists were in the final drives to capture Chungking in the west and Canton in the south, thus absorbing all of mainland China.) The key points of the White Paper were that the Kuomintang Party under Chiang Kai-shek had sunk into such ineptitude and corruption that it had lost the support of the Chinese people, that its army no longer had the will to fight and that it was incapable of making effective use of United States material aid. It said that Chiang's "reactionary" clique refused to carry out reforms which could put the Nationalist government on its feet. Also, the Nationalists had wasted two billion dollars in United States aid since V-J Day and there was nothing more the United States could do to stop the Communists in China except to go to war against them. As this was out of the question, the United States would henceforth concentrate on preventing a communized China from overrunning the rest of the Far East.

The cold war thus continued its juggernaut course across Eurasia and, through guerrilla actions, into many parts of the undeveloped world. Important weapons in this war were the propaganda outputs from both sides, aimed to persuade and magnetize public opinion in all countries. Although the pervasiveness of these efforts may have originated in the great emphasis the Soviet Union had always given to propaganda, the United States by this time was responding with its own equally intense propaganda apparatus. By the very massiveness of combined expenditures and effort, propaganda had obviously become a major battle arena. In this sort of combat it was difficult to tally winning points or to demonstrate that this or that new story or press release had won over a new group of former neutralists. Rather, like erosion by rain or wind, results came only through a long succession of efforts.

Thus, when the Department proposed to utilize the Dairen consulate's experience for maximum propaganda advantage, we recognized it as a valid objective. It would be one more story in the American output calling attention to Russia's arbitrary and antagonistic actions. It would also alert other nations to the probable difficulties of dealing with an emergent Communist China.

CHAPTER XII

CLOSING
THE CONSULATE
(SEPTEMBER 1949)

A telegram telling us that the State Department had decided to close the consulate came on the 2nd of September. We were told to keep this information secret until "the necessary arrangements can be made."

Simultaneously, the courier service recalled to its new Asian headquarters in Bangkok the two couriers who had been waiting—it seemed for months—at Hong Kong to get to us. (When a Russian ship became available, they were to travel to Vladivostok and thence to Dairen. The same two men had not waited there, of course: but the courier service always kept two men ready for traveling to us whenever the flash would come.) Now, with no prospect of couriers again, we really felt cut off and fundless.

The reason for the Department's decision at this particular time to close the consulate was its realization, after the accumulation of many incidents throughout Communist China, that the problems facing all its posts there were now unsolvable and that no easing of the difficulties could be expected in the foreseeable future. Within the next half-year the United States was to close all of these posts, one by one, and remove the staffs. Dairen was among the first of these retreats. Each had its peculiar problems. If the stories were combined, they would make an intriguing account of the complexities of dealing with the Communists. For example, on September 30 the Department closed its consulate at Hankow, the industrial city in the center of the country. The Communists prevented the staff from leaving, however, until many months later. A most dramatic tale is that of the consulate at Tihwa, located in Sinkiang, the extreme western province of China, where my long-time friend, John Hall Paxton, was in charge. It was closed on October 3. The Communists had not yet arrived there, but it was no longer possible for the Department to send in a plane. To escape, the staff had to go by truck along the edge of the Takla-Makan Desert, and then by horseback and on foot over the 18,000-foot passes of the Karakorum Mountains into northern India, 2500 miles in two and a half months. It was one of the most difficult odysseys in the history of the Foreign Service.

Although our own relations were theoretically with the Russians, we could not be sure that the closing of our consulate would be any easier than elsewhere in China. We did have the advantage that Dairen was a port, which eliminated the extra difficulties of overland travel. The Department's request for our advice on the factors involved in the "necessary arrangements" showed it was indeed aware of the barriers to overcome. Its telegram read in part:

> Department is particularly anxious all possible measures be taken to assure departure of loyal Chinese employees and families simultaneously with the Americans. Could Chinese staff be evacuated before announcement is made of closing? Inform Department re difficulties of obtaining exit visas for Chinese and American staff, transportation facilities available, proposed routes of travel, recommendations on possibilities of selling, evacuation or storage of Government-owned property. What do you recommend re effects of British officers stored in their building? Couriers will not be sent to Dairen. Closing instructions will follow soonest after receipt of your recommendations.

This telegram would have caught me by surprise except that a week before, a Moscow embassy telegram to the Department was repeated to Dairen. It was the only indication that discussion of closing the consulate had revived. The Moscow telegram had said:

> If Department decides to close Dairen, Embassy strongly assumes our actions will be planned carefully with view to:
>
> 1. minimum impairment of U.S. dignity and prestige.
> 2. maximum propaganda publicity and diplomatic exploitation of reasons for withdrawal to disadvantage of Russians and Chinese Communists.

Embassy believes achievement of these ends could be accompanied by notification to Russian Foreign Office at appropriate time re U.S. decision to close consulate on account of unreasonable and onerous restrictions and vexations imposed by Russian-dominated regime (including pertinent details) and failure of Russian government to give assurances requested in our note to Foreign Office June 9 that our consulate staff would be treated in accordance with international law and practice. Our note should be given full publicity due course.

Embassy also recommends that serious consideration be given to use U.S. Navy vessel for withdrawal of Consulate staff and effects, and that our intention to dispatch such vessel for this purpose be included in proposed note to Russian Foreign Office. Evacuation by this means would not only have advantages from standpoint of U.S. dignity and prestige but would also simplify otherwise difficult transportation problems. It might also enable U.S. to save faithful alien employees from unhappy fate at hands of Chinese Communists.

It might be well to inform Russians that the use of a naval vessel is necessary to obviate known difficulties and delays now prevailing with respect to ordinary means of travel into and out of Dairen area. Whether

Russians would place obstacles in way of implementation of such a plan is problematical. Although the last request for permission to send a courier to Dairen on U.S. naval vessel [apparently early 1947] was turned down by Russian Foreign Office on ground of alternative facilities via Vladivostok, Russians this time would have difficulty suggesting feasible alternatives, and, furthermore, might view final "withdrawal" voyage in different light from previous requests for periodic courier service. If Russians should flatly refuse to permit vessel to enter Port Dairen, arrangement for off-shore embarkation similar to that which took place on withdrawl of our mission from Albania in 1946 might be feasible.

The Department's decision to close the consulate set off a new spate of telegrams which should be interesting to students of the intricacies involved in a diplomat's profession. The best method of reporting them is to summarize their texts in sequence, almost in diary form. (I also give the dates of the chief telegrams to keep the chronology clear.)

September 3.

I telegraphed the Department:

    1. Transport alternatives:
        a. Russian ship to Vladivostok, then Russian plane to Tokyo or Trans-Siberian R.R. to Moscow or Russian ship to somewhere. Plane difficult due to our possibly large party and personal effects. Cost exhorbitant. No government-owned property worth sending via Vladivostok.
        b. Foreign freighter calling here under Russian charter. Impossible for consulate to see captain to arrange passage. No time for Department's representatives to try to contact such ship before departure to Dairen and not

certain, even if passage were arranged, Russians would allow us to use it. Russians might do so, however, if this is made a part of initial discussions with them re consulate closing.

   c. Diversion of special ship by Department. This is cheapest, due size of party and considerable amount of office and house furniture and equipment good enough for use by American post at first port of call. Whether Russians able to prevent use of such ship legally or would do so anyway is beyond consulate's knowledge.

2. Department should inform if confidential files should be destroyed or taken; also non-confidential.

3. Due lack of funds, consulate must sell jeep with trailer, Oldsmobile, transmitter, radios and coal supply in order to close properly. Please authorize. No other inventory items to be sold due to bad market.

4. If we go via Vladivostok, Moscow embassy must arrange to pay all our expenses there and onward transportation as we will arrive without funds.

5. Moscow should arrange laissez-passer for Americans to take personal effects out of Dairen and in and out of Vladivostok without customs examination; also for Russians to recognize us as couriers. Consulate will issue usual courier letter.

6. Regardless of transport used, consulate will try to take out effects of British officers now stored in British consulate and assume British government will pay costs, but Department should verify we should do this.

7. Chinese staff consists of two Chaos, chauffeur and messenger, who with families total fourteen Chinese. Not known, however, if chauffeur and messenger will wish to go.

8. All Chinese are without passports except Radio Clerk Chao who has expired Chinese Nationalist passport. He and Head Clerk Chao and family all have new Nationalist passports in courier mail waiting to come to Dairen, but these, of course,

can not now be received. All must therefore use some sort of certificate which Russians will recognize in lieu of passport.

9. Without couriers to accompany them, sufficient funds or passports, it is useless now to try and get two Chaos out ahead of Americans.

10. Russian delays re transit visas through Vladivostok for both Chinese and Americans, plus other difficulties that route, well known.

11. Re exit visas from Dairen, if decision is left to Chinese police, answer will be refusal re our Chinese staff (and possibly also for Americans). Local Russian authorities will not override that refusal unless specifically instructed to do so by Moscow.

12. Thus, consulate believes best manner of closing consulate is to broach it first to Russians at either Washington or Moscow. Consulate will thereupon inform local Russians re closing and apply for exit visas. However, consulate should know type of transport to be used and how exit visas are to be used.

13. Specifically, we want from Russians:
   a. Permission to leave Dairen on whatever transport Department decides.
   b. Exit visas for all of staff who wish to leave.
   c. Recognition of certificates for Chinese in lieu of passports.
   d. Recognition of Americans as couriers.
   e. Laissez-passers for Americans to avoid customs examination.
   f. Transit visas through Vladivostok if we go that route.

14. Consulate is unable to suggest effective approach to Russians to ensure we get all of above. Problem of exit visas given in consulate telegram of August 12; background of Russian military occupation of Dairen given in telegram to Moscow January 1 and repeated to Department.

15. Closure of this consulate can receive considerable publicity on basis of isolation of consulate, uncooperation of Russians and exposed position of consulate staff. Although propaganda along these lines possibly effective in U.S. and

non-Communist Asia, it is uncertain if Russian government will consider this aspect important.

16. However, Russia's position with Chinese public throughout China possibly could be hurt by propaganda emphasizing its anomolous military position in Dairen, for instance:

    a. Continued military occupation due to artificial excuse of waiting for Japanese treaty.

    b. Diplomatic relations with Chinese Nationalists but no Nationalist officials allowed here.

    c. Legalities of origin and present status of Kwantung administration never explained.

    d. Russians try to make local population believe Kwantung administration is ruling Dairen and disclaim all responsibility for such things as an exit visa. Yet, Kommandatura is unchanged and no decreases in Russian personnel. When Russians give order, officials of administration obey.

17. If exit visas are refused to Chinese staff, it would seem Department has legitimate basis for publicizing points in preceding paragraph. However, it would appear to Russian advantage to "persuade" Chinese police to issue visas and arrange for all of staff to leave Dairen quietly. Thus, when the proper official of Department (or Moscow embassy) discusses with Russians the closing of consulate and arrangement of visas, American use or non-use of publicity might be a bargaining point.

18. Moscow embassy suggestion should be given careful consideration, namely, if Russians hesitate to arrange for Chinese police to issue exit visas for our passportless Chinese staff, it is possible they could be persuaded to do so if pointed out that closure of consulate and removal of all staff thus can be quietly managed by sending in chartered freighter. If no visas for them, Moscow suggestion of naval vessel pertinent. If naval vessel of adequate size used, it could have useful propaganda effect not only here but throughout Manchuria.

19. Consulate hopes Department can arrange in ten days the two separate but related problems of

type of transport for us and exit visas for Chinese staff.

20. Basis for consulate's desire for haste is probability Russia will recognize new central government of Chinese Communist party in Peking as soon as organized. Perhaps Department aware this is not imminent; locally, it is constantly forecast. Since Chinese Communists regard Dairen as extension of Manchuria, we expect to be confined to our quarters [house arrest] after Russian recognition of Peking government, the same as apparently is being done to our Mukden staff. Although some element in Russian-Communist relations may postpone such drastic action we cannot count on it. As our provisions exhausted and we are bankrupt, we foresee long, difficult period before Department could arrange our departure. Since decision now made to close consulate we are anxious to leave before such recognition.

(I have given these quotations from the telegrams as the Department's code room wrote them up for circulation among the pertinent officers. The way I actually sent them from Dairen, using the last few sentences of the foregoing telegram as an example, was about like this: "Tho some element Rus Com relats may postpone such drastic action no count on it prd Provisions exhausted we bankrupt we foresee long diffic prd before Dept cld arrange depart. Since decision now made close Con we anxious go before such recog prd." This odd language was due, obviously, to the extremely high cost of our messages, for I cut words to the knucklebone.)

As background to the last point of my telegram, I shall recapitulate what I have said earlier. Russia claimed that the 1945 Sino-Soviet Treaty permitted them to keep troops in Dairen as long as a state of war existed between it and Japan i.e., until a peace treaty was signed. This interpretation Nationalist China had denied. By keeping its troops in Dairen without the sovereign power's permission, Russia, under international law, was in *de facto* control of the city; this meant it was responsible for the physical safety of the inhabitants, including the consulate staff.

This situation would not necessarily change when Russia shifted its diplomatic recognition from the Nationalists to the Communists. A change would occur, however, if the recognition was accompanied by new treaty agreements, such as the Chinese Communists' formally agreeing to the continued presence of Russian troops in Dairen in return for Russia's agreeing to the complete jurisdiction of the Chinese over the civil administration of the city (and over foreign consulates) without any vetoes from Russian officials. I took for granted that a new treaty along such lines would accompany Russian recognition, or follow soon afterward.

In this new situation, the United States would have to accept the Chinese jurisdiction even though it did not itself extend diplomatic recognition to the new Chinese government. No longer would the consulate have the American embassy in Moscow interceding in its behalf with the Russian Foreign Office.

No matter how chancy the conditions had been for us under the Russians, they were certain to be infinitely worse under the new Chinese Communist government. The Communist police had consistently displayed a rabid enmity toward us, and the refusal of the local Communist authorities to have any contact at all with the consulate was so absolute that we would be left utterly without protection.

Before the Department could reply to my long telegram of September 3, I alerted it to a new development in Dairen which might reduce the time margin available for evacuating the staff. A three-day conference had been announced for the reorganization of the government of Dairen city, beginning September 23. The heads of the area departments of the Communist party in China were invited to participate in formulating the changes and, interestingly, the propaganda. This let loose a surge of rumors which predicted that, prior to that date, the Russians would open diplomatic relations with the Peking government. Other rumors said the Chinese Communists were planning to detach the Dairen municipal government from the rest of the Kwantung administration, thus affecting the international status of the city rather than its purely municipal political structure.

Whatever the outcome of the conference itself, so far as I could judge the result would be harsh for the consulate.

On top of this particular worry, a new series of incidents with the Chinese police had erupted, either due to the announcement of this projected change of government or merely as another recurring wave of malice. Police surveillance of the consulate office and residence and of the officers, whether walking or driving, was stepped up to an intensity we had never before experienced.

September 8

I telegraphed. By now I realized that nothing much was going to happen within the time span of the ten days I had originally urged for our leaving Dairen:

> When restraints placed on local Chinese Communists are removed by Russian diplomatic recognition of Peking, consulate will be as exposed as Mukden consulate. Lack of supplies and funds, plus precedent of long record of unpleasant incidents in which helplessness of consulate proved, are expected to make consulate's position worse than that of Mukden post. Nothing in experience of Mukden to indicate Department can arrange departure of staff quickly under such conditions.

> Although in July it was decided not to close consulate, the mechanical problems involved have been before Department for many months. In past, Moscow embassy often was hampered by difficulty in getting appointment with a responsible official in Russian Foreign Office. Accordingly, consulate recommends Department itself take up the problem

of departure of Dairen staff at most effective level in Washington within twenty-four hours after receipt of this telegram.

Until notified to contrary by Department, consulate will plan on departure of staff by one route or another within ten days. Since Department has now decided to close consulate and because of announcement of prospective reorganization of Dairen city administration, Department should not postpone for any reason departure of staff.

And that, indeed, was a strong telegram to send to the Department—as any Foreign Service Officer will testify. Yet it was justifiable, as the threatened imminence of crisis with the Chinese Communists was real enough, and the recent increase of harrassments by the police equally real.

September 9

The Department instructed Ambassador Kirk in Moscow to call personally on the Russian Minister of Foreign Affairs, Vishinsky, and explain that the Dairen consulate was being closed due to obstacles to its normal functions and proper operation; these obstacles included the near-impossibility of effecting transfers of personnel, maintaining courier service and sending supplies and funds. Vishinsky was requested to instruct the Dairen officials to facilitate the closing of the post and departure of the staff. The Foreign Office was asked if it preferred the consulate staff to depart on a foreign vessel under Russian charter, an unarmed American naval vessel or a Russian vessel. Specific mention was made of a Panamanian freighter then in Dairen harbor as a possible means of withdrawing the staff. When Kirk made his call, Vishinsky said the urgency was apparent because of the ambassador's offer to come personally at any time to receive the answer of the Foreign Office; this answer "would be given as rapidly as possible."

The disappointing factor here was that no attempt was made to have the ambassador "bargain" or "negotiate" for the departure of our Chinese staff with us, regardless of whether this would have been a futile effort. Requesting nothing more than an urgent reply was indeed a weak-kneed approach, considering the range of playable cards in the Department's hand, as already indicated.

It took twelve days even to get the "urgent" reply.

And during that time much happened.

Also on September 9 came a telegram from the Department giving a fine example of bureaucracy in action. It read in its entirety:

"If unable to evacuate government property, can you recommend the consulate of a friendly power which would accept custody?"

This, after nearly a year and a half of telegrams from us emphasizing that the American consulate was the sole foreign post in the Dairen world except for the Russian consulate! Obviously, it was from some remote officer in the hierarchy who was now called on to look at Dairen for the first time. I constantly had the fear that our closing would be left in the hands of such staff officers, with resultant confusions and delays. Hence, my "strong" telegrams that would force attention from the top men in the Department. And that attention we did receive. Without waiting for the Department's authorization, Culver already had begun efforts to sell the jeep, which was our most saleable item. We were dismayed to find that the limited circle of persons or organizations that could afford it were afraid even to discuss its purchase with the consulate, although the public did not know yet of our closing. I began to realize that clearing out would not be easy.

September 10

The Department telegraphed instructions for guidance in terminating our work. It was four (!) pages long. The highlights were:

> You are authorized to evacuate or sell motor vehicles, typewriters and other office machines, office and household furniture. In your discretion, evacuate or destroy seals, fee stamps, blank passports, blank certificates of identity registration, cryptography material, stationery bearing official insignia, letter heads, files and archives. Furnish Department with certificates on items destroyed. Evacuate all accounts.
>
> Maintain radio contact until departure. If impossible to evacuate radio, destruction is authorized. Do not permit radio equipment to fall into Communist hands intact.
>
> In view of shortage of funds your post, could Department transfer needed amounts for local needs by telegram through local bank or Moscow bank? If necessary and feasible, inform Department of amount. Also inform Department amount of funds needed at Vladivostok or other port after departure from Dairen, so Department can arrange transfer of funds to that point if necessary.
>
> If unable follow completely the procedure outlined this telegram, you are authorized proceed with most feasible means to close office at your discretion. Keep Department informed and indicate when last message sent.
>
> If possible, ascertain next destination of Panamanian vessel now in port.
>
> If SCAP clearance forthcoming immediately, could German refugees depart on this or other vessel?

September 12

I sent the next telegram:

Consulate has not yet discussed with Chinese staff their evacuation because consulate not yet announced closing of post and will not do so until Department so instructs or until it is obvious, based on information from Moscow embassy, it is unwise to delay. However, consulate is planning definitely to evacuate two Chaos and family, but not chauffeur and messenger unless it is decided after talking with them it is likely they will be treated badly by police after consulate departs.

Useless to try any transfer of funds to consulate via local Russia state bank due lack of its facilities to handle such exotic transaction.

Panamanian ship still not docked. French ship rumored here also. Even with Russian permits to leave on foreign freighter it will be necessary to make arrangements with captain to accept us as passengers. If and when I am allowed to talk with a freighter captain, I shall emphasize all of us willing go deck passage if no accommodations. If ship is going direct to some distant port like Singapore, I shall try to persuade him to stop in Korea or Taiwan and shall guarantee that Department will pay his owners cost of such diversion. Once out of harbor I shall wireless Department.

After it is certain consulate staff can leave on some foreign ship in harbor, I shall try to arrange for Germans leave on it also."

September 14

My telegram:

Consulate informed Chinese staff today re closing of post, but instructed them not to repeat this information. No other publicity given re closing.

Verified that two Chaos definitely want to go with us.

Talks with chauffeur and messenger indicate they probably able withdraw into general Chinese population without too serious difficulty with police. Hence, consulate did not suggest possibility their evacuation. They will be discharged on closing of post.

* * *

Within twenty-four hours the Chinese Communist police arrested Head Clerk Chao.

September 16

My telegram told some of the story:

Last night 7 p.m. Chinese police from station for this district called at consulate residence and summoned Head Clerk Chao to accompany them. I did not learn of this until two hours later and then sent Gleysteen to police station to inquire as to reasons for police action. Police told him they had asked Chao a few questions and released him before 8 p.m. However, Chao did not return. It is assumed he is in hands of police, whether Russian or Chinese not known. This morning I sent letter to Kommandant asking on what ground Chao detained. I urgently requested a reply today by letter or interview. However, only reply was a telephone call by a junior officer who said Kommandant refused to send letter to me or grant interview, insisting matter is for the Chinese police and Russians have no responsibility. I then wrote that consulate could not accept a telephone call as an official answer and again requested a reply by letter or interview. Consulate is unable to suggest action to secure Chao's release because Russians are, I am sure, either acting on direct instructions from Moscow or else will not release him except on receipt of such instructions. I fear if his arrest is not protested effectively and immediately Russians will be in still better position to prevent evacuation of Radio Operator Chao.

Note that consulate's telegram of August 12 asking Department's views on Russian-Chinese police relations not answered.

In event I do obtain interview with Kommandant, I shall say:

1. It is consulate's opinion Russians are responsible for all actions against American consulate whether carried out by Russians or through Chinese police.
2. Latter are regarded as branch of Russian administration.
3. Application of Russian authority in Dairen city is evident from presence of Russian troops, Kommandatura, and Russian-controlled civil administration.
4. Russian relations with Chinese Nationalists have remained unchanged inasmuch as Russian embassy is still in Canton and Russian consulate general continues to function in Dairen; in contrast, Russia has closed its posts in Communist China.
5. There has never been any public announcement that Russians have turned over control of Dairen city to Kwantung administration.

Culver gave me a memo which describes the particulars of Head Clerk Chao's arrest:

Shortly after 7 p.m. a policeman from Fenglin station entered my side of the house through back entrance. He asked cook to summon Chao. When Chao appeared, policeman informed him he was wanted at police station to fill out his *curriculum vitae*. Chao said he already had done this. Policeman suggested the former copy might have been lost, and would Chao please come down again to fill another form. Policeman spoke in most courteous way. Chao said he would like to go upstairs first. He then told Radio

Operator Chao he was wanted at police stat.on for a routine matter, but if he did not return by eight o'clock inform Paddock or me. He then went downstairs and left house with the policeman.

Radio Operator Chao informed Paddock at about 8:30.

At 9:45 Paddock agreed I should go to Fenglin station to find out what I could about Chao. I walked down with my two dogs. At station only one man there. I asked where Chao was. Man replied that several routine questions had been put to Chao and then he was released before eight o'clock and should have gone home. I said he was not at home, but feeling I could not learn any more from this policeman I returned to the house.

Radio Operator Chao has suggested police deliberately tricked him out of consulate residence, probably had him fill out routine forms and then dismissed him. On way home he was probably picked up by political police (the policeman at Fenglin station talked to me with such an air of gravity he sounded as if he had memorized what he was supposed to say).

At present, the domestic servants in both our households know consulate is to be closed. The messenger first told the wife of your Number One Boy (who is the nephew of the messenger, which I learned for the first time today!) and through this means the news spread through the house.

It is possible the police arrested Chao to beat us to the draw. On the other hand, it is unlikely the Chinese police could have taken this type of drastic action affecting the American consulate without Russian cognizance and approval, if not on direct Russian orders. Therefore, it is likely Kommandatura already has information on the impending closure of the consulate via Russian Foreign Office."

We did not know whether the police acted against Chao because someone on our staff had carelessly or intentionally alerted the police to the consulate's closing, or whether the action was taken on the basis of information from Moscow (Ambassador Kirk's interview with Vishinsky had taken place five days earlier, about the right length of time for the news to reach Dairen), or whether specific instructions from Moscow had initiated the arrest. The reason was immaterial. The job was done.

We tried to ascertain the cause for Chao's arrest but never gleaned a single detail beyond the fact of his arrest. Culver called at the police headquarters several times but was rebuffed. We could not find out which police were imprisoning him, Russian or Chinese. Nor did we hear anything about how he was being treated. The embassy in Moscow did send a "strong" note to the Russian Foreign Office about Chao, but Washington took no action. The reply from the Foreign Office, ten days later, rejected Russian responsibility for the arrest of Chao: "Questions concerning Chinese citizens enter into the competence of the Chinese authorities." It did not, however, define "Chinese authorities." The Kwantung administration did not have the remotest connection with the Chinese Nationalist government, still recognized by Russia as the sovereign power in Dairen. Nevertheless, the Kremlin had spoken and its word was fiat without regard to legalities.

Head Clerk Chao had seemingly disappeared. With most political arrests throughout the Soviet empire, the hapless ones simply vanish from the earth as if they had never been—unless, some time in the future, they may be released. The mystery, however, remained: Why did the normally cautious Chao leave, apparently willingly, with the policeman that evening and without informing Culver or me (for we were both in our quarters)? I probably would have insisted that he wait until the next day. And if he really had to go then, I would have sent him in the car with Culver, who would have waited outside the station—the procedure we had followed in the past. The careless impulse—totally out of character—that had made Chao go out in the night with the policeman was unfathomable.

Only later did the possibility occur to us that this was the final act of a faithful employee who believed there was nothing the consulate could do further to help him and did not want to cause us additional troubles. That indeed was in his character.

It made a fitting testimonial to the early career of an outstanding man. I remembered now the commendation written about Chao by A. Sabin Chase, who was the American consul in Dairen at the time of Pearl Harbor when the post was closed. (Chao was then the consulate's messenger.)

> Chao has had a record of more than twenty years of extremely faithful and efficient service for the American government. He consistently has worked to improve his qualifications and his usefulness to the consulate, such as teaching himself to typewrite. He improved his English to such an extent that, aside from his duties as messenger, he was utilized for work which approached that of a typist and assistant file clerk. In all my experience I have never known a more capable, loyal, and dependable employee of the Foreign Service.

> After the outbreak of the Japanese war, the Japanese police at Dairen subjected the Chinese employees of the consulate and the Chinese servants of consular officers to very harsh and inhuman treatment. They were all confined with us on the premises of the consulate and, with the exception of the cook who made a daily trip to the market under a police escort, they were not allowed to leave the premises from December 8 until the departure from Dairen of the consular officers on April 7, 1942. They were not tortured or subjected to severe physical abuse by the police, but were constantly cross-examined, taunted, bullied, reviled for their association with the consulate and cuffed—in short, generally tormented in every way short of serious physical mistreatment. Their children were not allowed to attend school, and sick members of their families had the greatest difficulty in obtaining medical attention. I was able to discharge my chauffeur at the end of December; he

was jailed for three months. The other employees and servants were all given to understand they would spend similar periods in jail for investigation following our departure from Dairen.

Following their usual practice, the police were especially suspicious of Chao and singled him out for particularly abusive treatment because they were aware of the fact we valued and trusted him especially. He and his family were continually questioned and threatened and subjected to indignities. The severity of his treatment increased as a result of the false statements regarding him made by Mrs. A.M. Lewis, a clerk of the consulate whose pro-Japanese conduct and practice of spying for the police on other members of the staff are described in separate reports to the Department.

Throughout all this mistreatment Chao displayed the most examplary courage, patience, and loyalty to the consulate. The day before my departure he told me he fully expected to be jailed for a long period and that he would be fortunate if he escaped with his life. He told me with great earnestness that the only two things that mattered to him were the welfare of China and of the United States, that he was but one of four hundred million Chinese and that he would be proud to sacrifice himself for China and the United States. He said that when the war was over, if he were still alive, he would greatly like to be given employment again at the American consulate.

And the Japanese police did arrest him immediately and tortured him badly. He was kept in prison for a year. When released, it was months before he could walk again. Nevertheless, when consul Benninghoff arrived at Dairen in 1946 to reopen the consulate, Chao stood there on the dock, waiting to resume his duties, though he surely knew that working for the "enemy" Americans would be as perilous under the Russians as it had been under the Japanese.

So now the Russians or Chinese Communists had arrested him. I took for granted that the same cruel treatment would be repeated. In their constant propaganda the Russians vilified "fascist beasts," but what was the difference between the one and the other? A police state is a police state.

Chao's apparant epitaph came with the Department's telegram of September 28, obviously written by some junior officer:

> The Department agrees not to close the office until every effort to obtain the release of Chao is exhausted. In this connection the Department requests Embassy Moscow to report any further results by its representatives and you should continue your local efforts to obtain his release. The Department, appreciating your desire to depart soonest, commends your loyalty to the Chinese staff, but likewise realizes it may be forced eventually to abandon Chao, in which case the decision will be made by the Department.

* * *

The pressure of work in closing out the consulate was increased, this month of September, by the news of two repatriation ships coming for the Japanese. How many Japanese were still in Dairen I did not know.

We were not involved with the Japanese. But the Germans and other foreigners were desperate to receive exit visas to leave on those ships. For over half a year, both the Russians and the Chinese police had promised them that they could leave any time a ship was available. It became patently clear that this was a false promise, because at least some of the weekly freighters would have been willing to take a few, and all of the Dairen foreigners would have been happy to go even by deck passage. Yet no one was allowed to make contact with the captains. It had been a year now since any group had left, except for Poles and Czechs returning through Siberia.

The American consulate had become, in June, the official agent for the Germans. So, when I heard about the Japanese repatriation ships, I asked SCAP again for clearances for the entire group to travel on them. These came immediately, including clearances for the group of miscellaneous foreigners, which I also had requested.

There were many telegrams about the succeeding events, as well as letters from me to the Kommandant.

My telegram of September 28 to the State Department tells the story:

> All foreigners, including Germans, refused exit visas. Thus, none will be able to go on the repatriation ships. Representatives of the German group were told officially by Chinese police that their names had been sent to the Northeast Administration Committee in Mukden. This Committee has sent their names to the Central Revolution Committee in Peking. Only after Peking gives permission will local foreigners be allowed to leave Dairen. The recurrent claims of the Russians to have no responsibility over the Chinese police in this matter have been reported before.

> I wrote yesterday to the Kommandant for verification of above and asked information on following points:

> 1. If true, on what basis is Peking allowed by the Russians to decide on the matter of exit visas, or any other question in Dairen, since Russia's diplomatic relations with Nationalist · China remain unchanged, as evidenced by the continued functioning of the Russian Consulate General in Dairen, and since Russia has announced its military occupation of Dairen would continue until Japanese peace treaty signed?
> 2. On what basis are Russian citizens able to travel freely in and out of Dairen to Vladivostok and Manchuria but citizens of other countries are unable to leave the city?
> 3. On what basis is Kommandant able to give permission in his own name to the Japanese residents of Dairen to be repatriated when he

denies similar permits to citizens of other
countries?

Consulate reaffirmed its former assertions that Russia
is responsible for all exit visas. No answer to the letter
is expected. This telegram is repeated to Nanking
Embassy which should pass it to French Embassy. It
is hoped French will accept their responsibility of
initiating vigorous protests in Moscow concerning this
group of German residents in China who are prevented by Russia from using repatriation facilities
specifically authorized for them by SCAP. In Dairen
all action re Germans is taken by Consulate in name
of French Embassy.

(My letter to the Kommandant was a monotonous drone
from my many earlier letters, but one writes such notes as a
matter of course to "establish a file." If a loophole does appear,
then one has these references to past notes to buttress one's
case.)

The repatriation ship of September 28 did not take out the
Americans either. We had been hoping the Russians would see it
as an easy solution to the problems and one that would not
have affected their local prestige or protocol or whatever with
the Chinese.

The French embassy in Nanking did take up the matter of
Russian exit visas for the German group. A long series of
telegrams were exchanged between us. The French asked me for
a list of all the Germans, giving their names and other data. I
replied there were seventy-six covered by my certificates of
identification; two others were not leaving Dairen due to family
reasons. To telegraph all the data requested would cost five
thousand dollars. The French did not press the point.

The Germans and the foreigners continued their weary
rounds: constantly calling at the Russian and Chinese offices to
keep their cases alive and always hoping some break might
appear which could aid them. The Russian and Chinese clerks
receiving these petitioners no doubt enjoyed watching them

grovel helplessly in front of their desks, beseeching a signature on a piece of paper, a situation not unknown in non-Communist petty-bureaucratic establishments.

* * *

Meanwhile, the Russians were trying to jam our radio reception of the telegrams sent to us twice a day by the U.S. Information Service station, now located in Taiwan. They would begin jamming just before the time of the broadcasts to Dairen and stop immediately afterwards. The last sentence of my telegram reporting this new annoyance read, "Russians fail to jam Taiwan only because Russian equipment is bad, although Taiwan plant also is poor."

Closing out the consulate continued its stumbling way.

September 21.

I telegraphed:

> Apparently no answer in Moscow to Ambassador Kirk's informing Russian Foreign Office re closing of consulate, although arrest of Chao might be regarded as one form of answer. Surveillance of consulate office and residence, our auto and of officers is ever more intensive and blatant. Russians perhaps stalling in order to turn over the problem to Chinese later. Danger of further arrests of Chinese staff exists.

> I suggest consideration be given to retaliatory measures re this area, such as obstructing further soybean transactions with Japan and, if possible, discourage British, French and other ships coming here under Russian charter. Refer to my August 31 telegram asking if position of consulate sufficiently analogous to Russian mission Japan to justify and to warrant pressure in that direction, such as documentation by SCAP re arrival and departure of

Russian personnel, couriers and visitors. Russians contend Dairen is subject to military control pending Japanese peace treaty; hence, Consulate must submit to Russian military regulations. U.S. is at head of military occupation of Japan until peace treaty signed and Russians there presumably obliged to abide by military regulations. It would seem that if consulate personnel are prevented from moving in and out of "free port" of Dairen similar restrictions could be applied to Russians in Japan.

Regardless of route which Russians finally may permit, office will not be closed until specifically informed by Department no further efforts being made to obtain release of Chao.

Also, unless local or Moscow Russians promise no examination of official mail and personal luggage of Americans and no restrictions as to departure of Radio Operator Chao with us, we will refuse to leave until Department instructs my acquiescence re such examinations and abandonment of Radio Operator Chao.

Also on September 21, although we did not learn of this for several days, Mao Tse-tung proclaimed the People's Republic of China. His procedure involved submitting a plan of government for approval to the "Chinese People's Political Consultative Conference," then in session in Peking, thus postponing for a few days the formal establishment of his new government.

On September 24 the consulate received a circular telegram sent to all American posts around the world, signed by President Truman: "We have evidence that within recent weeks an atomic explosion occurred in USSR."

The cold war had moved to a new plateau.

September 24

My telegram:

Department's concern re Consulate's finances appreciated, but Consulate knows of no practical solution except physical transport of funds to Dairen. If effort is made to transmit money via Moscow it is estimated 100,000 rubles needed for average monthly expenses due to artificially high official exchange rates. Russian obstructions make it doubtful if money would reach us in worthwhile time.

Efforts to sell government property so far unsuccessful.

Consulate will send letters tomorrow to Russian Consulate General and Kommandatura stating Department is arranging immediate departure of staff and Consulate will close at date of my departure. Also, I shall report call of Ambassador Kirk on Foreign Minister Vishinsky informing him Consulate would be closed. This action is made necessary in order to move openly to dispose of salable Government property. Local authorities presumably long ago heard of closing from Moscow or at least from informers on our staff. There is little advantage to conceal it longer from general public.

September 24.

For Department's information consulate has concluded following to facilitate immediate departure:

1. All postwar archives, including confidential files and accounts now packed in pouches which we will take from Dairen regardless of route used.
2. Blank passports, fee stamps, rubber stamps, USIS material destroyed.
3. Seals, cryptographic material, stationery, forms, radio equipment destroyed except what is in current use.
4. Good office furniture will be stored uncrated in Bryner godown unless Department authorizes storage in British Consulate building.

5. Government-owned house furnishings will be crated if and when money available ($100 needed) and stored.
6. Office machines will be sold if possible, otherwise stored; all are old.
7. 67 drums of gas and oil will be sold or else permission of municipal authorities requested to destroy or, most probably, just left.
8. Effects of British officers will be taken with us regardless of route used.
9. Chauffeur and messenger will be paid two months salary lump sum and two months severance retirement.
10. If Head Clerk Chao not freed, consulate will pay wife two months lump sum, four months severange and four months partial payment for annuity. His services ceased end of September 15, date of arrest.

September 24.

We heard from embassy Moscow that it had received a note from Vishinsky stating he had sent instructions to the Kommandant of Dairen to facilitate the closing of the consulate and the departure of the consulate employees. This was the first indication that the Russians, apparently, were not going to obstruct, or at least hinder, our departure.

September 25.

My telegram to the State Department:

As a result of Moscow's telegram I today sent letter to the Kommandant. Following is summary:

Ambassador Kirk in personal call September 10 informed Vishinsky of Consulate's closing and requested Russians facilitate departure of staff and give their preference as to transport for their departure: Russian ship, foreign freighter under Russian charter, or unarmed American naval vessel. Russian Foreign Office note of September 22 in reply said appropriate instructions had been sent to you. Since no preference is given in note, I assume it is immaterial which type of transport is used. Thus, I now request the Kommandatura either itself to arrange passage for Consulate staff on one of foreign freighters here or to allow me to contact captains personally. If Russian ship to Vladivostok is leaving earlier it is satisfactory with me to go that route. Ambassador pointed out to Vishinsky that Gleysteen and I would be traveling as couriers; official mail thus exempt from examination. Also, our personal luggage should be exempt. Radio Operator Chao is to go with us. The question of the release and departure from Dairen of Head Clerk Chao is being taken up by Embassy Moscow. Reply by letter or interview is requested.

September 27.

Kommandant today in interview said departure of Americans of Consulate staff would be arranged on foreign freighter due here "in first days of October," but he does not know destination of freighter. Matter of examination of official mail and personal luggage not yet decided. Departure of Radio Operator Chao is for Chinese police to decide, not Russians, I said it is certain Department would not permit me to leave if official mail is subject to examination; personal luggage, however, is matter of international courtesy and I could not insist on exemption. Also, I am absolutely unable to go without Radio Operator Chao. However, I said I would make application for exit visa for him at Chinese police, recognizing it as a branch of the Russian administration in Dairen. Although Kommandant was definite about our departure on freighter, Department should note it presumably still is necessary for captain to agree to take us. I hope matters now arranged for departure, but many opportunities for Russians to delay departure until Chinese Communist Party reorganizes city government.

CHAPTER XIII

CLEANING UP
TO CLEAR OUT
(SEPTEMBER–OCTOBER 1949)

In late September came the first break in our efforts to close up the Dairen consulate. I telegraphed the State Department:

September 27

> Consulate today sold its vehicles, oil products, office machines, miscellaneous supplies for local currency approximately equal to $4500. This is roughly their replacement value. Nothing salable left. This amount enables consulate to handle all its obligations incidental to closing with enough left over for perhaps six weeks operation.

> I particularly commend Gleysteen for his initiative and tact during period when he successfully threaded his way around pitfalls of Russian and Chinese Communist go-betweens demanding cuts, Communist buyers welshing on their promises, constant efforts by Communist agents to get "squeeze," behind-the-scenes attempts of secret police to keep consulate isolated and boycotted—all, however, balanced by indomitable urge of one big-time Russian executive to ride in the Oldsmobile. Although all accounting regulations ignored in this package deal, Gleysteen succeeded in gaining for consulate adequate funds and all concessions necessary for operation of consulate until closing time, if evacuation is soon.

Culver's master stroke in selling all our salable property was indeed as razzle-dazzle, harebrained and devious as the telegram indicated. All efforts to come to grips with a buyer, any buyer, for any of the various items remained fruitless because police scared away prospective customers. At one time we made a firm agreement for the sale of the jeep and trailer, but the buyer failed to arrive with the money at the scheduled hour. The assistant manager of the Dairen Trading Company, a state-owned export-import trust, agreed to buy the gasoline and oil. All details were settled; but he also failed to show up. Due to a police-enforced boycott the consulate was truly under economic seige.

Then, somehow, without any evidence at hand, Culver sensed that some high Russian official far in the background was mad for our Oldsmobile—and it was obvious to him that this official had the power to flout the boycott. Culver teased the bait of the beautiful car while an astounding group of both Russian and Chinese would-be agents, hangers-on, and cutthroat artists roiled the waters. Culver never met the avid would-be buyer; we never even learned who he was. Aside from haggling over the price, the official insisted he wanted nothing but the car. Yet as Culver continued to dangle the bait, he agreed to buy more and more of our items in a package deal. In the end, he bought the whole consular line of goods lock, stock, and barrel.

At one stage the prospective buyer threatened, through the go-betweens, merely to exercise his power to confiscate the car, which he could have at any time, adding that he could prevent anyone else from buying the car anyway. So what would we do if we could not sell the car and he saw to it that we could not take it away with us on the ship? My answer for Culver to take back was that at the time of our departure I myself would drive the Oldsmobile to the dock, unload my baggage from it and then personally drive it off the dock into the water. It was that kind of business fray.

The official had probably worked out an arrangement for the go-betweens to relieve him of the non-Oldsmobile items. Nevertheless, the total price was an enormous sum in Dairen.

Based on local standards we decided he was paying the equivalent of $20,000 for the car alone, evidence, if evidence were needed, that Russia's top officials did have plenty of cash at hand for their pleasures.

Our formal sales agreement with one Wang Ta-shan listed:

1 Oldsmobile sedan, 1947 year.
1 Willys-Overland Jeep and Trailer.
38 drums of Mobil gasoline.
30 drums of Standesol.
1 electric generator.
2 General Electric refrigerators.
3 calculating machines.
6 typewriters.
  Miscellaneous equipment, including electric light bulbs, lubricants and anti-freeze for the automobiles, carbon paper, cardboard file holders, iron stoves, glue, erasers, toilet paper, insecticides (and even broken waterjugs!)

We retained only those items that could be stored for several years without deterioration.)

The terms of the sale specified that the consulate could continue to use, up to the time of our departure, the Oldsmobile, one refrigerator and the electric generator.

When the sale went through, Culver was paid in local paper currency (4,000,000 yuan!). He rushed non-stop to the foreign-exchange market. Before the dealers could catch on to what was happening, he went from stall to stall, changing the whole amount into gold bars. Our major worry had been that even if we did sell our goods, the local authorities would find some way to prevent us from exchanging the yuan. This might well have happened if Culver had not moved so fast, sweeping through the marketplace before the police there realized that this visit of his was, verily, a buccaneer's raid.

That night Culver and I had enormous fun as we celebrated the end of our financial worries. We admired the mound of gold bars; then we stacked them in pretty patterns and finally threw them into the air. Converting the gold bars back into yuan to meet our current expenses on a day-to-day basis proved no problem. The balance that was left we took out with us.

This vast supply of cash had come to us just as our financial troubles were fast climaxing into a true crisis. The rate of exchange on our dollar bills, which had always fluctuated, had again somewhat stabilized during the summer at 2000 yuan for one dollar. Then in September the rate suddenly dropped to 1000 yuan. Although the rate had been nearly this low before, we believed, because of the timing, that it was another pressure on the consulate for it doubled the cost of operating the post.

Recounting this delightful event—our getting lots of money—reminds me about another. Culver and I were currently in the midst of a daily routine of enjoying fine wines and champagne for lunch and dinner, having an excellent cocktail before hand, a liqueur afterwards, and then a highball—the way every gentleman lives if he can afford it. In our case, now, it was more a question of when we had the time for such pleasures.

As I reported before, we had been reduced to concocting cocktails made of pre-filtered Siberian spirit and maple syrup. And until the present rash of telegrams broke our routine, we had developed the pattern of playing gin rummy in the evenings before dinner. A cocktail, even that garish mixture, had been an integral part of the one relaxed time of the day for us.

To relate this story I must explain that in the rather large godowns, or storage rooms, surrounding our consulate compound were many miscellaneous boxes, bales and other things left over from the Bryner days. They were primarily trade goods which the company had not been able to ship out and which had stayed on in assorted piles. An elderly White Russian, Nazaroff, was caretaker of these goods. A quiet, highly honorable man, he lived alone in small quarters at a corner of the compound.

One day in August, quite by accident, Nazaroff mentioned to us that Mrs. Bryner's wine cellar had been stored in the godowns when she left for the United States before the war. Culver and I climbed over piles of goods, and Nazaroff showed us two large cases, about five feet by three by three. We opened one and, sure enough, there was a fine miscellany of bottles, all packed copiously in straw for shipment. We wanted to take some bottles home right away but suddenly sensed how wrong this would be. Nazaroff had guarded these goods faithfully all these years for the Bryners; it would have distressed him to see us take them in this cavalier way. Like true gentlemen we put the bottles back and told him we would telegraph Mrs. Bryner for authorization to buy them from her. We sent a telegram via the State Department offering a dollar a bottle and left it to the entity known as "Washington" to find her. It took three weeks for them to track her down, in San Francisco; she agreed to the "deal." (Later on, she told us of her amusement in getting reimbursed for wines she long had believed were lost or confiscated.)

By a ridiculous coincidence the telegram telling us we could go ahead with Mrs. Bryner's stock of wines arrived on the same morning as the Department's communication informing us that the consulate was to be closed.

We hired a pushcart and had the two beautiful boxes taken to our house. Then we lined up all the bottles, about a hundred of them—in a circle on the furniture and shelves around the living room. They formed the sort of collection a cosmopolitan European normally would have: a good range of wines, several brands of champagne, some whiskey, a variety of sherries and liqueurs. Fantastic, in Dairen!

Like gourmets we solemnly discussed with the cook what we were having for lunch (already two hours late), and selected the wine. For a quick aperitif we decided on a sherry: but which of the several different bottles? By eliminating the ones we knew to be too sweet or heavy, we came to one from a well-known brand that was labeled "Invalida." I said I had heard of that type. So with great ceremony the two of us opened the bottle and toasted the news of the closing of the Dairen consulate—then swallowed the weakest, sickliest, most nondescript liquor I have ever had. It was a sherry for, as it plainly said but we failed to realize, invalids. With all that liquor from which to choose we had taken the one that was undrinkable.

* * *

As the delays continued, I would wonder wistfully why the eager buyer of the Oldsmobile did not use his influence to get us out fast so he could take over his prize purchase. Perhaps he did not have that kind of influence; more likely, the subject of the consulate was handled so strictly within the framework of orders from Moscow that it was beyond local tampering.

The three-day conference for the reorganization of the Dairen city government ended without anything really happening, itself a rather startling development. Our fears of immediate troubles had been real enough, but now life was going on for everyone, including ourselves, the same as before: a letdown. We now assumed everything was in abeyance until the new government of the Chinese Communists would be organized in Peking. Russia would then recognize it officially; That would be the time when new troubles would start for us.

September 29

I sent another long, wrap-up telegram:

> After reviewing my interview with the Kommandant and after analyzing Russian and Chinese subterfuges and broken promises in refusing exit visas to foreigners, I am convinced real danger exists that consulate staff will be unable to leave "in the first days of October," as promised by him. It is definitely certain Radio Operator Chao unable to go under present circumstances. The runaround as to his exit visa already has begun. Following points pertinent:
>
> 1. No reason why Russians should ask us to await some particular, unnamed future ship, as foreign freighters in harbor now.
> 2. No reason why Kommandant should be unwilling give details re this ship. As a result, we are completely in Russian hands as to "unforeseen delays."

3. No way for Russians to know now if captain of this future ship will be able and willing to take us.
4. Most pertinent is subject of exit visas for foreigners. My opinion is that relations between Russians and local Chinese may have become so "touchy" on this matter that Russians may well believe only way for them to escape difficulties with the Chinese is to postpone departure for all foreigners for time being. This may include us.
5. No indication what future of Dairen will be after Chinese Communist government is formed in Peking. Local press states chairman of Kwantung administration exhorted Dairen Municipal Conference to be prepared to obey gladly all laws of the new government as soon as formed.
6. American government's helplessness re Mukden staff has provided effective, prolonged propaganda story to enhance Chinese Communist Party prestige. If similar situation develops here, it probably will be of propaganda value to both Communists and Russians.

To prevent any chance of consulate staff remaining here beyond formation of CCP Government, probably by October 4, it is recommended Department act on following lines:

1. If Department has itself definite information (that is, no need to query various posts) of foreign freighter arriving here by October 4, Department is requested to establish by wireless with captain that he agrees to accept consulate staff as passengers. It is necessary for him to agree before arrival, as once in Dairen he is isolated.
2. If no information of such a ship at hand or if no agreement with captain in twenty-four hours, Department is requested to instruct Embassy Seoul to arrange special freighter to come Dairen in order arrive here by October 4. It is unimportant how small ship may be.
3. Department is requested to have Embassy Moscow inform Foreign Office (and to have

consulate do the same with Kommandant) along following lines:

a. Department appreciates assurances of Kommandant that local Russians will facilitate departure of Consulate staff and that it will arrange evacuation in first days of October.

b. However, it is noted that Russian plans, as reported to Consulate, are vague: no specific information re name or destination of vessel, no assurances as to exemption of official mail or personal luggage of officers and no assurances to permit Radio Operator Chao to leave.

c. Department reiterates its position that Russia, as *de facto* military occupying power of Dairen, is responsible for these assurances.

d. Because it seems no definite Russian arrangements yet made for transportation of Consulate staff from Dairen, Department has itself arranged for special ship to call at Dairen by October 4 to evacuate Americans and Chao (or else has arranged with captain of a freighter to accept staff as passengers).

If impasse should then arise so that Russians refuse to admit the ship or to allow us to board it or to refuse departure of Chao, it will be necessary for Department finally to take a definite and public stand on status of Dairen. It is realized Department's ability to protest on behalf of Consulate was weakened when it did not raise the issue at time the Russians first claimed no responsibility concerning Chinese police harassment of Consulate. A review of Consulate's telegrams will show, however, the Russian position at Dairen is vulnerable and that Department should be able to exploit it effectively.

Now I must editorialize. Perhaps it was unfair of me to imply the Department could now be blamed for not having acted when the Russians first began to claim they had no responsibility over the Kwantung administration and its Chinese police. The initial illustrations of this Russian policy did not involve the consulate itself but affected the foreigners trying to obtain exit visas. And the first incidents concerning the consulate were not serious. I did not realize then that they formed the beginning of a series of such events. Nevertheless, rather early it was obvious the consulate staff was in trouble and possibly in danger when the Russians unilaterally shifted their responsibility for the consulate to their puppet Kwantung administration. Yet at no time did the Department tackle the illegalities and weaknesses of the Russian position and explore what possible pressures might make the Russians reverse their new stance. After certain of our incidents in Dairen, it would instruct Embassy Moscow to protest. This was done, however, in a routine fashion, merely one in a series of protests the embassy always was making to the Foreign Office regarding frictions between Americans and Russians around the globe. The Russians, at least concerning the Dairen incidents, treated the notes as unimportant because the Department never showed determination, or the desire, to use pressure to back up its notes. The lower officials in Washington handling these cases apparently believed naively, that writing a "strong" note to the Russians would receive the same serious attention as sending a similar note to a democracy, for instance to the British Foreign Office.

September 30

I felt obliged to send another long telegram to impress the Department with the need for action. I pointed out that my earlier telegram of September 21 concerning Head Clerk Chao was sent when there was still hope of effecting his release; now I realized this was impossible unless the Department utilized some other means than it had so far, namely, the single note to the Russian Foreign Office. I also pointed out that my telegram of September 27 was sent when I still believed the departure of Radio Operator Chao could be arranged; now I realized it was definitely impossible to get an exit visa for him "unless the

Department is able to force the Russians to order the Chinese police to issue it." I did not suggest how the Department could "force" the Russians, but my experience in the Foreign Service was that the measures were at hand in the network of Russian-American relations if only the right officials would seek them. The fate of two loyal employees was in the balance. My telegram continued:

Thus, we are at following impasse:

1. The one Chao cannot be freed and the other cannot leave Dairen.
2. If latter is left behind he will be seized immediately by police.
3. If Gleysteen and I remain, he probably will be arrested anyway.
4. If we remain, the local authorities soon will place even more restrictions on us, whether on basis of Dairen's incorporation into new Peking government or other excuse.
5. We are not prepared for siege in Mukden style as stores long ago exhausted.
6. Although Kommandant promised transport "in first days of October," it is now realized there is little reason to believe he will keep his promise.
7. No assurance of exemption of official mail from customs examination, as well as personal luggage of Americans.

It is believed advisable for Department to scrap all previous decisions and instructions re Dairen, review pertinent consulate telegrams and decide on next course of action. As stated in previous messages, consulate considers Russian position in Dairen to be vulnerable. It is difficult to believe that examination of that position would not reveal lever that would force Russians to let Radio Operator Chao go.

Hopefully, Department will reply to this telegram within twelve hours after receipt. Consulate is still convinced our deadline is date when new Peking government is established and Russians grant it recognition (locally, this is believed to be imminent almost hourly, although Department may have more exact information). Thus, consulate's suggestions of September 29 are still in order.

In retrospect today these urgently insistent telegrams of mine sound rash for a field officer to send to the august State Department, such as asking for a reply to a complex telegram in twelve hours. However, the crisis was on in full force and I certainly did not want our cause to be lost due to delays by some minor official in the Department. When I did get back to Washington, no one criticized my stridency.

During this week the "People's Conference" in Peking completed the organization of the new government, electing Mao as Chairman on September 30.

On October 2 Russia recognized the Peking government and broke off diplomatic relations with Nationalist China.

And still no changes were made or announced for a new legal basis, or new formal ties, between the Russians and Communists in Dairen. It was another letdown—though we probably would not have benefited from a change. The Russian military procedures remained unchanged. Russian soldiers, rather than Chinese police, continued to patrol the sections nightly where Russian citizens lived. Yet withdrawing the Russian troops from Dairen would, of course, be a simple matter physically: merely moving them across the city limits into the Port Arthur Naval Base area. The wives even could continue living in Dairen.

A secret conference of high Russian officials was reportedly called for the following week in Port Arthur. We now transferred our fears to the changes that might follow this conference.

Meanwhile, the Department had made contact with the old and prestigious British Far East trading firm of Butterfield & Swire, based in Hong Kong. It was asked to divert one of its small coastal ships to Dairen. This was important news because it showed the Department at last was ready to have its own diverted or chartered ship come here just for us. No more waiting for the Russians to arrange our transportation. No more hoping to contact the elusive owners and captains of freighters. I liked to think the approach to Butterfield & Swire was the result of my insisting on fast action by the Department. It never did reply to my telegram in the twelve hours, but the timing indicated that that was when they decided to charter a ship.

October 3

Telegram from Hong Kong:

Diversion of *Soochow* not practical. Diversion of *Hupeh* arrangeable provided there is assurance of early departure from Dairen. *Hupeh* is coal burner and if delayed at Dairen it could run out of fuel and water. Failing *Hupeh*, Butterfield & Swire suggest *Shansi*, due sail from Taku Bar (Tientsin) October 19. Please confirm reasonable assurance Dairen authorities will not delay *Hupeh* beyond time required embark passengers and load freight.

October 5.

My telegram to Hong Kong and the Department:

Consulate staff can embark with few hours' notice. However, unable give assurances as to possible delays arising from local authorities. As emphasized in previous telegrams, they act only on basis of orders from Moscow. Thus, it would seem Department is in better position to answer Hong Kong telegram than consulate.

October 6

I telegraphed the Department:

What is present status of Department's plans to evacuate consulate staff? Last information re Butterfield & Swire ships was Hong Kong telegram dated October 3. Target date of evacuation was October 4. Consulate is at loss why ships in Korea are so few that all plans must center on Hupeh for which arrangements must be delayed for consultation with Hong Kong and Tientsin.

The poor old coal-burning *Hupeh* was indeed timorous. First it was coming, then postponed, then coming again, then not. All this was repeated to the Moscow Embassy, which notified the Russian Foreign Office of each change. This shower of notes did produce a reply on October 7, which stated formally that the Foreign Office had no objection to a Butterfield & Swire ship calling at Dairen in connection with the closing of the Consulate. This was the first positive assurance the Russians really were going to permit us to leave, a step considerably more firm than their note using the vague phrase "to facilitate our departure," always open to subsequent interpretations.

The *Hupeh* was finally and surely scheduled for the early morning of October 8. At dawn I rushed up to our attic window. There, coming into sight, was a ship that fitted the description. But when it approached the harbor entrance at nine o'clock we recognized it as a Russian coastal vessel—just as Radio Operator Chao gave me a telegram saying the *Hupeh* was not coming after all. Instead, the *Shansi* would arrive on the 18th. It was a black day for us.

I had been sending notes regarding each of these changes to the Kommandant. In each message I reiterated my assumption that Radio Operator Chao would be leaving with us.

Actually, since the one interview with the Kommandant on September 27, when he assured us transportation on a foreign freighter "in the first days of October," there had been no word from him about anything at all: certainly not about his vague freighter. Nor was there word about other details of our embarkation, such as customs examination.

October 8

I sent another telegram to the Department stating that:

> . . . regardless of whatever assurances the Kommandant might give that official mail will not be examined at customs, it must be realized there may be trouble with the Chinese without opportunity to take pouches back to Consulate for burning. To be freer to meet contingencies and because it is believed unwise to postpone action longer, Consulate today burned its files, both classified and unclassified. There remains only packet containing copies of current material which Department does not have, copies of consulate's letters to local authorities and the consulate's accounts. This represents, however, the seven months of accumulated outgoing mail to Department since last couriers. Thus, matter of customs examination is still important.

Now is the time to interject some other ongoing perplexities in which the consulate was concerned.

From the beginning of our evacuation plans I had carefully avoided any suggestion to the Russians that the ship might also be available to the German group and the miscellaneous foreigners. That obviously would have complicated our own arrangements with the Russians and in the end might preclude our leaving. And, of course, though I had done favors for the Germans, I had no legal responsibility for any of them; technically, it was up to them to obtain their own exit visas and to arrange their own passage out of Dairen.

I did, however, have two American visa cases, and for these I could write notes to the Kommandant urging that they be allowed to leave on the evacuation ship.

One was a White Russian, Mrs. Anna Slenkina, whose relatives in the United States had sponsored her application for an immigration visa and had guaranteed to SCAP her transportation costs from Japan to the United States. These details had been fixed only recently; now she had all necessary documentation except the exit visa.

The other case was Mrs. Schumann and her three children. Although classified as an ordinary member of the German group, her background set her apart from the others with respect to documentation. For one thing, she had a German diplomatic passport. For another, she had been a Russian citizen until her marriage. Since she had left Russia legally at that time, she was a Real Russian, not a White Russian. Furthermore, she fortunately still had her old Soviet identification papers from Vladivostok.

When the decision was made to close the consulate, I immediately worried about what might happen to her because of her association with Culver and me. She gave us lessons every day and came to the house rather regularly for lunch or dinner. Also, she had been living in the "Patch house," to which I had had her move a half-year earlier to protect the building while waiting for the new American clerk who never came. It could well be that after the consulate was closed she might be in trouble, for she had been too close to us Americans.

I myself now sponsored her to obtain both the SCAP clearance and an American transit visa to travel from Japan through the United States to Germany. That is, I provided the money for the costs for her and the children. Actually, I was lending her the money; she repaid the loan on her arrival in Germany.

So now both women were steadily calling at the Russian and Chinese offices to try to receive exit visas. It was touch and go. Mrs. Slenkina stood the better chance because an immigration visa allowing her to join relatives and to live in the United States was something the local officials could comprehend. However, with Mrs. Schumann they never quite understood how she had been able to separate herself from the rest of the German group by her travel documents. And they were not willing to give special consideration to someone whom the Chinese obviously considered almost a member of our consulate staff. In fact, as the tensions with the police built up from early September—the arrest of the one Chao and the uncertain fate of the other—it became obvious she too could be in danger of arrest. This undoubtedly would be compounded if she did not get away with us and remained behind.

Shortly after Chao's arrest I advised Mrs. Schumann and the children to leave the Patch house and go to live in the building where the rest of the Germans were huddled together. She did not want to go. It was a dismal place, and the atmosphere was rife with group tensions and acrid cliques. However, I felt there would be an extra degree of safety for her among all the others, rather than living alone in the Patch house if she did not get away with us. The German building was already so crowded, I had to call in the heads of the group and insist that they find a room for her and the children. They complied because I was still their only link with the outside world.

Several days before our "false date" of sailing on the *Hupeh* Mrs. Schumann and Mrs. Slenkina did receive their exit visas. It was done strictly on the personal order of the Kommandant himself, thus overriding the Chinese refusals. A persuasive and charming person, Mrs. Schumann had been able on one occasion to get inside his office and convince him she was indeed a Real Russian—while all other officials had been insisting on treating her as a White Russian/German. It was a moment of jubilation for all of us when we learned that she could leave.

However, when the women and the male heads of the German community learned that Mrs. Schumann had received an exit visa and would be leaving on the *Hupeh*, they rushed moblike to the visa office, insisting that if she were able to go they all must go. They raised such a ruckus that the visas of both women were cancelled. And then, of course, the *Hupeh* did not come.

Eventually, the Kommandant gave his direct, personal order again and the visas were reissued. This time I told the two women not to mention the new visas to a soul, not even to Mrs. Schumann's children. Never was a secret more carefully kept.

As for the German group as a whole, the details of transport after they succeeded in getting out of Dairen had been established by now. I had written a formal letter to "The German Community," saying, in summary:

> The funds for your repatriation have been provided by the West German Economic Council at the request of the Tripartite Powers. Your repatriation will take place, from whatever port you reach after leaving Dairen, by a single chartered plane of the Trans-Ocean Airlines Corporation. The entire flight to Germany is expected to take seventy-two hours. The plane seats fifty passengers and thus it will be necessary for the children and perhaps some adults to sit on the floor. Each person must reduce his hand baggage so that the total amount normally carried on such a plane will not be exceeded. The plane will pick you up within twenty-four hours. No one will be allowed to leave the group at any time between the port of disembarkation and Germany. Permission for you to leave Dairen is for the Community itself to arrange with the local authorities. Due to the type of freighters now coming to Dairen it is likely you will have to be prepared to travel deck passage or in the hold and to take your own food. SCAP has granted your entry into Japan as a group but each individual must carry a Certificate for entrance into Germany issued by the consulate in the form prescribed by the French embassy in Nanking. Tentative arrangements also have been made for heavy baggage not carried on the plane to be shipped as a unit by sea. This will remain unverified until after your arrival at the port of disembarkation from Dairen. All persons unfortunately must be prepared for the total loss of all baggage not actually carried on board the plane.

It was going to be a rough three-day trip to Germany on that plane. Presumably, the excitement of leaving behind the tribulations of Dairen would carry them through. But it still was as uncertain as ever when they could get away. It could be a month or a year from now.

An inordinate number of telegrams were sent regarding the storage of the consulate's office equipment and household furniture, all of it dating from prewar days, but most in rather good condition. We first planned to store it in the Bryner godowns, but after many telegrams it turned out the Bryner Company was going to charge the American Government $828 per year for 115 cubic meters of space. I pointed out that we were paying only $600 rent for their entire office and godown compound plus one of the largest houses in Dairen. I added: "Since the storage of U.S. property would be the chief protection of Bryner compound a nominal fee of $10 a year would be proper. Also, Bryner has decided not to furnish further funds to the caretaker, Nazaroff, thus leaving him without protection in relation to local authorities. To pay current taxes caretaker used some of his own money."

All this left a bad taste in the mouth, although from a profit point of view, Bryner was right to cut its ties here as there was obviously no likelihood of reopening the office. Nazaroff was a person I was sorry to leave behind, but as an elderly White Russian it was possible the police would ignore him. I had been paying his salary from funds provided by Bryner: I now gave him the balance in a lump sum. As we had not been able to sell our winter's supply of coal, I gave part to the German community for use in their building and part to Nazaroff, since he could sell it for living expenses.

The Department, after more telegrams, received authorization from the British for us to store the government property in their building. I also learned for the first time that the British had placed their consulate officially under the protection of the Russian commander-in-chief for Manchuria in 1945!

The British now said they had been grateful for my help and requested that I do what I could to remove the Communist slogans that had been painted on the garden walls so many months ago and to arrange for necessary repairs. The Department said it informed the British it might be impossible to do anything . . . "but apparently the British Foreign Office does not wish to approach Russians regarding this." (Why not, I never could guess.) It added, "In view of British assistance to

American interests elsewhere in China, please do what you can." I had the repairs made but did not bother about the slogans. Maybe they are still there.

As for the 122 boxes of the personal effects of the British officers stored there since Pearl Harbor, I already had informed the Kommandant I would take them with me, no matter which route was used for the evacuation. I had known one of the officers when we were both stationed in Batavia/Djakarta, Indonesia, and I was determined to get his teapots to him.

* * *

The recital of efforts to save Radio Operator Chao affords a textbook illustration of Communist police control methods in action. On October 3 I telegraphed the Department a summary of the consulate's efforts to obtain an exit visa for him:

1. September 27.   I told Kommandant in interview Chao would apply to Chinese police for exit visas, even though I continued to regard police as branch of Russian administration in Dairen.
2. September 28.   Chao, accompanied by Gleysteen, called at Kwantung administration police headquarters and was referred to subordinate Dairen municipal police and thence to police station for our residential area. There on several succeeding days they were told to come back another time because the proper official was not there. On last visit Chao was told, "It is not certain if he ever will be here."
3. September 29. Consulate wrote Kommandant asking him to request the proper authorities to accept and expedite visa application. No answer. Impossible to arrange another interview with Kommandant.
4. September 30. Gleysteen called alone at Kwantung administration headquarters. He was not allowed past guard but did talk with a minor official who reiterated that application must be made at local station.

5. October 1. Chao went to police station alone due to belief that maybe Gleysteen's presence may have heretofore prejudiced previous efforts. He was unable to see official in charge and was told all government offices were closed for three days in honor of new Chinese Communist government in Peking. This was first time Chao had been out of house alone for many months except for occasional, enforced visits to police.

6. Thus, Russians disclaim responsibility for Chao's visas and Chinese police refuse even to permit him make application.

October 8

I telegraphed:

Chao states he left house on his own decision the nights of October 6 and 7 to contact police. On second night he signed four statements under threat to personal safety. In summary, these were:

1. He works for American imperialism.
2. American consulates are in China for aggressive purposes.
3. He will tell all he knows re Dairen consulate.
4. He will not tell of these interviews.

I do not blame him for his actions. Without signing the statements his position is hopeless; perhaps this way he has chance to survive. His next meeting is for October 10. The possibility exists, of course, that Head Clerk Chao has signed by now similar statements. Neither Chao ever had contact with confidential material.

Possibly, this is a build-up for spy charges similar to ones made against Mukden consulate. Department should note that Mukden spy story has been of immense propaganda value to both Russians and Chinese Communists; it is still used regularly in political classes at factories, etc. The temptation to them to repeat their success is obvious.

The Department had telegraphed several days earlier:

> If evacuation ship plans already reported to you materialize and if Chaos unable to leave aboard such ship, Department reluctantly of opinion that your and Gleysteen's departure should not be delayed if exit permits to the Chaos not forthcoming. Publicity is only lever which might be effective in this situation, but Department is of opinion such pressure would not result in favorable action re either Chao, would probably have undesirable effect by further jeopardizing your departure and possibly would make more difficult the position of the Chaos when they have to remain in Dairen. Pressure through SCAP believed impossible.
>
> When time comes to leave, you should, therefore, make payments to the one and the family of the other in accordance with instructions sent in separate telegram.

I had kept Chao continually informed of the messages to and from the Department as, of course, it was wrong to leave him in the dark to build up false hopes. I had told him of this telegram, which he recognized as saying his case was hopeless. That is the time when he finally went out to meet with the police and thereupon signed the statements.

There was nothing further that could be done to protect Chao. He knew he would be arrested when we left.

Chao was quite a remarkable personality. I had come to recognize he possessed a great deal of inner strength. He never once became emotionally upset or bewailed his fate or, as he could have done, condemned the United States government for not keeping its promise to transfer him from Dairen at the end of his six-month tour of duty. I am sure he could have received his Dairen exit visa then, at the end of December, but the Department had procrastinated about sending an American as a replacement. At the time, I thought I had prodded the Department as much as I could to transfer him. In retrospect, I blamed myself that I had not used more forceful language or had made such a fuss that action would have been taken. I, too, had procrastinated—and the realization hurt.

Chao was a true patriot. He had walked a thousand or more miles from Shanghai to Chungking to fight the Japanese. He was always faithful to China, but different standards were applied in Dairen.

* * *

Now, for some ten days, an eerie lull settled over us. The Butterfield & Swire ship *Shansi* was to arrive from Taku Bar in the morning of the 18th—then the 19th and then the 21st—chock-full of refugees from Tientsin and Peking. Culver and I set aside blankets for deck passage. We still worried that Russian-Chinese political developments might prevent our going, but we did have that one telegram from Moscow indicating the Foreign Office had agreed to the ship's coming for us. No verification, naturally, from the Kommandant—nor, for that matter, any word from him about anything at all.

Our false departure date for the *Hupeh* had rushed us to clean out all the paper work, travel certificates to the German community and other details necessary before leaving.

Culver finished up some long press reports which analyzed the new Dairen city government and listed the new officials of the Kwantung administration. He prepared a paper entitled "Miscellaneous Data on the Post-War Kwantung Economy"; it was a detailed survey, the last one on the area, obviously, except for future propaganda pieces of the Communists.

A "Dairen Industrial Exhibition" now opened. The announced purpose was to strengthen "Sino-Russian Friendship." However, the displays were arranged to exalt Russian science and Russian industrial management methods and to convince the Chinese that the industrialization of China was dependent on Russian techniques and aid.

One telegram I sent reported that all local real estate owners had been ordered in August to "register" their property; taxes were now levied on the basis of this new registration. Actually, there had been no taxes of this type in the past two years and so the present charges were for all of 1948-49. The rates were levied per square meter without regard to the actual value of the building on the property. As most households were unable to pay the extremely high amounts demanded, the taxes usually were confiscatory.

Since the Department's first news to us that the consulate would be closed, at least we had not been receiving more telegrams about couriers trying to reach us through Mukden or proposed efforts for Culver to go there and make contact with Angus Ward. The Mukden staff still remained cut off from the world: now a period of some ten months. Except for the Communists' announcement in June that Ward and his staff were accused of espionage and the one telegram Ward had been able to send to the Department, there had been, afterwards, only a few not very informative messages from him. It was an extraordinary position for an official representative of a government, perhaps unique in modern diplomacy. In other incidents or quarrels involving diplomats the men would be expelled from the country or, if not that, tried and put in jail—not held incommunicado month after month, no one knowing under what physical conditions, no one knowing exactly why.

It was now seven weeks since the Department's decision to close the Dairen consulate. We were anxious to get going, at long last, before a fate like the Mukden staff's could befall us—possible still if some new, sudden twist in Sino-Soviet dealings would place us in the hands of the Chinese Communists in Dairen.

CHAPTER XIV

FAREWELL
TO DAIREN
(OCTOBER 21, 1949)

I sent my final letter to the Kommandant on October 20.

Good God! How many letters had I sent him in the last year and a half? And only once did I ever get a reply. Less than half a dozen times was I able to have an interview with him, although I was always in there trying. And each of these concerned matters already settled in Moscow. In fact, at these meetings he would carefully read from a pad in front of him what someone in the back office apparently allowed him to say. He would answer my questions by looking down and repeating some phrase from the pad. On one occasion I realized the notes on the pad were not even in his own handwriting. Other questions he would write down, promising me answers that rarely came.

The signal importance of the Russian Kommandant of Dairen had been obvious to me from the start; the ambiguity of his position I realized only gradually. I slowly became aware that the Kommandant himself was merely a front man, a mouthpiece, without too much power of his own. All major decisions concerning the American consulate, as well as the local population, were actually made by his superiors in Port Arthur or, far beyond it, somewhere within the hierarchy of governmental power in Moscow. Yet somehow, now that I was leaving Dairen, I saw the Kommandant as the very symbol or crux of the consulate's peculiar and uneasy relations with the Communist bureaucracy, whether Russian or Chinese. It was as if there was nothing truly human about any of them: they seemed robots wound up as functionaries serving power structures designed to accommodate plans, not people.

Now, in this last letter to the Kommandant, I said that the *Shansi* was due to enter Dairen port the next day at daybreak and that the consulate staff would be ready to proceed to the harbor at any time after 7 a.m. I repeated what had become a standard paragraph in the succession of letters:

> As the consulate has made no effort to obtain trucks for the transportation of our effects, I trust the Kommandant already has arranged for them. The consulate is informing Mrs. Schumann that it will send to her quarters one of the trucks for her baggage and that the consulate will send its automobile to take her and the children to the port.

(Mrs. Slenkina was to meet us at the port entrance).

At the time of the *Hupeh* misfire I already had informed the Kommandant there would be six diplomatic pouches, some twenty-two wooden boxes, our miscellaneous hand baggage and the 122 boxes of personal effects belonging to the former British consular officers. In addition, the Department had requested me to take with us, if possible, four boxes of possessions of Mrs. Bryner, now an American citizen.

The Kommandant had never promised the trucks, but neither had he said they would not come. As always, he was a void of information. The coming or not coming of the trucks was one of the uncertainties of the morrow.

Before the false sailing of the *Hupeh* there had been too much pressure for me to make official farewell calls. Now, however, I called on the Russian consul general. He was a nice enough old gentleman but had proved useless in any important matter except when occasionally acting as a channel of communication to the people who could make decisions. (My chief memory of him is the many times he would say, "But, my dear colleague, this really is not in my competency.") He usually was flanked by a blank-faced official, whom I took to be his KGB shadow.

I also made a farewell call on the Kommandant. I asked him as a personal favor to me if he would assist in arranging for Chao's return to his home in Shanghai. But he shrugged and said he had "no jurisdiction." And he was right. He was probably not allowed to breathe without an order to do so from Moscow. As so often before when I faced Communist officials in Moscow and elsewhere. I considered what it takes for a man to rise to the higher levels of their bureaucracy. The basic rules are simple enough. Never say anything that an informer can report, never put anything into writing except as a record to protect oneself, always let somebody else make the decisions. How do things ever get done? But they do. Somewhere someone has to say "yes" or "no."

I wondered if he was the one who had bought the Oldsmobile, but I decided that even he, a major general, was not high enough to be able to drive an American car without fingers pointing at him as "a running dog of imperialism." (It must have been a really top man in Port Arthur, maybe the ranking general, maybe the head of the KGB.) Our parting was coldly, mechanically polite—without good wishes for the future.

The next morning because of fog we could not see the harbor from our attic window. We had given ourselves until noon to wait for action from the Russians—such as telling us the ship was here, that it was time to go aboard, that the trucks were coming . . . something. When the fog lifted at ten o'clock, there in all its white beauty was definitely the 3000-tons *Shansi*, at one of the piers.

Almost simultaneously, two Chinese policemen barged through the front door. With the roughest manners they announced they had come to "investigate" Radio Operator Chao and tried to push past me and Culver to the stairs. To be technical about this, they were correctly in Culver's side of the house and intended to go to Chao's room, the place I had agreed earlier the police could go. I told them that the consulate was still officially open and Chao was still a government employee. After a ten-minute violent argument I telephoned, in their hearing, the Kommandatura and said I felt certain the Russian authorities did not wish the consulate to have a grave incident on our last day in Dairen. The officer who answered replied that the military police would be sent immediately. They arrived in a few minutes and quickly moved the Chinese policemen out of the house; proof again as to who had the power in town. It was the only time in our series of police confrontations I had called on the Russians for help.

Were the Chinese police really so itchy to get their hands on Chao they could not wait? It was a disheartening episode.

There was a further deliberate wait to see if the Russians were going to send the trucks. All our personal effects were ready to go. Confidential mail was stowed in pouches with wax seals impressed with the insignia of the United States government. The consulate's pouches and boxes were set. Also Mrs. Bryner's. The cases at the British consulate were organized for instant loading. Mrs. Slenkina presumably already was at the port entrance waiting for us. Mrs. Schumann was standing by in her room in the German building. The chauffeur was on duty with the Oldsmobile. (The jeep had been turned over a few days before to the agent of the mysterious high official who had bought our equipment.)

I did not have the patience to wait until noon. At 11:30 I picked up the telephone to call the Kommandatura to ask about the trucks. But the phone was dead. For several months when four of our five phones had been cut off, Culver and I had a running joke as to when the last one would go. (Would this or that crisis be the one to do it?) Now, at the most improbable of all times, it had happened. What possibly could be the reason?

I drove to the Kommandatura and asked to see the Kommandant. On every other occasion when I had tried to see him without an appointment I always was sent away with a curt "Write a letter." Today, he received me immediately and gave me all the data which he could have told me the day before, during my official farewell visit.

He said that the harbormaster would settle with me all details about truck transportation and entry into the port area, that passage through the police barrier to get to the port area already was arranged for me. He assured me that official baggage and our personal luggage would not be examined at customs; the 122 boxes of the former British consular officers would, however, be examined. I made no issue of the British boxes, merely stating that I knew the British embassy at Moscow had obtained the consent of the Foreign Office for me to take the crates, but that I did not know what had been decided as to their examination at customs.

I hied back to the house to get Culver and go to the harbormaster. Until this interview with the Kommandant I had tried not to let myself become emotionally convinced we would get out of Dairen. Now we were leaving, and apparently without difficulties.

I gave to Chao his last message to send for us: "I am embarking on *Shansi* with Gleysteen. Will wireless from ship at sea." (The day before I had received the Department's last message: "With closing of Consulate Dairen, Department desires to commend you and Gleysteen upon splendid service you have rendered under extreme difficulties and conditions of personal hardship.")

The harbormaster was friendly and cooperative. I had asked for three trucks but he suggested six in order to move everything to the port in one trip. He insisted that each truck should have eight coolies: an excessive number, but at this point I was not arguing about anything. The cost of the trucks and coolies could not be determined until we were finished with them; Culver would return to the harbormaster's office to pay the bill. He said the trucks would be ready in fifteen minutes, three to go to the British consulate and the others to the consulate residence.

It was unbelievable, this speed. Culver and I rushed to the different points to make certain all was in readiness. Everybody and everything going to the port in one grand caravan was an excellent idea.

After the "fifteen minutes" became two hours Culver went back to the harbor master, who told him the trucks had "just left." We waited some more. Then I sent Culver and the chauffeur to drive around town to see if they could spot them. The trucks were found on a side street, idling under some trees. Culver told the drivers to follow the consulate car. Five minutes later, however, the six trucks had become "lost."

At four-thirty on the nose—four hours after the harbormaster said the trucks would be ready in fifteen minutes—the column of trucks drove smartly to the British consulate and to our residence. The boxes were loaded in jig time.

The farewells with the household staff suddenly were emotional. Informers or not, they had been good and resourceful servants.

I wanted to embrace Radio Operator Chao, but he formally put out his hand. Perhaps that was the best way. What could one say or do for one who could be in a Communist prison that night?

And I remembered once again, all too painfully, that other Chao, Head Clerk Chao, to whom we were unable to say goodbye. (When I was back in Washington, I tried to find out what had been done by the Department itself in behalf of the two Chaos, other than sending fruitless notes from the Moscow embassy to the Russian Foreign Office. Although everyone had been sympathetic, no one had really done anything. No important person, such as the Secretary of State, was apparently approached with the subject of evacuating the two Chinese employees of the Dairen consulate. Lower officers are often cautious not to trouble the top men with details: that is the way with bureaucracies. Yet the long record of dealing with the Russians had already proved that if someone high enough, such as the Secretary, personally takes up with them a matter like this one of the Chaos, they may accede. Blaming our inaction on the turmoil of the collapse of all of our posts in China was not enough reason. I have always believed that the Department failed to save the Chaos through ineptitude and indifference. Since the consulate was closing, this might have been a sufficient diplomatic "new element" for the Department to effectuate the means for both Chaos to leave with us. After all, Head Clerk Chao had spent his lifetime working for the American government. And Radio Clerk Chao, in accepting the Dairen assignment from our State Department, had entrusted the American government with his very life.)

Our caravan of the Oldsmobile, the Ford with the police that was always at my heels and the six trucks now drove to the German building. I had tried to keep Mrs. Schumann (and also Mrs. Slenkina waiting at the port) quietly informed during the day, but the delays had been a great strain on her. She was desperately worried that something could happen which would force us to leave for the ship without her. She had remained in her room all this time, having a hard time keeping her fidgety children inside and under control.

Which were more startled at the appearance of our long caravan: the children or the other German inmates? It would be hard to say. In three minutes the coolies had loaded the small amount of the Schumanns' possessions and we were off, Culver and the children rode in the Oldsmobile, but Mrs. Schumann and I stood precariously at the back of one of the trucks. We looked ridiculous there, but I was not going to lose those elusive vehicles another time.

We reached the port at five o'clock, only thirty minutes after the trucks had come for us. At a customs window near the entrance the effects of Mrs. Slenkina were now examined with great thoroughness, but not those of Mrs. Schumann, which were opened later inside. Apparently, the distinction was that the former was a White Russian but the latter was a Real Russian. (Although she had a German diplomatic passport, her governing document, at least here, was the old Soviet identification paper she had used on her departure from Vladivostok as a bride some eighteen years earlier.) It was another illustration of the hairline between "spheres" of jurisdiction.

As the trucks and the Oldsmobile drove into the long shed beside the *Shansi*, a most significant incident happened. The faithful Ford—my shadow, my hound dog—turned and drove away up the street. It was the one sure sign that, come what may, we were going to be able to board the *Shansi.*

Inside the shed were a dozen Russian and Chinese officials. It was difficult to determine their individual functions, for they never sorted themselves out as to which ones were customs men, which immigration, which openly police and which covertly something else. Also, no one person seemed in charge. They were stern-faced, but no more so than other officials in town. Their first act was to allow Mrs. Slenkina to go aboard.

Culver went to the harbormaster's office to settle the bill for the trucks and coolies. At the official rate of exchange the amount would have come to $1500. However, we paid with the local currency we had bought at the exchange market, the total amounting to $80. (By local standards the former was the true equivalent of what ordinary people would have had to pay.)

The shed itself was completely empty. The coolies spread out the consulate's boxes in one area, the British ones in another and Mrs. Schumann's to one side. Then the whole forty-eight of them moved off against the wall and sat on their haunches the rest of the time, waiting to load our things on board.

I kept the Oldsmobile and the chauffeur at hand, just in case. In Dairen, I had learned so well, anything could happen anytime.

Through the one open door of the shed, where the gangway was, I could see a portion of the lower deck of the *Shansi*—so clean and white, so very alluring. It became apparent to us that there were no passengers at all on board. Where were all those refugees from Tientsin? (Later, the captain merely shrugged and said that no one had received an exit visa at Tientsin. So Dairen was not alone in struggling with such troubles.)

With the consulate's effects, I pointed out to the inspectors the different piles of official pouches, boxes with official equipment, my personal baggage, Culver's baggage. Customs examination immediately was waived for all except Culver's.

Now arose an old problem in the Foreign Service—the difference between an American Special Passport (Culver's) and a Diplomatic Passport (mine). The latter is used for all personnel to whom the State Department has assigned full diplomatic status. The former is used for other government employees (although today it is seldom issued to persons traveling in Communist countries). Culver was affected because, although he had passed the written examinations for entry into the Foreign Service before coming to Dairen, he had not yet been appointed as a "career" officer. On his return to Washington, after passing the oral examinations, he would receive designation as a Foreign Service Officer. In the meantime, his official status was "Vice Consul of Non-Career"—the lugubrious title then in use.

There was no real reason for me to protest the examination of Culver's baggage since the officials had valid arguments for their action; also, the Department had allowed this examination at many boundaries around the world. However, at the end of a day of frustrations it is usually the unimportant detail which goads the spirit of resistance. Both of us had had our luggage examined in Vladivostok; both of us had reached Dairen together. Always our baggage had been treated as a unit. Why allow a change now?

My protest resulted in a half-hour of argument, the most non-stop practice I had had in using my Russian language. (Mrs. Schumann would have been amused or even proud of my sudden fluency, had she not been too tense with worry that she might yet be prevented from going aboard.) Eventually, some-one scurried off for the approval of somebody; in the end, Culver's shirts and shoes were not examined. He then went on board with our sealed pouches of official mail.

It was now seven-thirty.

The officials next examined Mrs. Schumann's effects, carefully, checking every item and taking an inordinate length of time. Also, a woman official, whom I had not noticed before, took the whole family off to an alcove, where they had to take off their clothes. The seventeen-year old Edmund had his own male attendant.

But finally the Schumann family was allowed to board the

ship with all their possessions intact. It was a poignant moment when they turned and walked up the gangway.

The rest of the consulate's boxes were now cleared and carried aboard.

Meanwhile, other officials were concerned with the examination of the four medium-sized boxes belonging to Mrs. Bryner. When opened, the contents proved to be one box of piano sheet music and three of books in several languages, including many published in Russian before the Revolution of 1917. I was informed that the music could be taken but not the books.

The boxes had no official status; I did not protest their right to forbid our taking the books. I insisted, however, that I be given: (1) a copy of the customs regulations governing this action, (2) a receipt for the boxes and (3) assurance that the officials would be responsible for returning the boxes to their former storage place in the Bryner godown. They refused all three points unequivocally. I then said I would myself go back into town with the boxes and put them in the godown. The plan flustered the officials and was never refused outright.

This new argument lasted nearly an hour. I enjoyed emphasizing in my surprisingly fluent Russian that customs authorities elsewhere in the world always have copies of regulations at hand and that invariably a correct receipt is given for any item left in official hands. Failure to give such a receipt would be regarded as irregular confiscation for the personal profit of the inspector. Such action concerning the property of an American citizen would be cause for the embassy in Moscow to request an official explanation. After I had repeated all this for the eighth time, the customs officials suddenly acceded. Without further ado, the coolies carried the boxes on board.

During all this time there was the background turmoil of the opening and examining of the 122 British boxes. The only tools available were two broken hatchets, two crowbars and some hammers without claws. Not one nail puller. In their treatment of these excellently crafted boxes (prepared originally for shipment to London) and the carefully packed contents the officials acted like irresponsible children. Dishes and other fragile objects were pulled out and then shoved back any old way. Silver spoons were bent, to test them for something or other. My pleas for care only made the officials more suspicious. We could not imagine what they were looking for. The items that caused most interest and were passed from hand to hand were some souvenir pamphlets of the last British coronation and some children's drawing books complete with childish scribblings. (Fortunately, the subject of books leaving Dairen had already been settled.)

I stood by disconsolately, watching the devastation. The shed had grown dark, and the lights were turned on—merely a couple of weak bulbs dangling from the ceiling. This gave a dramatic play of shadows over the shattered British boxes, turning the shed into a sort of stage scene, as if for Shakespearean actor-kings to declaim over some lost battlefield.

A contrasting drama could have been enacted at the deck railing of the pure white ship that serenely floated beyond the gangway next to the dismal shed. There British officers in their trim whites, insouciant and bored, appeared from time to time to chat with each other and idly gaze at the Dairen harbor. This might have been the proper setting for a Noel Coward play.

At ten o'clock sharp, and with only half the British boxes examined, the officials said they were finished. This sudden announcement left my mouth hanging open; I was expecting several hours more of their brutal inspection. They motioned to the coolies; and all the boxes were taken into the hold in a matter of minutes. Later, at sea, I wirelessed the American consulate in Hong Kong to inform the British that when the *Shansi* arrived there they should have a responsible person at hand to oversee the unloading of these appetizing boxes, which would be wide open to any pilfering stevedore's hands.

In farewell, the Russian officers and I formally shook hands all around: the customs men, the immigration men, the port personnel, the KGB men, the unexplained bystanders. We were not buddies, but I had been talking Russian to them all these hours. By now, at least we were "professional colleagues."

Then I, too, walked up the gangway, and away from Dairen. Within less than an hour the ship had cleared the dock and was out in the open sea.

Suddenly we understood why the inspection procedure in the shed had gone on for so long and always at a snail's pace, why the officers insisted on the useless project of examining the British boxes and why, without warning, the investigation had stopped exactly at the hour of ten o'clock. And also why there had been the long delay that day in getting us to the port, the foolish waiting for the trucks and then "losing" them.

The authorities did not want us to go through Dairen harbor until after dark. They did not want us to see their secrets! From the beginning, of course, they could merely have told the captain he was not allowed to sail until ten o'clock, which he would have accepted as a port regulation. So all day long they had stalled and stalled—and one unnecessary casualty was those beautifully crafted and packed British boxes.

As the ship's steward brought us sandwiches, we all stood at the rail, not looking back at the lights of Dairen but out forward, toward freedom. The steward asked if we would like a drink. Mrs. Slenkina said it had been years since she had had a martini and she was aching for the taste of one, so that is what we all asked for. The steward quickly obliged, but in making this unfamiliar exotic cocktail he shook it too hard in the shaker. It was not a "real" martini, yet somehow that nugatory drink made the right sort of farewell to Dairen.

After a while, Mrs. Slenkina suddenly laughed and pointed to the glass buttons on her dress. The dress looked nondescript and so did its buttons. She told us now that they were her diamonds. The Chinese customs officials had confiscated jewelry from her, she said, and also a large amount of British and American currency, they gave no receipt or even a reason; they just took them. Nor was she allowed to send them to Dairen friends. But anyway, using one of the oldest tricks in the smuggling trade, she had brought her diamonds past the inspection.

We stayed up for hours, enjoying the ocean and the air—happy to be outside the Communist sphere of informers and away from the confrontations with traffic police and all of the unanswered pleas to the Kommandant. In fact, I never even went to bed; at dawn I was watching the shoreline and islands of Korea go by on the horizon.

In the early afternoon we reached Inchon, the port twenty-five miles from Seoul. There an officer of the embassy met the ship; he was to drive Culver and me to Seoul.

Mrs. Slenkina and Mrs. Schumann would remain on the ship until it reached Japan. I already had arranged with a friend at SCAP to help Mrs. Schumann and the children obtain transportation to San Francisco on a ship of the American President Line.

Our parting with Mrs. Schumann and her children was emotional, full of mixed feelings: sadness at this end to the close association of lonely people in an alien land, joyous relief that each of us was now bound for a new and freer life.

Driving from Inchon to Seoul at the horrendous speed of forty miles an hour was a frightening experience. It was my first time going faster than twenty miles in nearly a year and a half. The road seemed a death-trap jumble of automobiles, carts and people.

Seoul was a thriving, teeming, jubilant metropolis. Before the war Seoul and Dairen had held approximately the same number of people: six to seven hundred thousand. Now Dairen's population had a little over two hundred thousand whereas Seoul was pushing toward a million. The one was glum and dispirited, the other exciting and frantically noisy.

Fortunately for them, the carefree people of Seoul could not foresee the invasion from North Korea only eight months in the future, when they would be scattering in desperate flight. In the latter part of 1951 I came back in Korea as Political Officer of the Embassy, then located in Pusan. The population of Seoul was reduced to fifty thousand; it was a ghost city. Today, it is five and a half million—the eighth largest city in the world. The ups and downs of urban mankind are indeed beyond prediction or even comprehension.

Culver and I had some debriefing sessions with the embassy officers. Then we held several press conferences with the Korean reporters and the foreign correspondents stationed in Seoul. The Department had instructed us to tell the full story of our stay in Dairen. It was stimulating to talk openly about matters we had kept suppressed for so long.

The wire services carried the interviews with us to the American press; the national news magazines gave accounts too. The whole story, however, was compressed into a few paragraphs, and there were no follow-ups. The original plan of the State Department to organize "maximum publicity" for the Dairen consulate's story was not carried out. To the State Department and to the news media, obviously, our tale was just one more incident in the drama of the collapse of Nationalist China and the swift rise to power of the People's Republic of China. The American public, already convinced of Russian treachery and Chinese Communist aggressiveness, probably needed no further propaganda prodding. The cold war's battlelines were by now deeply entrenched.

But for me personally, Dairen had been a rare and fascinating experience. Always I shall recall the city with a complex collection of vivid memories; in time even the unpleasant episodes may acquire a patina of feelings that are not really enmity against the Russians and Chinese Communists, but rather a degree of tolerance: the Kommandant's expressionless face as he told me "No," the panoramic view of city and harbor from the steep hill above our house, the Chinese residents' hostile or fearful glances at the town's two hated Americans, Mrs. Schumann's good-humored patience at my stumbling Russian lessons, her children's laughter and bounce, the bold Oriental characters of the Communistic slogan-scribbling on the British consulate's walls, the wildflowers blooming freely and profusely on Iron Mountain, that single naked light bulb shining in a lonely Soviet police station in the countryside, the calm and industrious demeanor of the two doomed Chaos, the worn old coins of the world displayed in glass cases in stalls at the foreign-money-exchange market, the decrepit and decaying buildings—once-luxurious hotels and business residences from a prosperous era—now teeming with ever-hungry, ever-insecure tenants, policemen ranting at the chauffeur alongside our shiny gray Oldsmobile that sported the American flag, the perpetual and painstaking coding and decoding of telegrams to and from Washington and Moscow, the desperate look of stranded Europeans who wished to go home, the odd excitement of the townspeople among the typhoon's debris, some favored Chinese objet d'art sold to me for a song to earn dollars for Mao, Culver's glee over the success of his "business deal" with the unknown top Soviet official which induced him to buy all our salable goods including the broken waterjugs, the all-night bridge party on New Year's Eve, goat cheese, warm beer, and illicit firecrackers at the consulate's Fourth of July celebration, our playful tossing of gold bars, the many experiments with the Siberian brew followed by the unexpected pleasure of acquiring a whole stock of fine wines, our one remaining telephone cut off at last—and that lingering, final look back at the city and its lights while our ship drew away from the port. Fare thee well, Dairen!

EPILOGUE

The entire German group in Dairen did get away two months after we left, on an exceedingly crowded ship to Japan. The remaining foreigners also were able to leave then. The German men interned in Siberia all returned to Germany, except for three who had died. Mrs. Schumann's husband, one of the first to be released, had just reached Germany and was waiting for her and the children when their ship docked in Bremen. He rejoined the German diplomatic service; the family lived in Bonn, Brussels, and Lisbon before he retired.

Culver Gleysteen was made a regular Foreign Service Officer upon his return to Washington. I was best man at his wedding soon afterwards. His assignments have been Bonn, Djakarta, the United States Naval War College, the State Department in Washington and Moscow (twice). He is currently American Consul General in Leningrad; his fluency in Russian long ago matched his ability in Chinese.

Within a few months I was posted to the Canadian National Defence College and then had assignments in Korea, Malta, Laos, Philippines, followed by two General Assemblies of the United Nations and then retirement.

No information has ever surfaced as to the fate of the two Chaos.

Six weeks after our departure from Dairen, Consul General Angus Ward and all his staff and their families were released from Mukden. Their isolation had lasted twelve and a half months. From them, directly, the world heard their full story at last.

On November 20, 1948, Chinese Communist soldiers without warning cordoned off the Mukden consulate office and both residence compounds, simultaneously cutting telephones, electricity, and water. The Communist Military Control Committee sent a letter to Ward claiming he had failed to surrender his radio station, despite his earlier suspension of all radio traffic and despite his previous offer to place the radio equipment under seal or guard. Ward and twenty consulate employees were forcibly kept inside the office building: there a single bucket of water served for a period of thirty hours. Only two weeks later, on December 4, were the Americans allowed to go between the office and their residences, and then only a few for one trip a day. Electricity and running water were finally restored on December 24, but not at the staff residence compound until much later. Chinese visitors who happened to be in the houses at the time of the Communist seizure of the buildings were held with the Americans for several months. An aged German national who chanced to be reading in the USIS library was held at the consulate for a year, even his appeals for clothing from his home going unheeded.

In June some of the restrictions were lessened. However, on the 20th the Mukden press charged the consulate staff with spying. Five days later Ward was allowed to send a telegram to the State Department. Thereafter, the isolation was resumed, although telegrams occasionally were received and sent. In September Ward was accused of hitting a Chinese employee on a trumped-up charge. During all these months medical services were refused, members of the staff were occasionally beaten, cesspools at the houses overflowed. The Chinese clerks were not allowed to leave either, and were badgered and threatened constantly. In November of 1949 the Communists staged a perverted sort of trial; they gave suspended sentences and then ordered the Americans' deportation.

The Mukden story was far more complex and the rigors of confinement harsher than this summary indicates. A continuing major news story, it generated world-wide interest. As the staffs of the other American posts in Communist China were gradually released over a period of half a year, similar accounts of difficulties were told.

These stories justified Culver's and my fears, in Dairen, that we too, might be caught up in some Mukden-type happening if we lost Russian "protection," and were turned over to the unrestricted jurisdiction of the Chinese Communists.

Russia and the new Chinese Communist Government at Peking signed a "Treaty of Friendship, Alliance and Mutual Assistance" on February 14, 1950, four months after we left Dairen. It specifically cancelled the 1945 Treaty with Nationalist China. Concerning Port Arthur Naval Base Area (excluding Dairen), the 1950 Treaty stated the Russian troops would leave immediately after the conclusion of a peace treaty by Russia with Japan or, in any case, not later than the end of 1952. (No peace treaty was signed and the withdrawal of the Russians was postponed in 1952 for another two years. Finally, in 1954, it was agreed that the troops would leave by May 31, 1955—and this was done. With a straight face, the 1950 treaty actually referred to Port Arthur as having been a "jointly used naval base," a situation which the 1945 treaty with the Chinese Nationalists had specified but which the Russians had never allowed to operate.)

As for Dairen, no mention at all was made in the 1950 treaty about the Russian troops there. It merely said the question of the port of Dairen would be examined after the conclusion of a peace treaty with Japan (which of course was never signed). Meanwhile, the administration of Dairen was to be wholly in the hands of the Communist Chinese Government. (Quite probably, the Soviets maintained some form of control over Dairen until their troops finally left the surrounding area.)

Today China has been opened up to foreign visitors, and some of them may have been allowed to go to Dairen. James Reston is the only person I know who has written about a visit there. The *New York Times* columnist spent a single day in Dairen in August 1971. He reported that the Communist authorities told him that Dairen now has sizable electrical and locomotive industries, that it now ranks next to Shanghai as the most important port in China, and that the population of "metropolitan" Dairen numbers four million. (No matter what the boundaries of the "metropolitan" area may be, that seems a startling figure.)

Obviously, Dairen at last has achieved its rightful place as the commercial entrepôt and port for goods going into and out of the huge area of Manchuria, a region containing fertile agricultural lands, rich minefields and important concentrations of industry. During the half-century (1898-1950) when Dairen had been detached from Manchuria while under Russian or Japanese control, Manchuria itself had often been, for a large part of the time, in the midst of military or political turmoil. Thus, even when the transportation routes to Dairen had been open, the amount and type of trade were frequently restricted. When full peace finally came to Manchuria and the barriers to commerce were removed, Dairen quickly grew into a major city, surpassing its prominence in the days of Japanese entrepreneurship and colonization.

Peace is always an effective catalyst for economic development regardless of the strange ideologies in control.